Close-up

COMPANION C1

Jennifer Heath

SECOND EDITION

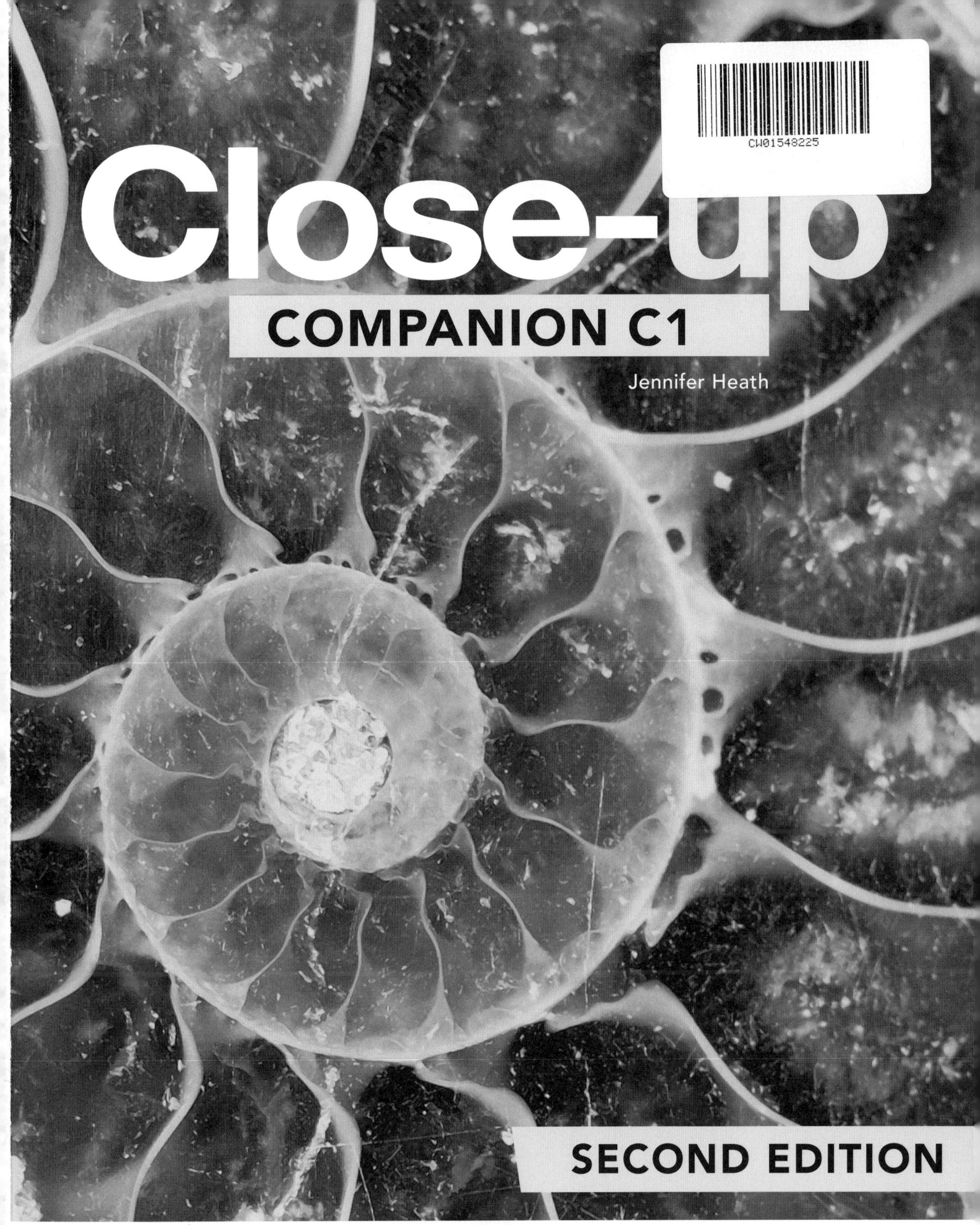

NATIONAL GEOGRAPHIC LEARNING

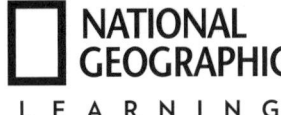

Australia • Brazil • Mexico • Singapore • United Kingdom • United States

Close-up C1 Companion, Second Edition
Jennifer Heath

Publisher: Sharon Jervis
Project Manager: Jon Ricketts
Editorial Development: Liz Gardiner
Cover designer: Ken Vail Graphic Design Ltd
Compositor: MPS Limited

© 2016 National Geographic Learning, a Cengage Learning Company

ALL RIGHTS RESERVED. No part of this work covered by the copyright herein may be reproduced or distributed in any form or by any means, except as permitted by U.S. copyright law, without the prior written permission of the copyright owner.

"National Geographic", "National Geographic Society" and the Yellow Border Design are registered trademarks of the National Geographic Society ® Marcas Registradas

For product information and technology assistance, contact us at
Cengage Learning Customer & Sales Support, cengage.com/contact
For permission to use material from this text or product,
submit all requests online at **cengage.com/permissions**
Further permissions questions can be emailed to
permissionrequest@cengage.com

ISBN: 978-1-4080-9587-4

National Geographic Learning
Cheriton House, North Way, Andover, Hampshire, SP10 5BE
United Kingdom

National Geographic Learning, a Cengage Learning Company, has a mission to bring the world to the classroom and the classroom to life. With our English language programs, students learn about their world by experiencing it. Through our partnerships with National Geographic and TED Talks, they develop the language and skills they need to be successful global citizens and leaders.

Locate your local office at **international.cengage.com/region**

Visit National Geographic Learning online at **NGL.Cengage.com/ELT**
Visit our corporate website at **www.cengage.com**

Photo credits
Cover image: © Geanina Bechea/Shutterstock,

To access the Close-up C1 Companion audio go to **ngl.cengage.com**

Search for **Close-up C1** with **ESL/ELT** selected from the dropdown menu. Then click on the **Student Companion Site** link

To access the Grammar and Vocabulary section Answer Keys go to **ngl.cengage.com**

Search for **Close-up C1** with **ESL/ELT** selected from the dropdown menu. Then click on the **Teacher Companion Site** link (Teacher access only)

Printed in China by RR Donnelley
Print Number: 03   Print Year: 2017

Contents

Unit	Page
Note to Teachers	4
Terms & Abbreviations	4
Key to pronunciation and phonetic symbols	4
1 Scaling the Heights	5
Vocabulary	5
Grammar	13
2 Like Comment Share	18
Vocabulary	18
Grammar	25
3 Just for the Health of It!	29
Vocabulary	29
Grammar	37
4 Lights, Camera, Action!	40
Vocabulary	40
Grammar	47
5 Eat Up!	51
Vocabulary	51
Grammar	58
6 Living Planet	61
Vocabulary	61
Grammar	69
7 Eureka!	73
Vocabulary	73
Grammar	80
8 Money Mad	84
Vocabulary	84
Grammar	91
9 All That Jazz!	94
Vocabulary	94
Grammar	100
10 Modern Living	104
Vocabulary	104
Grammar	111
11 Sports Crazy!	115
Vocabulary	115
Grammar	123
12 Fast Forward	128
Vocabulary	128
Grammar	134
Alphabetical Word List	137

Note to Teachers

Close-up C1 Companion provides students with everything they need to understand the vocabulary and grammar in the *Close-up C1 Student's Book*.

In the vocabulary section, words and phrases are listed in order of appearance together with their parts of speech and IPA. Each entry includes a clear explanation of the headword, an example sentence, derivatives (appropriate for the level) and the Greek translation of the word or phrase as it is used in the context of the Student's Book. For some entries there are special notes. These include antonyms, synonyms and expressions. At the end of the word lists for most sections, there are word sets that help students learn related words or phrases more easily. There are also *Look!* boxes with notes on usage. The vocabulary section ends with a variety of tasks that practise many of the new words and phrases of that unit.

In the grammar section, there are comprehensive grammar explanations in Greek with plenty of topic-related example sentences. The grammar section ends with tasks that practise the grammar of that unit.

At the back of the book, there is a complete list of all the words and phrases in the companion in alphabetical order with their entry number. This helps teachers and students to locate words easily, for example, if they want to refer to a word they learnt in another unit, or if they come across any difficulties.

Finally, *Close-up C1 Companion* is accompanied by audio, which contains the accurate pronunciation of each headword. You can find the audio here: ngl.cengage.com

Terms & Abbreviations

Terms / Abbreviations		Όροι / Συντομεύσεις
n	noun	ουσιαστικό
v	verb	ρήμα
phr v	phrasal verb	περιφραστικό ρήμα
adj	adjective	επίθετο
adv	adverb	επίρρημα
det	determiner	προσδιοριστικό
pron	pronoun	αντωνυμία
prep	preposition	πρόθεση
conj	conjunction	σύνδεσμος
expr	expression	έκφραση
excl	exclamation	επιφώνημα
Opp	opposite	αντίθετο
Syn	synonym	συνώνυμο
abbr	abbreviation	συντόμευση

Key to pronunciation and phonetic symbols

Consonants					
p	pen	/pen/	tʃ	chain	/tʃeɪn/
b	bad	/bæd/	dʒ	jam	/dʒæm/
t	tea	/tiː/	f	fall	/fɔːl/
d	did	/dɪd/	v	van	/væn/
k	cat	/kæt/	θ	thin	/θɪn/
g	get	/get/	ð	this	/ðɪs/

Vowels and diphthongs					
iː	see	/siː/	ɜː	fur	/fɜː/
i	happy	/ˈhæpi/	ə	about	/əˈbaʊt/
ɪ	sit	/sɪt/	eɪ	say	/seɪ/
e	ten	/ten/	əʊ	go	/gəʊ/
æ	cat	/kæt/	aɪ	my	/maɪ/
ɑː	father	/ˈfɑːðə/	ɔɪ	boy	/bɔɪ/
ɒ	got	/gɒt/	aʊ	now	/naʊ/
ɔː	saw	/sɔː/	ɪə	near	/nɪə/
ʊ	put	/pʊt/	eə	hair	/heə/
u	actual	/ˈæktʃuəl/	ʊə	pure	/pjʊə/
uː	too	/tuː/	ʌ	cup	/kʌp/

1 Scaling the Heights

page 5

1.1 **scale the heights** (expr) /skeɪl ðə haɪts/
be very successful • *The athlete scaled the heights when he won gold in all his races.*
❖ φθάνω στα ύψη, επιτυγχάνω κάτι

1.2 **achievement** (n) /əˈtʃiːvmənt/
sth sb succeeds in doing • *Getting into university was a great achievement.*
➢ achieve (v) ❖ επίτευγμα

1.3 **overcome** (v) /əʊvəˈkʌm/
manage to deal with a problem or a feeling • *He overcame his fear of flying and went by plane to London.* ❖ ξεπερνώ

1.4 **obstacle** (n) /ˈɒbstəkl/
sth in your way • *Her main obstacle when she moved to Munich was not knowing any German.* ❖ εμπόδιο

1.5 **bivouac** (v) /ˈbɪvuæk/
camp in a temporary shelter which is like a small tent • *When the storm began, we bivouacked in the cave entrance.* ❖ διαμένω σε καταυλισμό

Word Focus — page 6

1.6 **bare-bones** (expr) /beə bəʊnz/
having only the simplest and most important parts • *He lived on a bare-bones budget while he was a student.* ❖ τα πιο βασικά

1.7 **tandem** (adj) /ˈtændəm/
built for two people • *Two people can ride this tandem vehicle.* ❖ για δύο

1.8 **staggering** (adj) /ˈstæɡərɪŋ/
unbelievable; amazing • *The banker earns a staggering two million dollars per year.*
❖ απίστευτος

1.9 **top-notch** (adj) /tɒp nɒtʃ/
excellent; of the highest quality • *Major football teams rely on top-notch sponsors to finance them.* ❖ κορυφαίος

1.10 **acclaim** (n) /əˈkleɪm/
public praise • *The film received worldwide acclaim and won many awards.*
➢ acclaim (v) ❖ αποθέωση

Reading — pages 6-7

1.11 **secure a deal** (expr) /sɪˈkjʊə ə dɪəl/
arrange an agreement • *The businessman secured a deal with an advertising agency.*
❖ εξασφαλίζω μια συμφωνία

1.12 **exclusive** (adj) /ɪksˈkluːsɪv/
not shared • *This exclusive arrangement means that only your company name will be on the team's shirts.* ➢ exclusivity (n)
❖ αποκλειστικός, προσιτός μόνο σε λίγους

1.13 **expedition** (n) /ekspəˈdɪʃn/
a journey to explore a place • *The expedition to the North Pole was a dangerous journey.*
➢ expeditionary (adj) ❖ εξερευνητική αποστολή

1.14 **inspire** (v) /ɪnˈspaɪə/
make sb want to do sth • *Watching the Olympics inspired Martin to become an athlete.*
➢ inspiration (n), inspirational (adj) ❖ εμπνέω

1.15 **pursue one's dreams** (expr)
/pəˈsjuː wʌnz driːmz/
follow one's ambitions • *Bob is pursuing his dreams to become an actor by going to drama school.* ❖ κυνηγώ/ακολουθώ τα όνειρά μου

1.16 **runner-up** (n) /ˈrʌnə ʌp/
sb who finishes second in a race or competition • *The runner-up was disappointed not to win.* ❖ δεύτερος (αγωνιστής), επιλαχών

1.17 **ultimate** (adj) /ˈʌltɪmət/
most extreme • *Climbing Mount Everest is the ultimate challenge for a mountaineer.*
➢ ultimately (adv) ❖ απόλυτος

1.18 **descent** (n) /dɪˈsent/
action of going down • *The descent from the summit to the foot of the mountain took three hours.* ➢ descend (v) ❖ κάθοδος
✎ Opp: ascent

1.19 **remarkable** (adj) /rɪˈmɑːkəbl/
impressive • *The remarkable performance by the team got them into the final.* ➢ remark (v)
❖ αξιοσημείωτος

1.20 **corporate sponsor** (n) /ˈkɔːprət ˈspɒnsə/
a business that pays for a show, sports event, etc. in exchange for the right to advertise at that event • *The corporate sponsor for the team is Telecom.* ❖ εταιρικός χορηγός

1.21 **essentials** (pl n) /ɪˈsenʃlz/
necessary things • *Two essentials for a good report are clarity and organisation.*
➢ essential (adj) ❖ τα απαραίτητα

1.22 **vision** (n) /ˈvɪʒn/
an idea of what sb thinks sth should be like • *The architect's vision was to create an energy-saving building.* ➢ visionary (n, adj) ❖ όραμα

1.23 **quest** (n) /kwest/
search • *The explorers went on a quest for the mythical city of El Dorado.* ❖ αναζήτηση

1.24 **summit** (n) /ˈsʌmɪt/
highest point of a mountain • *They climbed up to the summit of the mountain.* ❖ κορυφή

1.25 launch (v) /lɔːntʃ/
throw into the air • *The boy ran fast to launch his kite into the air.* ➢ launch (n) ❖ εκτοξεύω

1.26 highlight (n) /ˈhaɪlaɪt/
best moment • *The highlight of the year was our school trip to the Natural History Museum.* ➢ highlight (v) ❖ το πιό σημαντικό ή εντυπωσιακό μέρος ή στιγμή ενός γεγονότος

1.27 gender (n) /ˈdʒendə/
being male or female • *She faced gender prejudice in the male-dominated board room.* ❖ γένος, φύλο

1.28 barrier (n) /ˈbærɪə/
sth that prevents you from doing sth • *The language barrier between Carlos and Sandra led to many misunderstandings.* ❖ εμπόδιο

1.29 go on (to do) (phr v) /gəʊ ɒn/
continue or move to the next thing • *After finishing school, she went on to study at university.* ❖ προχωρώ (σε κάτι άλλο)

1.30 crush (v) /krʌʃ/
beat completely • *PAOK crushed Olympiakos 5–0.* ➢ crushing (adj) ❖ συνθλίβω, συντρίβω

1.31 snatch (v) /snætʃ/
grab • *Greece snatched the victory when they scored a goal in extra time.* ❖ αρπάζω

1.32 pocket (v) /ˈpɒkɪt/
take possession of • *He won the final of the darts competition and pocketed a thousand pounds.* ➢ pocket (n) ❖ τσεπώνω

1.33 home turf (n) /həʊm tɜːf/
the place sb comes from or lives in • *Panathinaikos won on their home turf at OAKA, but they must play CSKA in Moscow next week.* ❖ έδρα

1.34 ground-breaking (adj) /graʊnd ˈbreɪkɪŋ/
important and new • *The ground-breaking research could mean a cure for cancer.* ❖ πρωτοποριακός

1.35 industrial (adj) /ɪnˈdʌstrɪəl/
related to factories • *The factory is in an industrial area near the port.* ➢ industry (n), industrialist (n) ❖ βιομηχανικός

1.36 instant (adj) /ˈɪnstənt/
immediate • *David Bowie's new song was an instant hit, reaching the top ten overnight.* ➢ instantly (adv) ❖ άμεσος

1.37 mind-blowing (adj) /ˈmaɪnd-bləʊwɪŋ/
very impressive • *His mind-blowing 100-metre sprint was a new world record.* ❖ πολύ εντυπωσιακός

1.38 stunt (n) /stʌnt/
a dangerous action done to entertain people • *He did a stunt where he jumped over ten cars on a motorbike.* ❖ κόλπο, επικίνδυνο ακροβατικό τέχνασμα

1.39 leap (v) /liːp/
jump • *She ran and leapt over the wall.* ➢ leap (n) ❖ πηδώ

1.40 beam (n) /biːm/
a long piece of wood or metal used in building • *There are large beams across the ceiling that hold up the roof.* ❖ δοκάρι

1.41 suspend (v) /sʌsˈpend/
hang • *The light is suspended in the centre of the room by a wire.* ➢ suspension (n) ❖ κρεμάω

1.42 patroller (n) /pəˈtrəʊlə/
a guard; a police officer • *The night patroller stopped a man who looked drunk.* ➢ patrol (v, n) ❖ φρουρός, περίπολος

1.43 fearlessness (n) /ˈfɪələsnəs/
lack of fear • *She showed total fearlessness when she calmly landed the damaged plane.* ❖ αφοβία

1.44 enable (v) /ɪnˈeɪbl/
make it possible for sb to do sth • *Good marks enabled him to get into university.* ❖ επιτρέπω, δίνω δυνατότητα

1.45 hail (v) /heɪl/
acknowledge, claim to be • *Bolt is hailed as the fastest man on Earth, having won many gold medals.* ❖ αναγνωρίζω

1.46 execute (v) /ˈeksɪˌkjuːt/
perform • *The tennis player executed the service perfectly.* ➢ execution (n) ❖ εκτελώ

1.47 tumble (v) /ˈtʌmbl/
fall with a rolling movement • *Doug fell over and tumbled down the grassy hill.* ➢ tumble (n) ❖ πέφτω, κατρακυλώ

1.48 vertical (adj) /ˈvɜːtɪkl/
straight up • *They looked up the vertical cliff and wondered how to climb it.* ➢ vertical (n), vertically (adv) ❖ κάθετος

1.49 face (n) /feɪs/
a side of a mountain • *The rocky face of the mountain was difficult to climb.* ❖ όψη, πλευρά

1.50 gaping (adj) /ˈgeɪpɪŋ/
big and wide • *There was a gaping hole in the road where the workman had dug it up.* ➢ gape (v) ❖ φαρδύς, που χάσκει

1.51 crevasse (n) /krɪˈvæs/
a deep crack in ice, especially in glaciers • *The man broke his leg when he fell into a crevasse in the glacier.* ❖ σχισμάδα

1.52 spontaneous (adj) /spɒnˈteɪnɪəs/
not planned; decided at that moment • *Many of the comedian's jokes were spontaneous in reaction to the audience.* ➢ spontaneity (n) ❖ αυθόρμητος

1.53 upbringing (n) /ˈʌpbrɪŋɪŋ/
the way your parents look after you and teach you to behave when you are growing up • *His upbringing in the UK and Dubai made him open to other cultures.* ➢ bring up (phr v) ❖ ανατροφή

On the road to success

acclaim	inspire
ground-breaking	overcome
hail	quest

Vocabulary pages 8-9

1.54 discriminate (v) /dɪsˈkrɪmɪneɪt/
treat a person or group differently from another in an unfair way • *Racial discrimination is a terrible thing.* ➢ discrimination (n) ❖ κάνω άδικη διάκριση

1.55 distinguish (v) /dɪsˈtɪŋgwɪʃ/
notice or understand the difference between two things; make one person or thing seem different from another • *What distinguishes me from my twin is that I am taller.* ➢ distinction (n) ❖ ξεχωρίζω

1.56 baby boomer (n) /ˈbeɪbi ˈbuːmə/
sb born during a period when more babies are born than usual • *The baby boomers of the 1960s were a lucky generation.* ➢ baby boom (n) ❖ κάποιος που γεννήθηκε σε περίοδο υψηλής γεννητικότητας

1.57 bring about (phr v) /brɪŋ əˈbaʊt/
make sth happen • *What brought about the change in his attitude?* ❖ προκαλώ
✎ Syn: cause

1.58 evolution (n) /ˌevəˈluːʃn/
gradual development • *The evolution of the computer has been rapid.* ➢ evolve (v), evolutionary (adj) ❖ εξέλιξη

1.59 revolution (n) /revəˈluːʃən/
a complete change in ways of doing things • *The technological revolution has completely changed the world of communications.* ➢ revolutionise (v), revolutionary (adj) ❖ επανάσταση

1.60 entrepreneur (n) /ˌɒntrəprəˈnɜː/
sb who starts a business • *The entrepreneur started a successful online store.* ❖ επιχειρηματίας

1.61 founder (n) /ˈfaʊndə/
sb who establishes a business, organisation, school, etc. • *Steve Jobs was one of the founders of Apple.* ➢ found (v) ❖ ιδρυτής

1.62 realise one's ambitions (expr) /ˈriːəlaɪz wʌnz æmˈbɪʃənz/
succeed in doing what you want to do • *She realised her ambitions when she became a doctor.* ❖ πραγματοποιώ τις φιλοδοξίες μου

1.63 accrue (v) /əˈkruː/
increase over a period of time • *The Hollywood star accrued a fortune over the years.* ❖ μαζεύω, συσσωρεύω

1.64 industrious (adj) /ɪnˈdʌstrɪəs/
hard-working • *The industrious employee produced three reports in one week.* ❖ εργατικός, φιλόπονος

1.65 accomplish (v) /əˈkʌmplɪʃ/
succeed in doing sth • *He accomplished his career goals by the age of fifty.* ➢ accomplishment (n) ❖ εκπληρώ, πετυχαίνω

1.66 insist (v) /ɪnˈsɪst/
say firmly • *She insisted on turning off the TV even though I wanted to watch the film.* ➢ insistence (n), insistent (adj) ❖ επιμένω (να γίνει κάτι)

1.67 persist (v) /pəˈsɪst/
continue doing sth even though it is difficult • *He persisted in arriving late for work so he was asked to leave.* ➢ persistence (n), persistent (adj) ❖ επιμένω (να κάνω κάτι)

1.68 resolve (v) /rɪˈzɒlv/
solve or end a problem or difficulty • *They resolved their differences and now get on marvellously.* ➢ resolution (n) ❖ λύνω

1.69 troubleshooter (n) /ˈtrʌblʃuːtə/
sb who is employed to come into an organisation to deal with a problem • *They want to employ a troubleshooter to make the company more efficient.* ➢ troubleshooting (n), troubleshoot (v) ❖ κάποιος που λύνει τα προβλήματα, που διορθώνει το κακό

1.70 admit defeat (expr) /ədˈmɪt dɪˈfiːt/
accept that you have failed and give up • *The athlete had to admit defeat when he finished fourth.* ❖ παραδέχομαι την ήττα

1.71 bold (adj) /bəʊld/
not afraid • *The bold student made a speech at the demonstration.* ➢ boldness (n) ❖ τολμηρός, θαρραλέος

1.72 gutsy (adj) /ˈgʌtsi/
brave and determined • *The gutsy boy did a stunt on his skateboard.* ➢ guts (pl n) ❖ τολμηρός

1.73 mediocre (adj) /miːdiˈəʊkə/
not very good • *The mediocre film received neither good nor bad reviews.* ➢ mediocrity (n) ❖ μέτριος

1.74 honourable (adj) /ˈɒnərəbl/
honest and fair; deserving praise and respect • *If you lose, it would be honourable to congratulate the winner.* ➢ honour (v, n) ❖ έντιμος, αξιότιμος

1.75 noble (adj) /ˈnəʊbl/
moral in an honest, brave and unselfish way • *It was noble of him to forgive his enemies.* ➢ nobility (n) ❖ έντιμος, αξιοθαύμαστος

1.76 vain (adj) /veɪn/
too proud of oneself • *Rob is so vain that he is always telling us how clever he is.* ➢ vanity (n) ❖ ματαιόδοξος

1.77 virtuous (adj) /ˈvɜːtʃʊəs/
good and honest • *The virtuous woman never cheated or told a lie.* ➢ virtue (n) ❖ ενάρετος

1.78 merciless (adj) /ˈmɜːsɪləs/
having or showing no mercy • *The merciless school bully took everyone's lunch money.* ➢ mercy (n) ❖ ανελέητος, αμείλικτος

1.79 **pitiless** (adj) /ˈpɪtɪləs/
cruel and having no pity • *His pitiless cruelty made her cry.* ➢ pity (v, n) ❖ ανελέητος

1.80 **ruthless** (adj) /ˈruːθləs/
without pity, feeling or guilt • *The ruthless businessman sacked ten employees to save money.* ➢ ruthlessness (n) ❖ αδίστακτος

1.81 **selfless** (adj) /ˈsɜːlfləs/
caring about other people more than about yourself • *It takes a selfless person to volunteer to help sick children.* ➢ self (n), selflessness (n) ❖ ανιδιοτελής
✎ Opp: selfish

1.82 **crafty** (adj) /ˈkrɑːfti/
clever and dishonest • *That crafty man cheated me out of twenty pounds.* ➢ craftiness (n) ❖ πανούργος

1.83 **cunning** (adj) /ˈkʌnɪŋ/
clever at planning to get what you want, especially by tricking other people • *It was cunning of you to get me to do your homework.* ➢ cunning (n) ❖ πονηρός, πανούργος

1.84 **sly** (adj) /slaɪ/
deceiving people in a clever way to get what you want • *Don't trust her; she's very sly.* ❖ πονηρός

1.85 **touchy** (adj) /ˈtʌtʃi/
too sensitive; easily upset • *Katy is very touchy, so she'll get cross if you ask her age.* ➢ touch (v) ❖ ευαίσθητος, εύθικτος

1.86 **sentimental** (adj) /sentɪˈmentl/
easily affected by emotions such as love in a way that seems silly to others • *Being sentimental, she cries whenever she sees a romantic film.* ➢ sentiment (n) ❖ συναισθηματικός

1.87 **upbeat** (adj) /ˈʌpˌbiːt/
hopeful and happy • *The dance music created an upbeat mood at the party.* ❖ αισιόδοξος

1.88 **fair** (adj) /feə/
right and just; not taking sides • *To be fair, you deserved to get punished because you cheated.* ➢ fairness (n) ❖ δίκαιος
✎ Opp: unfair

1.89 **impartial** (adj) /ɪmˈpɑːʃl/
not taking sides • *The football commentator wasn't impartial and clearly supported Panionios.* ➢ impartiality (n) ❖ αμερόληπτος, αντικειμενικός
✎ Opp: partial

1.90 **objective** (adj) /əbˈdʒektɪv/
based on facts; not influenced by personal feelings • *It is hard to be objective when judging your own family.* ➢ objectivity (n) ❖ αντικειμενικός
✎ Opp: subjective

1.91 **timid** (adj) /ˈtɪmɪd/
shy and afraid • *The timid child was too shy to say hello.* ➢ timidity (n) ❖ δειλός

1.92 **cautious** (adj) /ˈkɔːʃəs/
avoiding risk • *He was very cautious as he drove slowly along the icy road.* ➢ caution (n) ❖ προσεκτικός

1.93 **impetuous** (adj) /ɪmˈpetʃuəs/
acting suddenly and without thinking • *The impetuous player kicked the ball without aiming and missed the goal.* ❖ ασυγκράτητος, παράτολμος

1.94 **rash** (adj) /ræʃ/
careless or unwise; not thinking what the result of one's actions may be • *It was rash to swim where you know there are sharks.* ➢ rashness (n) ❖ απρόσεκτος, ριψοκίνδυνος

1.95 **reckless** (adj) /ˈrekləs/
doing sth dangerous and not worrying about the risks and the possible results • *The reckless driver caused a serious accident.* ➢ recklessness (n) ❖ ριψοκίνδυνος

1.96 **candid** (adj) /ˈkændɪd/
open, honest • *His candid manner made everyone trust him.* ➢ candour (n) ❖ ειλικρινής

1.97 **headstrong** (adj) /ˈhedstrɒŋ/
determined to do what you want without listening to others • *She is a headstrong child who rarely listens to good advice.* ❖ ισχυρογνώμων, πεισματάρης

1.98 **obstinate** (adj) /ˈɒbstɪnət/
determined to act in a particular way despite what anyone else says • *I can't understand your obstinate refusal to go to university.* ➢ obstinacy (n) ❖ ισχυρογνώμων, πεισματάρης

1.99 **stubborn** (adj) /ˈstʌbən/
determined not to change your opinion, ideas, plans, etc. • *Jack is far too stubborn to change his mind.* ➢ stubbornness (n) ❖ πεισματάρης

1.100 **adaptable** (adj) /əˈdæptəbl/
able to change in order to be successful in new situations • *She'll settle down quickly in her new home as she's adaptable.* ➢ adapt (v), adaptation (n) ❖ προσαρμοστικός

1.101 **considerate** (adj) /kənˈsɪdərət/
kind; thinking of others • *It was very considerate of you to help me move house.* ➢ consider (v), consideration (n) ❖ διακριτικός, αβρός

1.102 **modest** (adj) /ˈmɒdɪst/
not talking too much about yourself or being too proud of yourself • *The actor was being modest when he said he didn't deserve so much praise.* ➢ modesty (n) ❖ μετριόφρων
✎ Opp: immodest

1.103 **triumphant** (adj) /traɪˈʌmfənt/
successful • *He felt triumphant when he won the gold medal.* ➢ triumph (n) ❖ θριαμβευτικός

1.104 **apprehensive** (adj) /æprɪˈhensɪv/
worried or nervous about the future • *He felt apprehensive about spending a lot of money on a car.* ➢ apprehension (n) ❖ διστακτικός

1.105 **conceited** (adj) /kənˈsiːtɪd/
too proud of oneself • *You are conceited if you think you are the only person who matters.*
➢ conceit (n) ❖ αλαζονικός

1.106 **ignorant** (adj) /ˈɪɡnərənt/
not knowing things that you should know • *Only an ignorant person wouldn't know where the Parthenon is.* ➢ ignorance (n) ❖ ανίδεος, αμαθής

1.107 **inflexible** (adj) /ɪnˈfleksɪbl/
unwilling to change • *The manager is inflexible in his opinion of candidates without university degrees; he refuses to employ them.* ➢ inflexibilty (n)
❖ άκαμπτος, ανένδοτος, αμετάβλητος
✎ Opp: flexible

1.108 **blow sb away** (phr v) /bləʊ ˈsʌmbədi əˈweɪ/
impress sb • *The amazing painting blew me away.* ❖ εντυπωσιάζω

1.109 **break through** (phr v) /breɪk θruː/
manage to get past sth that is in your way • *The demonstrators broke through the police barriers.* ➢ breakthrough (n)
❖ καταφέρνω να περάσω από εμπόδιο

1.110 **come up against** (phr v) /kʌm ʌp əˈɡenst/
face a problem • *The builders came up against a problem when they found water underground.* ❖ αντιμετωπίζω

1.111 **pull sth off** (phr v) /pʊl ˈsʌmθɪŋ ɒf/
succeed in doing sth • *We didn't think we would get to the summit, but we pulled it off!*
❖ καταφέρνω

1.112 **fall through** (phr v) /fɔːl θruː/
not happen • *The plans for the trip fell through because nobody could come.* ❖ αποτυχαίνω

1.113 **get ahead** (phr v) /ɡet əˈhed/
make progress • *He got ahead in his career and became department manager.*
❖ προοδεύω

1.114 **hang on** (phr v) /hæŋ ɒn/
wait • *Don't leave. Hang on a minute and I'll come with you.* ❖ περιμένω

1.115 **knuckle down** (phr v) /ˈnʌkl daʊn/
start working or studying hard • *We have to knuckle down and study for our exams.*
❖ αρχίζω σκληρή δουλειά

1.116 **go for it** (expr) /ɡəʊ fɔː ɪt/
decide to do sth • *If you want to be in the team, just go for it and sign up.* ❖ αποφασίζω να κάνω κάτι

1.117 **have (got) a lot of one's plate** (expr)
/hæv (ɡɒt) ə lɒt ɒn wʌnz pleɪt/ have a lot to do • *I can't come out this weekend as I've got a lot on my plate.* ❖ έχω πολλή δουλειά

1.118 **work around the clock** (expr)
/wɜːk əˈraʊnd ðə klɒk/
work day and night • *They had to work around the clock to prepare the car for the race.*
❖ δουλεύω όλο το εικοσιτετράωρο

1.119 **by a mile** (expr) /baɪ ə maɪl/
by far • *That was the funniest film I've ever seen by a mile.* ❖ κατά πολύ

1.120 **be under fire** (expr) / bi ˈʌndə faɪə/
facing criticism • *The coach was under fire for the sixth defeat of the season.* ❖ βάλλομαι, επικρίνομαι, κατακρίνομαι

1.121 **go without a hitch** (expr)
/ɡəʊ wɪðˈaʊt ə hɪtʃ/
happen without any problems • *There was no violence between fans and the game went without a hitch.* ❖ συμβαίνει χωρίς προβλήματα

1.122 **get there** (expr) /ɡet ðeə/
succeed; arrive • *He got there in the end, passing his driving test on the third attempt.*
❖ πετυχαίνω

1.123 **persevere** (v) /pɜːsɪˈvɪə/
keep trying • *You should persevere and finish the course you are on even if you find it hard.*
➢ perseverance (n) ❖ επιμένω, συνεχίζω την προσπάθεια παρά τα εμπόδια

1.124 **do the trick** (expr) /duː ðə trɪk/
solve a problem; provide what is needed
• *Changing the battery did the trick and now this gadget works again.* ❖ φτιάχνω

1.125 **go all out** (expr) /ɡəʊ ɔːl aʊt/
try one's hardest • *The team went all out and won the league cup.* ❖ τα δίνω όλα

1.126 **do one's best** (expr) /duː wʌnz best/
try as hard as you can • *We did our best in the exams and hopefully we have all passed.*
❖ κάνω το καλύτερο δυνατό

1.127 **get the green light** (expr) /ɡet ðə ɡriːn laɪt/
be told you are allowed to do sth • *When you get the green light from the boss, you can apply for a rise.* ❖ παίρνω το πράσινο φως

1.128 **go places** (expr) /ɡəʊ ˈpleɪsɪz/
likely to become famous or successful • *That young actor is going places and will be famous one day.* ❖ ανεβαίνω, προοδεύω

1.129 **wise up** (phr v) /waɪz ʌp/
realise the truth about a situation • *You should wise up and see that he is cheating you.*
❖ ξυπνώ, συνειδητοποιώ

1.130 **a no-brainer** (n) /nəʊ ˈbreɪnə/
sth very easy to do or understand • *The first question on the test was so easy, it was a no-brainer.* ❖ κάτι το εύκολο

1.131 **dumb down** (phr v) /dʌm daʊn/
make sth easier to understand • *Let me dumb down these instructions for the average consumer.* ❖ απλοποιώ

1.132 **streetwise** (adj) /ˈstriːtwaɪz/
able to deal with life and dangers in big cities
• *Streetwise kids manage to avoid getting into danger in the street.* ❖ μάγκας, της πόλης, περπατημένος

1.133 box clever (expr) /bɒks ˈklevə/
behave in a careful and cunning way to get what you want • *He had to box clever when the police questioned him otherwise they would have found out the truth.* ❖ συμπεριφέρομαι έξυπνα

1.134 bright spark (expr) /braɪt spɑːk/
sb who says or does sth that they think is clever but is stupid • *Who's the bright spark who didn't lock the door before leaving the building?* ❖ εξυπνάκιας

Sport

corporate sponsor   runner-up
crush   snatch
home turf

Grammar   pages 10-11

1.135 dominance (n) /ˈdɒmɪnəns/
being more important or powerful than sb/sth else • *What is the reason for the dominance of Germany in Europe?* ➢ dominant (adj) ❖ κυριαρχία

1.136 worthy cause (n) /ˈwɜːði kɔːz/
an organisation or aim that deserves support • *The children's hospital is a worthy cause that many people donate to.* ❖ αντάξιος σκοπός

1.137 preoccupied (adj) /priˈɒkjupaɪd/
thinking about sth else • *He looked preoccupied, so I asked what the matter was.* ➢ preoccupy (v), preoccupation (n) ❖ απορροφημένος

1.138 disturb (v) /dɪˈstɜːb/
interrupt; bother • *Please don't disturb me while I'm talking on Skype.* ➢ disturbance (n) ❖ ενοχλώ

1.139 property (n) /ˈprɒpəti/
a quality or power that sth has • *One of the most important properties of copper is that it is a good conductor of electricity and heat.* ❖ ιδιότητα

1.140 obedience (n) /əˈbiːdiəns/
doing what you are told • *Obedience training for dogs is essential so they listen to your instructions.* ➢ obey (v), obedient (adj) ❖ υπακοή
✎ Opp: disobedience

1.141 breed (v) /briːd/
keep animals in order for them to produce babies with particular qualities • *These horses have been bred to race.* ➢ breed (n) ❖ εκτρέφω

1.142 jaw (n) /dʒɔː/
the bones of the face that contain the teeth • *A crocodile has very powerful jaws.* ❖ γνάθος, σαγόνι

Listening   page 12

1.143 be up to scratch (expr) /biː ʌp tʊ skrætʃ/
be satisfactory • *Your work is not up to scratch so please try harder.* ❖ είναι ικανοποιητικός

1.144 appealing (adj) /əˈpiːlɪŋ/
attractive • *We chose a restaurant where the dishes sounded appealing.* ➢ appeal (v, n) ❖ ελκυστικός

1.145 cheer sb on (phr v) /tʃɪə ˈsʌmbədi ɒn/
encourage sb with shouts • *The crowd cheered the player on as he approached the goal.* ❖ ενθαρρύνω

Speaking   page 13

1.146 depict (v) /dɪˈpɪkt/
describe sb/sth • *The writer depicts life in an English village 100 years ago.* ➢ depiction (n) ❖ απεικονίζω

1.147 aspect (n) /ˈæspekt/
the way in which a person, place or situation can be considered • *Let's consider the problem from a different aspect.* ❖ πλευρά, άποψη

1.148 come over (phr v) /kʌm ˈəʊvə/
make a particular impression • *She's a quiet person and comes over as shy.* ❖ δίνω την εντύπωση, περνιέμαι
✎ Syn: come across

Phrasal verbs

blow sb away   fall through
break through   get ahead
bring about   hang on
cheer sb on   knuckle down
come over   pull off
come up against   wise up
dumb down

Writing: a reference   pages 14-15

1.149 entail (v) /ɪnˈteɪl/
involve • *My job entails a lot of travel.* ❖ περιλαμβάνω, ενέχω

1.150 clerical staff (n) /ˈklerɪkəl stɑːf/
office employees • *The clerical staff were provided with new computers.* ❖ υπαλληλικό προσωπικό γραφείου

1.151 correspondence (n) /kɒrɪˈspɒndəns/
letters • *I receive little correspondence by post as most of my friends use email.* ➢ correspond (v) ❖ αλληλογραφία

1.152 **trait** (n) /treɪt/
a quality, good or bad, in sb's character • *His best personality trait is his kindness.*
❖ γνώρισμα, χαρακτηριστικό

1.153 **courteous** (adj) /ˈkɜːtɪəs/
polite • *The courteous waiter greeted us politely.* ➢ courtesy (n) ❖ ευγενικός
✎ Opp: discourteous

1.154 **under-privileged** (adj) /ˈʌndə-ˈprɪvɪlɪdʒd/
with fewer advantages than others • *Under-privileged children often lack opportunities to study.* ❖ άπορος, στερημένος

1.155 **tremendous** (adj) /trɪˈmendəs/
great • *This new financial support is tremendous news for the company.* ❖ τεράστιος

1.156 **asset** (n) /ˈæset/
sb/sth that is useful because they help you succeed • *The financial expert was an asset to the company as she saved it from closing down.* ❖ προσόν

1.157 **without reservation** (expr) /wɪðˈaʊt rezəˈveɪʃn/
with no doubt • *The manager happily recommended Francis' promotion without reservation.* ❖ χωρίς επιφυλάξεις

1.158 **appoint** (v) /əˈpɔɪnt/
employ • *The boss appointed a new assistant when Mrs Jones retired.* ❖ διορίζω

1.159 **personable** (adj) /ˈpɜːsənəbl/
attractive because you have a pleasant appearance and personality • *Everyone liked the personable young head teacher.* ❖ ευχάριστος

1.160 **attribute** (n) /ˈætrɪbjuːt/
quality; feature • *Good interpersonal skills are important attributes of a film director.*
➢ attribute (v) ❖ γνώρισμα, χαρακτηριστικό

1.161 **accomplished** (adj) /əˈkʌmplɪʃt/
very good at sth; skilful • *Margaret is an accomplished pianist.* ➢ accomplish (v), accomplishment (n) ❖ επιτυχημένος

1.162 **flair** (n) /fleə/
talent; a natural ability to do sth well • *He has a flair for languages and can speak French, Italian and Spanish.* ❖ ταλέντο, χάρισμα, κλίση

Common adjective endings

-ive
apprehensive
exclusive
objective

-y
crafty
gutsy
touchy

-less
merciless
pitiless
reckless
ruthless
selfless

-able
adaptable
honourable
personable
remarkable

-al
impartial
industrial
vertical

-ous
cautious
courteous
impetuous
industrious
spontaneous
tremendous
virtuous

Video 1: Extreme skydiving
page 16

1.163 **terminal velocity** (n) /ˈtɜːmɪnəl vəˈlɒsɪti/
fastest speed • *We measured the speed of the falling object when it reached terminal velocity.* ❖ τελική ταχύτητα (πτώσης)

1.164 **falcon** (n) /ˈfɔːlkən/
a small hunting bird • *The falcon dived down from the sky and caught a mouse.* ❖ γεράκι

1.165 **shuttlecock** (n) /ˈʃʌtlˌkɒk/
a small object you hit in the game of badminton • *The badminton player hit the shuttlecock with his racket.* ❖ μπαλάκι του μπάντμιντον

1.166 **bird of prey** (n) /bɜːd ɒv preɪ/
a bird that hunts animals • *Eagles are birds of prey that eat animals like rabbits.* ❖ αρπακτικό πουλί

1.167 **parachute** (n) /ˈpærəʃuːt/
a large piece of cloth which allows you to float to the ground from a plane • *The skydiver's parachute opened and he dropped slowly to the ground.* ➢ parachute (v), parachutist (n)
❖ αλεξίπτωτο

1.168 **challenger** (n) /ˈtʃælɪndʒə/
sb who competes for another person's title • *The challengers for the cup are Liverpool against the cup holder Manchester United.*
➢ challenge (v, n) ❖ διεκδικητής

1.169 **exceed** (v) /ɪksˈiːd/
go beyond • *He exceeded the speed limit and had to pay a fine.* ➢ excess (n)
❖ υπερβαίνω

1.170 **harness** (n) /ˈhɑːnɪs/
straps that fasten equipment to your body • *The instructor fastened the harness and checked that the parachute was correctly worn.* ➢ harness (v) ❖ ιμάντας, λουρί πρόσδεσης, χάμουρα (αλόγου)

1.171 **inflate** (v) /ɪnˈfleɪt/
fill sth with air so it becomes bigger • *The mechanic inflated the tyres on my car as they were a bit flat.* ➢ inflation (n), inflatable (adj)
❖ φουσκώνω

1.172 **lure** (v) /ljʊə/
attract • *I put a piece of cheese on the trap to lure the mouse.* ❖ δελεάζω

1.173 **resistance** (n) /rɪˈzɪstəns/
force that stops sth from moving or makes it move more slowly • *The air resistance on the skydiver prevented her from falling faster.*
➢ resist (v) ❖ αντίσταση

1.174 **acceleration** (n) /ækseləˈreɪʃn/
increase in speed • *The acceleration when the plane took off was impressive.*
➢ accelerate (v) ❖ επιτάχυνση

1.175 approach (n) /əˈprəʊtʃ/
the way you deal with sth • *Her approach with naughty children in the classroom is to find them something interesting to do.* ➢ approach (v)
❖ στάση, προσέγγιση

1.176 wobble (v) /ˈwɒbl/
move from side to side because you are not steady • *The gymnast lost points when she wobbled on the bar.* ➢ wobble (n) ❖ κουνιέμαι πέρα δώθε/με αστάθεια, ταλαντεύομαι

Vocabulary Exercises

A Complete the sentences with these verbs in the correct form.

| cheer do get go go have pursue realise scale secure work |

1 He _____ places if his book gets good reviews.
2 The fans _____ their team on for the whole match.
3 This new light bulb should _____ the trick.
4 Are you going to _____ around the clock to finish your project?
5 He _____ a lot on his plate and feels exhausted.
6 If you want to _____ the heights, you must be ambitious.
7 Do you think you can _____ the deal?
8 He went to drama school to _____ his dream of becoming an actor.
9 He _____ his ambitions to become a director by the time he was thirty.
10 Last night's performance _____ without a hitch.
11 As soon as I _____ the green light from my sponsors, I will start my research.

B Match.

1 The actor went   a down and start revising.
2 You must work hard to get   b deal off?
3 Let's knuckle   c on to have a successful film career.
4 Can you pull the   d up against?
5 Just hang   e me away.
6 Our plans for a picnic fell   f on and you'll get used to the job.
7 What problems did he come   g through because of bad weather.
8 Her singing voice just blew   h ahead in this company.

C Complete the word groups.

| fair mind-blowing noble ruthless sly stubborn timid |

1 staggering, remarkable, _____
2 honourable, virtuous, _____
3 merciless, pitiless, _____
4 crafty, cunning, _____
5 headstrong, obstinate, _____
6 apprehensive, cautious, _____
7 objective, impartial, _____

1 Grammar

1.1 Present Simple

Χρησιμοποιούμε τον Present Simple για:
γεγονότα ή γενικές αλήθειες.
→ The sun **rises** in the east.
ρουτίνες ή συνήθειες (συχνά με επιρρήματα συχνότητας).
→ Robbie often **goes** snowboarding in winter.
μόνιμες καταστάσεις.
→ She **is** a top-notch athlete.
προγράμματα, ώρες έναρξης/λήξης/άφιξης/αναχώρησης στο μέλλον.
→ The race **starts** at 9 am tomorrow.
αφηγήσεις (μια ιστορία, ένα ανέκδοτο, μια πλοκή, μια αθλητική αναμετάδοση κλπ.).
→ Bates **sprints** forward and **crosses** the finishing line.

Σημείωση: Κάποιες συνηθισμένες χρονικές εκφράσεις που χρησιμοποιούνται συχνά με τον Present Simple είναι *every day/week/month/spring, every other day, once a week, twice a month, in the morning/afternoon/evening, at night, at the weekend, in July, on Fridays, on Tuesday mornings* κλπ.
→ I use my iPhone **every day**.

Θυμήσου: Χρησιμοποιούμε συχνά adverbs of frequency (επιρρήματα συχνότητας) με τον Present Simple. Μπαίνουν πριν από το κύριο ρήμα, αλλά μετά από το ρήμα *be*.
→ She **often** chats with friends on Facebook.
→ My brother is **usually** cheerful.
→ I **rarely** go kayaking.

Συνηθισμένα adverbs of frequency είναι *always, usually, often, sometimes, rarely, hardly ever, seldom* και *never*.

1.2 Present Continuous

Χρησιμοποιούμε τον Present Continuous για:
πράξεις που συμβαίνουν την ώρα που μιλάμε.
→ He **is interviewing** young entrepreneurs for a TV programme.
πράξεις που εξελίσσονται γύρω από την ώρα που μιλάμε, αλλά όχι αυτή τη στιγμή.
→ **I'm doing** a project on gender barriers in the 21st century.
καταστάσεις που είναι προσωρινές.
→ **We're photographing** abandoned factories this week.
ενοχλητικές συνήθειες (συχνά με τα *always, continually, constantly* και *forever*).
→ My sister **is always sending** messages on her mobile phone.
να περιγράψουμε μια εικόνα.
→ In this picture the runners **are getting** ready for the race.
σχέδια και ότι έχουμε κανονίσει για το μέλλον.
→ **They're launching** a new social media campaign.
καταστάσεις που μεταβάλλονται ή εξελίσσονται στο παρόν.
→ Digital technology **is becoming** more and more popular.

Σημείωση: Κάποιες συνηθισμένες χρονικές φράσεις που χρησιμοποιούνται συχνά με τον Present Continuous είναι *now, at the moment, for the time being, this morning/afternoon/evening/week/month/year, today* κλπ.
→ **At the moment**, I'm working as a receptionist.

Θυμήσου: Τα stative verbs συνήθως δε χρησιμοποιούνται στους χρόνους διαρκείας (continuous) διότι περιγράφουν καταστάσεις (states) και όχι πράξεις. Για να μιλήσουμε για το παρόν, χρησιμοποιούμε τα ρήματα αυτά στον Present Simple.
→ This dog **doesn't belong** to me.
→ The athletes **look** exhausted.

1.3 Present Perfect Simple

Χρησιμοποιούμε τον Present Perfect Simple:
για κάτι που ξεκίνησε στο παρελθόν και συνεχίζεται ως τώρα.

1 Grammar

→ *I've had* this laptop for two years.

για κάτι που έγινε στο παρελθόν αλλά δε γνωρίζουμε ή δεν αναφέρουμε ακριβώς πότε.

→ Owen **has accepted** the job offer.

για κάτι που έγινε στο παρελθόν και το αποτέλεσμα επηρεάζει το παρόν.

→ He**'s won** a gold medal. That's why he's so excited.

για πράξεις που έχουν μόλις τελειώσει.

→ *I've just finished* the book on dog breeds.

για εμπειρίες και επιτεύγματα.

→ Jacob **has travelled** to India and China.

για κάτι που έγινε αρκετές φορές, ή επανειλημμένα στο παρελθόν.

→ She **has run** in several races but hasn't finished first yet.

με τον υπερθετικό των επιθέτων (superlatives), και με τις φράσεις *the first time/the second time* κλπ.

→ He's the most industrious young person *I've ever met*.

Σημείωση: Κάποιες συνηθισμένες χρονικές εκφράσεις που χρησιμοποιούνται με τον Present Perfect Simple είναι *already, ever, for, for a long time, for ages, just, never, once, recently, since 2009/October, so far, twice, seven times, until now, yet* κλπ.

→ I've known the Smiths **for ages**.

Θυμήσου: Χρησιμοποιούμε *have been* όταν κάποιος έχει πάει κάπου και τώρα έχει επιστρέψει. Χρησιμοποιούμε *have gone* όταν κάποιος έχει πάει κάπου και βρίσκεται ακόμα εκεί.

→ Dad **has been** to the office but he's at home now.
→ Dad **has gone** to the office and he'll be back in the evening.

1.4 Present Perfect Continuous

Χρησιμοποιούμε τον Present Perfect Continuous για:
πράξεις που ξεκίνησαν στο παρελθόν και είναι ακόμα σε εξέλιξη ή που έχουν συμβεί επανειλημμένα ως τώρα.

→ Larry **has been trying** to organise the new expedition.

πράξεις που έγιναν πολλές φορές στο παρελθόν και έχουν ολοκληρωθεί πρόσφατα, αλλά έχουν αποτελέσματα που επηρεάζουν το παρόν.

→ I'm tired because I**'ve been cycling** all morning.

να τονίσουμε τη διάρκεια μιας πράξης.

→ We**'ve been thinking** about climbing Everest for six months.

μια πράξη που είναι πρόσφατη ή που δεν έχει ολοκληρωθεί.

→ I**'ve been reading** about the falling share prices of Facebook.

Σημείωση: Κάποιες συνηθισμένες χρονικές εκφράσεις που χρησιμοποιούνται συχνά με τον Present Perfect Continuous είναι *all day/night/week, for years, for a long time, for ages, lately, recently, since*. Μπορούμε να χρησιμοποιήσουμε *How long…?* με τον Present Perfect Continuous σε ερωτήσεις, και *for (very) long* σε ερωτήσεις και αρνητικές προτάσεις.

→ Lisa has been filing correspondence **all week**.
→ **How long** has she been competing against male surfers?

1.5 Past Simple

Χρησιμοποιούμε τον Past Simple για:
κάτι που ξεκίνησε και τελείωσε στο παρελθόν.

→ Scott **reached** the South Pole on January 17, 1912.

ρουτίνες και συνήθειες που είχαμε στο παρελθόν (συχνά με adverbs of frequency).

→ My father always **watched** the Olympics on TV.

καταστάσεις του παρελθόντος.

→ He **wasn't** satisfied with his progress.

πράξεις που έγιναν η μία μετά την άλλη στο παρελθόν, για παράδειγμα όταν λέμε μια ιστορία.

→ Beth **jumped** on her bike and **cycled** towards the beach.

Σημείωση: Κάποιες συνηθισμένες χρονικές εκφράσεις που χρησιμοποιούνται συχνά με τον Past Simple είναι *yesterday, last night/week/month/summer, a week/month/year ago, twice a day, three times a month, at the weekend, in March, in the morning/afternoon/evening, at night, on Saturdays, on Sunday evenings* κλπ.
→ *I won the scholarship **two years ago**.*

1.6 Past Continuous

Χρησιμοποιούμε τον Past Continuous για:
πράξεις που ήταν σε εξέλιξη σε συγκεκριμένη χρονική στιγμή στο παρελθόν.
→ *I **was having** a discussion with my coach yesterday at 6pm.*
δύο ή περισσότερες πράξεις που ήταν σε εξέλιξη την ίδια χρονική στιγμή στο παρελθόν.
→ *I **was checking** my emails while Steve **was watching** the news.*
να δώσουμε το σκηνικό μιας ιστορίας.
→ *It **was getting** dark and the climbers **were feeling** apprehensive.*
μια πράξη που ενώ ήταν σε εξέλιξη στο παρελθόν, διακόπηκε από μια άλλη.
→ *She **was trying** to fix her snowboard when she fell.*
προσωρινές καταστάσεις στο παρελθόν.
→ *Jules **was doing** dangerous stunts for a film company back then.*

Σημείωση: Κάποιες συνηθισμένες χρονικές εκφράσεις που χρησιμοποιούνται συχνά με τον Past Continuous είναι *while, as, all day/week/month/year, at eight o'clock last night, last Tuesday/week/month/year, this afternoon* κλπ.
→ *The students were studying for their exam **all night**.*

1.7 Past Perfect Simple

Χρησιμοποιούμε τον Past Perfect Simple για μια πράξη ή κατάσταση που τελείωσε πριν από κάποια άλλη πράξη ή κατάσταση στο παρελθόν.
→ *She **had applied** for many jobs before she found one.*
→ *By the time the race began, it **had started** to rain hard.*

Σημείωση: Κάποιες συνηθισμένες χρονικές εκφράσεις που χρησιμοποιούνται συχνά με τον Past Perfect Simple είναι *before, after, when, already, for, for a long time, for ages, just, never, once, since 2011/September, so far, yet* κλπ.
→ *I had **never** been good at multi-tasking.*

1.8 Past Perfect Continuous

Χρησιμοποιούμε τον Past Perfect Continuous για:
πράξεις που ξεκίνησαν στο παρελθόν και ήταν ακόμα σε εξέλιξη όταν ξεκίνησε μια άλλη πράξη ή όταν έγινε κάτι.
→ *Kelly **had been paragliding** for years before she decided to stop.*
πράξεις που ήταν σε εξέλιξη στο παρελθόν και επηρέασαν μια μεταγενέστερη πράξη.
→ *Adam was tired as he **had been answering** calls all day at the office.*

Σημείωση: Κάποιες συνηθισμένες χρονικές εκφράσεις που χρησιμοποιούνται συχνά με τον Past Perfect Continuous είναι *all day/night/week, for years, for a long time, for ages, since*. Μπορούμε επίσης να χρησιμοποιήσουμε *How long…?* σε ερωτήσεις με τον Past Perfect Continuous και *for (very) long* σε ερωτήσεις και αρνητικές προτάσεις.
→ ***How long** had you been working on the report?*

1.9 *Used to* και *Would*

Χρησιμοποιούμε *used to* + bare infinitive (απαρέμφατο χωρίς *to*) για:
πράξεις που κάναμε συχνά στο παρελθόν, αλλά δεν κάνουμε τώρα πια.
→ *He **used to go** to the gym daily when he was younger.*
καταστάσεις που υπήρχαν στο παρελθόν αλλά δεν υπάρχουν τώρα.
→ *I **used to be** reckless as a teen but now I'm very careful.*

Χρησιμοποιούμε *would* + bare infinitive (απαρέμφατο χωρίς *to*) για πράξεις που κάναμε συχνά στο παρελθόν, αλλά δεν κάνουμε τώρα πια. Δεν το χρησιμοποιούμε για καταστάσεις.
→ *In the past, I **would take** photographs of track and field events.*

1 Grammar

Grammar Exercises

A Choose the correct answers.

1. Goods ___ more and more expensive.
   a get
   b are getting

2. If you add salt to water, it ___ below zero degrees.
   a freezes
   b is freezing

3. Karen ___ for the World Games at the moment.
   a trains
   b is training

4. Mark ___ about the weather day in day out!
   a always complains
   b is always complaining

5. The bus ___ at nine sharp every morning.
   a leaves
   b is leaving

6. Don't interrupt her while she ___ because she doesn't like it.
   a talks
   b is talking

7. You ___ pleased with yourself. What's going on?
   a sound
   b are sounding

8. They ___ now that they are getting older.
   a don't often go out
   b aren't often going out

B Complete the sentences using the Present Perfect Simple or the Present Perfect Continuous of the verbs in brackets.

1. He _____ (study) for the test all morning and wants to carry on.
2. He _____ (not contact) us yet with the details of the expedition.
3. Is this the first time you _____ (meet) a celebrity?
4. How long _____ you _____ (wait) for the letter to arrive?
5. Janet still _____ (not finish) her degree.
6. We _____ (not get along) very well lately.
7. _____ you ever _____ (be) to a match final?
8. He _____ (volunteer) at the hospital for years.

C Complete the sentences using the Past Simple or the Past Continuous of the verbs in brackets.

1. He _____ (win) three medals at the 2012 Olympics.
2. He _____ (commute) to work when he _____ (see) the accident.
3. While she _____ (carry out) research at university, she _____ (make) an important discovery.
4. Yesterday he _____ (seem) preoccupied all day.
5. I _____ (stop) the car, _____ (get out) and _____ (rush) to help the elderly man.
6. _____ you _____ (spend) the whole of yesterday at the library?
7. _____ the kids _____ (listen) to the teacher when you walked in?
8. We _____ (not like) the taste of the food at that top-notch restaurant.

D Circle the correct words.
1 Ken used to / would be an important political figure.
2 She used / would often go the cinema with her parents as a child.
3 He realised that Doug had arrived / had been arriving much earlier.
4 She had looked / had been looking for her keys when she found the diary.
5 Martin didn't use to / wouldn't like archaeology when he was younger.
6 Had he known / Had he been knowing about the deal for long?
7 What time had you agreed / had you been agreeing to meet?
8 I hadn't worked / hadn't been working there long when the company was sold.

Exam Task

For questions 1-12, read the text below and decide which answer (A, B, C or D) best fits each gap.

The 40-hour week?

In order to (1) ___ ahead in the corporate world, it is clearly necessary to be (2) ___. People (3) ___ for top posts, so logically the more dedicated are (4) ___. But how do employers judge dedication exactly? Unfortunately, rather than considering performance, employers often translate working long hours into commitment. This is often the case in the private sector in Greece, where many employers (5) ___ on getting more than the legally required 40-hour week. In Greece, this doesn't only apply to managerial positions but also to (6) ___ staff. A(n) (7) ___ number of employees work a 12-hour day, feeling required to do so in order to keep their job in a society where unemployment is on the increase. There are also many employees who deal with (8) ___ on laptops or tablets while commuting or at home. Many feel they will be under (9) ___ should they fail to put in long hours, or even replaced by someone who is prepared to work (10) ___ the clock.

The result is increasing dissatisfaction in a working population already hit by cutbacks and rising taxes. People still have ambitions to realise but many feel it is getting harder to (11) ___ their dreams when they are working such long hours for so few rewards. Perhaps it is time for employers to (12) ___ up and judge performance instead of the hours spent at a desk.

1	A	go	B	get	C	be	D	have
2	A	industrious	B	industrial	C	impetuous	D	timid
3	A	compete	B	achieve	C	overcome	D	accomplish
4	A	crushed	B	launched	C	leapt	D	appointed
5	A	insist	B	discriminate	C	pull off	D	distinguish
6	A	modest	B	clerical	C	considerate	D	candid
7	A	gaping	B	appealing	C	inflexible	D	staggering
8	A	barriers	B	correspondence	C	founders	D	property
9	A	fire	B	trick	C	hitch	D	green light
10	A	under	B	over	C	around	D	by
11	A	pocket	B	persevere	C	pursue	D	persist
12	A	scale	B	wise	C	get	D	hang

2 Like Comment Share

page 17

2.1 **comment** (v) /ˈkɒment/
give your opinion about sth • *I commented that her blog was worth visiting.* ➢ comment, commentary, commentator (n) ❖ σχολιάζω

2.2 **share** (v) /ʃeə/
use or look at sth with sb else • *I shared my photos with my friends by posting them on my Facebook page.* ❖ μοιράζομαι

Word Focus — page 18

2.3 **learned** (adj) /ˈlɜːnɪd/
having a lot of knowledge because you have studied a lot • *The learned professor knew all the ancient texts.* ➢ learn (v) ❖ πολυμαθής

2.4 **gruelling** (adj) /ˈɡruːəlɪŋ/
exhausting and extremely difficult • *The ten-kilometre run across the countryside in the rain was gruelling.* ❖ εξαντλητικός

2.5 **treacherous** (adj) /ˈtretʃərəs/
extremely dangerous • *The climb to the summit in the snowstorm was treacherous.* ❖ πολύ επικίνδυνος

2.6 **sever** (v) /ˈsevə/
cut • *He severed the rope with a sharp knife.* ❖ κόβω

2.7 **scroll** (v) /skrɒl/
move parts of a text on a computer screen up and down • *It was a long email so I had to scroll down to read all of it.* ➢ scroll (n) ❖ κυλώ, σκρολάρω

Reading — pages 18-19

2.8 **addictive** (adj) /əˈdɪktɪv/
so enjoyable you do not want to stop • *Video games can be very addictive and some people play them for hours.* ➢ addict (n), addiction (n) ❖ εθιστικός

2.9 **irritating** (adj) /ˈɪrɪteɪtɪŋ/
annoying • *His bad guitar playing is really irritating.* ➢ irritate (v), irritation (n) ❖ ενοχλητικός

2.10 **literary** (adj) /ˈlɪtərəri/
to do with literature • *He is a literary man and has many books in his library.* ➢ literature (n) ❖ λογοτεχνικός

2.11 **criticism** (n) /ˈkrɪtɪsɪzm/
disapproval; judgement • *The film received a lot of negative criticism in the newspapers despite being popular with audiences.* ➢ criticise (v), critic (n), critical (adj) ❖ κριτική

2.12 **confine (to)** (v) /kənˈfaɪn (tʊ)/
restrict (to) • *Reviews of his books are confined to serious literary journals. They are not published in daily newspapers.* ❖ περιορισμένος (σε)

2.13 **air one's views** (expr) /eə wʌnz vjuːz/
say one's opinion • *The journalist often airs his views on politics on morning radio.* ❖ εκφράζω τη γνώμη μου

2.14 **void** (n) /vɔɪd/
a gap; an empty space • *He looked over the rock face down to the dark void below.* ❖ κενό, χάσμα

2.15 **come in for** (phr v) /kʌm ɪn fɔː/
receive • *His views on education came in for criticism from parents.* ❖ γίνομαι αποδέκτης

2.16 **follower** (n) /ˈfɒləʊə/
sb who has an interest in sth • *He has hundreds of followers who read his tweets.* ➢ follow (v) ❖ οπαδός

2.17 **set out** (phr v) /set aʊt/
start doing sth in order to achieve a particular result • *I set out to write a short story but it ended up being a novel.* ❖ έχω ως στόχο

2.18 **reaction** (n) /riˈækʃn/
how you feel or what you do because of sth that has happened • *My reaction to the good news was relief.* ➢ react (v) ❖ αντίδραση

2.19 **provoke** (v) /prəˈvəʊk/
make sb angry • *The rise in taxes provoked a lot of anger.* ➢ provocation (n), provocative (adj) ❖ προκαλώ

2.20 **crawl** (v) /krɔːl/
move on your hands and knees • *The injured man crawled on his hands and knees to safety.* ➢ crawl (n) ❖ μπουσουλώ

2.21 **second to none** (expr) /ˈsekənd tʊ nʌn/
excellent; the best • *Lionel Messi's dribbling is second to none.* ❖ εξαιρετικός, χωρίς σύγκριση

2.22 **ordeal** (n) /ɔːˈdiːl/
a very difficult and unpleasant experience • *Breaking his leg was an ordeal for Grandpa.* ❖ δοκιμασία

2.23 **GCSE** (abbr) /ˌdʒiː siː es ˈiː/
a British exam taken by students in England and Wales when they are about 16 • *I am writing my GCSE exams at the end of the term.* ❖ Γενικό Πιστοποιητικό Δευτεροβάθμιας Εκπαίδευσης
✎ GCSE: General Certificate of Secondary Education

2.24 **adolescent** (n) /ˌædəˈlesnt/
a young person who is changing from a child to an adult • *Many adolescents fight a lot with their parents.* ➢ adolescent (adj), adolescence (n) ❖ έφηβος

2.25 **protest** (n) /ˈprəʊtest/
a strong objection • *There were loud protests against the unfair exam.* ➢ protest (v), protester (n) ❖ διαμαρτυρία

2.26 **screech** (v) /skriːtʃ/
shout unpleasantly and loudly • *The man's wife screeched at him to stop the car at the red traffic light.* ➢ screech (n) ❖ στριγκλίζω

2.27 **bitter** (adj) /ˈbɪtə/
angry and disappointed • *He felt bitter about not getting the promotion he thought he deserved.* ➢ bitterness (n) ❖ πικραμένος

2.28 **take sb aback** (phr v) /teɪk ˈsʌmbədi əˈbæk/
surprise sb • *The surprise visit by her cousin from Greece took Mary aback.* ❖ αιφνιδιάζω

2.29 **cheat death** (expr) /tʃiːt deθ/
stay alive in a very dangerous situation • *He cheated death when he survived the plane crash.* ❖ εξαπατώ το θάνατο

2.30 **bunch** (n) /bʌntʃ/
a group of people or things • *I invited a bunch of friends to my house to listen to music.* ❖ ομάδα

2.31 **spotty** (adj) /ˈspɒti/
having a lot of spots (or pimples) on your skin • *She used to be a spotty adolescent, but now she has a beautiful clear skin.* ➢ spot (n) ❖ γεμάτος σπυριά
✎ Syn: pimply

2.32 **cyborg** (n) /ˈsaɪbɔːg/
a being that is part human and part machine • *The cyborg in the film Terminator looks like a human on the outside but is a machine on the inside.* ❖ ανθρωπόμορφο ρομπότ

2.33 **anthropologist** (n) /ˌænθrəˈpɒlədʒɪst/
sb who studies the origins, development, customs and beliefs of the human race • *The anthropologist gave a lecture on the eating habits of early humans.* ❖ ανθρωπολόγος

2.34 **hours on end** (expr) /ˈaʊəz ɒn end/
many hours • *She watched TV for hours on end, sometimes for a whole day.* ❖ για ώρες

2.35 **interact** (v) /ˌɪntərˈækt/
if one person or thing interacts with another, they affect each other; talk or work together • *He interacts online with his friends and family.* ➢ interaction (n) ❖ αλληλεπιδρώ

2.36 **virtually** (adv) /ˈvɜːtʃuəli/
almost • *Virtually everyone I know has a mobile phone.* ➢ virtual (adj) ❖ σχεδόν

2.37 **breakthrough** (n) /ˈbreɪkθruː/
an important development • *A cure for cancer would be a breakthrough for the medical world.* ❖ σημαντική ανακάλυψη

2.38 **values** (pl n) /ˈvæljuːz/
ethical beliefs • *The values they try to teach their children are honesty and reliability.* ➢ value (v, n) ❖ αξίες

2.39 **miniature** (adj) /ˈmɪnɪtʃə/
tiny • *He has a miniature Batman car in his collection of toy vehicles.* ➢ miniature (n) ❖ μινιατούρα, μικροσκοπικός

2.40 **plug (into)** (v) /plʌg (ˈɪntʊ)/
connect a machine to an electricity supply • *Plug your mobile phone into the socket here to charge it.* ❖ συνδέω, βάζω στην πρίζα

2.41 **groggy** (adj) /ˈgrɒgi/
weak and ill • *He felt groggy after the rough ferry crossing.* ❖ αδύναμος

2.42 **distance** (v) /ˈdɪstəns/
make sb/sth less involved or connected with sb/sth else • *I hate violence and I try to distance myself from violent situations.* ➢ distance (n), distant (adj) ❖ απομακρύνω,-ομαι, απέχω

2.43 **unrivalled** (adj) /ʌnˈraɪvld/
better than any other • *She succeeded in solving the problem because of her unrivalled powers of concentration.* ➢ rival (v, n) ❖ απαράμιλλος, ασυναγώνιστος

2.44 **traumatise** (v) /ˈtrɔːmətaɪz/
shock sb so badly that they cannot work or think normally • *The terrible experience traumatised the child.* ➢ trauma (n) ❖ τραυματίζω

2.45 **sign up (for sth)** (phr v) /saɪn ʌp (fə ˈsʌmθɪŋ)/
put your name on a list for a course or activity because you want to take part in it • *Are you going to sign up for the course?* ❖ δηλώνω συμμετοχή

2.46 **cut (sth) off** (phr v) /kʌt ˈsʌmθɪŋ ɒf/
stop the supply of electricity or water or access to the telephone • *He couldn't pay his bill so the phone company cut him off.* ❖ κόβω (παροχή)

Vocabulary pages 20-21

2.47 **remark** (n) /rɪˈmɑːk/
a comment • *He made a rude remark about her hair.* ➢ remark (v), remarkable (adj) ❖ σχόλιο

2.48 **observation** (n) /ˌɒbsəˈveɪʃn/
a comment based on sth that was seen, read or heard • *His research involves the observation of animal behaviour.* ➢ observe (v), observer (n) ❖ σχόλιο, παρατήρηση

2.49 **defend** (v) /dɪˈfend/
protect sb/sth from attack • *He defended his decision to sell the house, explaining that he needed the money.* ➣ defence (n), defensive (adj) ❖ υπερασπίζω

2.50 **blast** (v) /blɑːst/
criticise very strongly • *The critics blasted the actor's terrible performance.* ➣ blast (n) ❖ κριτικάρω

2.51 **slam** (v) /slæm/
criticise severely • *The team was slammed by their furious coach for losing 6-0.* ❖ κριτικάρω

2.52 **relate** (v) /rɪˈleɪt/
have a connection • *He doesn't relate to anyone and he prefers to be alone.* ➣ relation (n) ❖ σχετίζομαι, επικοινωνώ

2.53 **morals** (pl n) /ˈmɒrəlz/
standards for good character and behaviour • *The murderer clearly has no morals; he doesn't feel sorry for what he did.* ➣ moral (adj) ❖ ήθη

2.54 **ideal** (n) /aɪˈdɪəl/
an idea that seems perfect and worth trying to achieve • *Working for world peace is an honourable ideal but difficult to achieve.* ❖ το ιδανικό

2.55 **burden** (n) /ˈbɜːdən/
sth that causes worry or trouble • *Owing money to the bank is a financial burden he cannot bear.* ➣ burden (v) ❖ βάρος, επιβάρυνση

2.56 **offend** (v) /ɒˈfend/
upset • *She offended him by laughing at his appearance.* ➣ offence (n), offensive (adj) ❖ προσβάλλω

2.57 **bother** (v) /ˈbɒðə/
annoy • *Don't bother me now – I'm busy.* ➣ bother (n), bothersome (adj) ❖ ενοχλώ

2.58 **resist** (v) /rɪˈzɪst/
stop yourself from doing sth that you want to do • *He can never resist a delicious ice cream.* ➣ resistance (n) ❖ αντιστέκομαι

2.59 **thrill** (v) /θrɪl/
cause sb to feel very excited • *The firework display thrilled us all.* ➣ thrill (n), thrilling (adj) ❖ συναρπάζω, συγκινώ

2.60 **phishing** (n) /ˈfɪʃɪŋ/
sending emails or having a website intended to trick sb into giving away personal information • *He was the victim of a phishing scam when his credit card was used by somebody else.* ❖ κλοπή στο Διαδίκτυο

2.61 **unsuspecting** (adj) /ʌnsʌsˈpektɪŋ/
not aware sth is going to happen • *She sold fake good to unsuspecting customers.* ❖ ανυποψίαστος

2.62 **scam** (n) /skæm/
a dishonest plan for making money • *Don't give them any money! It's a scam!* ➣ scam (v), scammer (n) ❖ απάτη, κομπίνα

2.63 **legitimate** (adj) /lɪˈdʒɪtɪmət/
lawful • *Amazon.com is a legitimate online store so you can safely order from it.* ❖ νόμιμος

2.64 **valid** (adj) /ˈvælɪd/
legally or officially acceptable • *To travel to Australia, you need a valid passport.* ➣ validate (v), validity (n) ❖ έγκυρος, σε ισχύ

2.65 **accessible** (adj) /əkˈsesəbl/
that can be entered, reached, used, etc. • *Their house is only accessible by a country road.* ➣ access (n, v) ❖ προσβάσιμος

2.66 **identity** (n) /aɪˈdentəti/
who sb is • *The police still don't know the identity of the thief.* ➣ identify (v) ❖ ταυτότητα

2.67 **loan** (n) /ləʊn/
money that sb or an organisation lends sb • *I'll need to ask my parents for a loan to buy some books.* ➣ lend (v) ❖ δάνειο

2.68 **max out** (expr) /mæks aʊt/
use all the money available • *I can't buy anything else because I've maxed out my credit card.* ❖ εξαντλώ, φτάνω στα όρια

2.69 **domain** (n) /dəʊˈmeɪn/
a web address • *The letters 'gr' signify that the domain is Greece.* ❖ διεύθυνση Διαδικτύου

2.70 **bring down** (phr v) /brɪŋ daʊn/
cause sb to lose power • *The financial scandal brought down the politician, who had to resign.* ❖ ρίχνω

2.71 **cut in** (phr v) /kʌt ɪn/
interrupt sb while they are speaking • *Do you mind if I cut in before you finish your comment?* ❖ διακόπτω

2.72 **get back at** (phr v) /get bæk æt/
take revenge • *She got back at him for his nasty comments by ignoring him all evening.* ❖ εκδικούμαι

2.73 **stir up** (phr v) /stɜː ʌp/
cause problems for sb else • *You stirred up some bad feeling when you were rude about the film star.* ❖ προκαλώ προβλήματα

2.74 **take to** (phr v) /teɪk tuː/
start liking sb/sth • *Mary and I took to each other as soon as we met.* ❖ αρχίζω να συμπαθώ, αποκτώ συνήθεια

2.75 **revenge** (n) /rɪˈvendʒ/
sth you do in order to punish sb because they have made you suffer • *He waited for years to take revenge on the bullies who had hurt him at school.* ❖ εκδίκηση

2.76 **detractor** (n) /dɪˈtræktə/
a critic • *Detractors said the comedy was so bad that nobody would laugh watching it.*
➢ detract (v) ❖ δυσφημιστής

2.77 **hat trick** (n) /hæt trɪk/
three goals scored by one player in one game • *Karagounis has scored three goals - that's a hat trick.* ❖ χατ τρικ

2.78 **corrupt** (adj) /kəˈrʌpt/
dishonest • *There are so many corrupt politicians and public servants in this country that I don't know how we'll get rid of them all.*
➢ corrupt (v), corruption (n) ❖ διεφθαρμένος

2.79 **under construction** (expr) /ˈʌndə kənˈstrʌkʃn/
still being made • *No one can visit my website yet because it is still under construction.*
❖ υπό κατασκευή

2.80 **go blank** (expr) /gəʊ blæŋk/
stop showing any pictures • *The TV screen went blank when the antenna broke.* ❖ σβήνω

2.81 **in confidence** (expr) /ɪn ˈkɒnfɪdəns/
on the understanding that you don't tell anybody else • *I'm telling you this in confidence so don't tell anyone else.* ❖ εμπιστευτικά

2.82 **out of context** (expr) /aʊt ɒv ˈkɒntekst/
repeated without saying in which circumstances it was said • *The celebrity was quoted out of context so he didn't actually mean what you think.* ❖ εκτός πλαισίου

2.83 **on occasion** (expr) /ɒn əˈkeɪʒn/
sometimes • *On occasion he goes for a walk but mostly he stays indoors.* ❖ πότε πότε

2.84 **at a guess** (expr) /æt ə ges/
probably • *At a guess I'd say she is under fifty but I really don't know.* ❖ υποθέτοντας, με πρόχειρο υπολογισμό

2.85 **guts** (pl n) /hæv ðə gʌts/
the courage to do something difficult
• *The bully didn't have the guts to actually fight, so he ran away.* ❖ έχω τα κότσια

2.86 **to sb's face** (expr) /tʊ ˈsʌmbədiz feɪs/
directly to sb • *She told him to his face how much she hated him and then walked off.* ❖ κατάμουτρα

2.87 **straight from the horse's mouth** (expr) /streɪt frɒm ðə ˈhɔːsɪz maʊθ/
from the source • *Spielberg told the reporter the name of his new film, so it's straight from the horse's mouth.* ❖ από το ίδιο του το στόμα

2.88 **sing like a canary** (expr) /sɪŋ laɪk ə kəˈneri/
reveal everything • *The thief sang like a canary and told the police the names of all his gang.* ❖ μαρτυρώ τα πάντα

2.89 **painfully** (adv) /ˈpeɪnfəli/
extremely and in an annoying or upsetting way
• *The construction of the website has been painfully slow.* ❖ ανιαρά

2.90 **wouldn't say boo to a goose** (expr) /ˈwədənt seɪ buː tʊ ə guːs/
used to describe a shy and quiet person
• *Bob is shy and wouldn't say boo to a goose.*
❖ τόσο ντροπαλός που δε μιλώ

2.91 **a little bird told me** (expr) /ə lɪtl bɜːd təʊld miː/
said by sb when they know who gave them the information being discussed but will not say who it was • *A little bird told me that you're getting married.* ❖ ένα πουλάκι μου είπε

2.92 **have a frog in one's throat** (expr) /həv ə frɒg ɪn wʌnz θrəʊt/
have difficulty speaking because your throat feels dry and you want to cough • *The lecturer drank some water because he had a frog in his throat.* ❖ κόμπιασε ο λαιμός μου

2.93 **cat's got your tongue** (expr) /kæts gɒt jɔː tʌŋ/
sth you say to sb when you are annoyed because they will not speak • *What's the matter? Has the cat got your tongue?*
❖ δε μιλάει, δε λαλάει

Phrasal verbs

bring down	set out
come in for	sign up (for sth)
cut in	stir up
cut off	take sb aback
get back at	take to

Grammar   pages 22-23

2.94 **install** (v) /ɪnˈstɔːl/
add software to a computer so it is ready to be used • *He installed the new computer game on his laptop.* ➢ installation (n) ❖ εγκαθιστώ

2.95 **itinerary** (n) /aɪˈtɪnərəri/
a plan of a journey and the route you will take
• *We prepared our itinerary before we left on our holiday.* ❖ διαδρομή, δρομολόγιο

2.96 **static** (adj) /ˈstætɪk/
unchanging • *The population figures have remained static for years with no increase or decrease.* ❖ στατικός

2.97 **evolve** (v) /ɪˈvɒlv/
develop • *Languages evolve when they take on words from other languages.* ➢ evolution (n), evolutionary (adj) ❖ αναπτύσσομαι, εξελίσσομαι

2.98 **advent** (n) /ˈædvent/
arrival • *The advent of mobile phones changed the way people interact.* ❖ έλευση

2.99 **a host of** (expr) /ə həʊst ɒv/
many; a lot of • *There is a whole host of reasons why I don't want to live in London.*
❖ πλήθος

2.100 **purist** (n) /ˈpjʊərɪst/
sb who believes that sth should be done in the correct way • *As a purist, he dislikes new words entering the language.* ➢ pure (adj)
❖ καθαρολόγος, δογματικός

2.101 **encounter** (v) /ɪnˈkaʊntə/
come across • *We encountered problems when the printer stopped working.* ➢ encounter (n) ❖ αντιμετωπίζω

2.102 **withdraw** (v) /wɪðˈdrɔː/
take out • *She withdrew enough money from the bank to pay for the week's food shopping.* ➢ withdrawal (n) ❖ αποσύρω, κάνω ανάληψη

Listening — page 24

2.103 **remains** (pl n) /rɪˈmeɪnz/
the body of a dead person • *The archaeologists dug up some human remains.*
❖ σορός, λείψανα

2.104 **out of bounds** (expr) /aʊt ɒv baʊndz/
beyond the place you are allowed to be • *The building site is out of bounds to members of the public.* ❖ εκτός (επιτρεπόμενων) ορίων

Speaking — page 25

2.105 **device** (n) /dɪˈvaɪs/
an object used for a particular purpose • *A tablet is a useful device for people who work while they are travelling.* ❖ συσκευή

2.106 **gadget** (n) /ˈɡædʒɪt/
a small device that does sth useful • *A USB stick is an essential gadget for computer users.* ❖ μικροσυσκευή, μαραφέτι

Computing
cyborg	install
device	interact
domain	scroll
gadget	

Writing: an essay (1) — pages 26-27

2.107 **reach** (n) /riːtʃ/
the distance that you can stretch out your arm to touch sth • *Put that bottle out of the reach of children.* ➢ reach (v) ❖ έκταση (χεριών), η απόσταση που φτάνει κανείς τεντώνοντας τα χέρια του

2.108 **broaden one's horizons** (expr) /ˈbrɔːdən wʌnz həˈraɪzənz/
learn more about the world • *Spending a year abroad as a student broadened his horizons.*
❖ διευρύνω τους ορίζοντες μου

2.109 **unprecedented** (adj) /ʌnˈpresɪdentɪd/
never having happened before • *PCs in every home was an unprecedented development in the 20th century.* ❖ πρωτοφανής

2.110 **confidential** (adj) /kɒnfɪˈdenʃl/
private • *Your medical records are confidential so they are not available to the general public.* ➢ confidentiality (n) ❖ απόρρητος

2.111 **identity theft** (n) /aɪˈdentɪti θeft/
illegal use of sb's personal details, especially in order to steal money from them • *He was a victim of identity theft when his credit card number was used by someone he didn't know.* ❖ κλοπή προσωπικών δεδομένων

2.112 **credit card fraud** (n) /ˈkredɪt kɑːd frɔːd/
using another person's credit card illegally • *The sales assistant who was arrested for credit card fraud had stolen 10 card numbers from unsuspecting customers.*
❖ απάτη πιστωτικών καρτών

2.113 **misinformation** (n) /mɪsɪnfəˈmeɪʃn/
wrong information • *He couldn't rely on the website because it was full of misinformation.* ➢ misinform (v) ❖ παραπληροφόρηση

2.114 **wary** (adj) /ˈwɜːri/
cautious • *Be wary of crossing the road here as there have been some nasty accidents.*
❖ επιφυλακτικός

2.115 **double-edged sword** (n) /ˈdʌbl-edʒd sɔːd/
sth that seems to be good but that can have a bad effect • *Researching online is a double-edged sword because although there is a lot of information, you don't know if it is correct or not.* ❖ δίκοπο μαχαίρι

2.116 **have sth at one's fingertips** (expr) /həv ˈsʌmθɪŋ ət wʌnz ˈfɪŋɡətɪps/
have what you need and be able to find or use it easily • *He knows a lot about history and has the facts at his fingertips.* ❖ έχω κάτι στη διάθεσή μου, έχω εύκολη πρόσβαση σε κάτι

2.117 **offset** (v) /ɒfˈset/
use sth that has an opposite effect so the situation remains the same • *The convenience of the mini-market must be offset against its higher prices.* ❖ αντισταθμίζω

Crime
corrupt	phishing
credit card fraud	scam
identity theft	

Video 2: Orangutan Language
page 28

2.118 native (adj) /ˈneɪtɪv/
used to describe plants and animals that live naturally in a place and have not been brought there from somewhere else ● *Kangaroos are native to Australia.* ➢ native (n) ❖ προέρχομαι από, ιθαγενής

2.119 coordinator (n) /kəʊˈɔːdɪneɪtə/
organiser ● *The event coordinator told everyone what to do.* ➢ coordinate (v), coordination (n) ❖ συντονιστής

2.120 voluntary (adj) /ˈvɒləntri/
done because you want to do it ● *Mary's participation at the canteen for the homeless is voluntary.* ➢ volunteer (v, n) ❖ εθελοντικός
✎ Opp: involuntary; compulsory

2.121 obligatory (adj) /əˈblɪgətri/
that must be done because of a law or regulation ● *There is an obligatory paper that has to be written as part of this course.* ➢ oblige (v), obligation (n) ❖ υποχρεωτικός

2.122 endangered (adj) /ɪnˈdeɪndʒəd/
at risk ● *Polar bears are endangered animals and will disappear if more of the ice cap melts.* ➢ endanger (v) ❖ απειλούμενος με εξαφάνιση

2.123 extinct (adj) /ɪkˈstɪŋkt/
no longer alive ● *Dinosaurs became extinct 65 million years ago.* ➢ extinction (n) ❖ εξαφανισμένο (είδος), εκλιπών

2.124 captivity (n) /kæpˈtɪvɪti/
when an animal is kept somewhere and is not free in the wild ● *The elephant was raised in captivity in the zoo when its mother was killed by hunters.* ➢ capture (v), captive (n, adj) ❖ αιχμαλωσία

2.125 primate (n) /ˈpraɪmeɪt/
a human, ape or monkey ● *Orangutans are among the most intelligent primates.* ❖ πρωτεύον θηλαστικό (πίθηκος κλπ)

2.126 stimulating (adj) /ˈstɪmjʊleɪtɪŋ/
causing enthusiasm and interest ● *After the talk, we had a stimulating discussion.* ➢ stimulate (v), stimulation (n) ❖ που διεγείρει το ενδιαφέρον ή τον ενθουσιασμό

2.127 mental (adj) /ˈmentəl/
to do with the mind ● *She does Sudoku to improve her mental abilities.* ➢ mentality (n) ❖ διανοητικός, νοητικός

2.128 conservation (n) /kɒnsəˈveɪʃn/
protection of the natural environment ● *The conservation of forests in Greece is very hard because of fires.* ➢ conserve (v), conservationist (n) ❖ διατήρηση και προστασία του περιβάλλοντος

2.129 regard (n) /rɪˈgɑːd/
respect ● *He has a high regard for athletes in the Paralympics.* ➢ regard (v) ❖ σεβασμός

Vocabulary Exercises

A Complete the sentences with these words.

| bird | boo | broaden | confidence | construction | context | end | guts | mouth | none |

1 I can't tell you what he said. He told me in _____.
2 His fictional style is second to _____.
3 She sat at the computer for hours on _____.
4 The actress was angry because the journalist quoted her comment out of _____.
5 I didn't have the _____ to do a parachute jump.
6 This news is straight from the horse's _____ so it must be true.
7 A little _____ told me you've got a new boyfriend.
8 He's so shy that he wouldn't say _____ to a goose.
9 This website is currently under _____.
10 Travel is the best way to _____ your horizons.

B Complete the phrasal verbs in these sentences.
1 The government came _____ for a lot of criticism over its policies.
2 She was taken _____ when she saw her neighbour on TV.
3 They set _____ to raise a thousand pounds but actually raised three thousand.
4 I'm sorry to cut _____, but there is a phone call for you.
5 The child took _____ swimming like a fish.
6 Financial scandals brought _____ the previous government.
7 The two mothers-in-law stirred _____ trouble all the time for the couple.
8 He refused to speak to her to get _____ at her for forgetting their anniversary.

C Complete the sentences with the correct form of the words.
1 I don't like this _____ programme.   IRRITATE
2 How many _____ do you have on Twitter?   FOLLOW
3 He finds surfing the Internet _____ and often cannot stop. ADDICT
4 She hates speaking in public because she's _____ shy. PAIN
5 There was a _____ discussion about the economy on TV last night. STIMULATE
6 _____ all my friends have a Facebook page.   VIRTUAL
7 She feels it is cruel to keep animals in _____.   CAPTIVE
8 A _____ wouldn't accept English words in the Greek language. PURE
9 Due to _____, research on the Internet has many problems. INFORM
10 We need a _____ to organise the whole show.   COORDINATE

D Circle the correct words.
1 I couldn't resist / provoke eating another piece of cake. It was delicious!
2 His unkind regard / remark was uncalled for.
3 The Green Party member made an interesting conservation / observation.
4 The survivors were lucky to thrill / cheat death.
5 The acclaimed / legitimate musician interpreted the piece beautifully.
6 Being stuck in the lift for over an hour must have been an advent / ordeal.
7 The scammer / detractor tricked people into revealing credit card details.
8 You should be unsuspecting / wary of clicking on links from unknown email senders.
9 The singer was blasted / bothered by the press for making a stupid statement.
10 I hate it when people lie to me to my face / mouth.

2 Grammar

2.1 Future Simple

Χρησιμοποιούμε Future Simple:
για αποφάσεις που παίρνουμε την ώρα που μιλάμε.
→ My eyes feel tired. I**'ll remove** my contact lenses.
για απλές προβλέψεις.
→ Languages **will continue** to change in the future.
για υποσχέσεις.
→ Yes, I**'ll come** to the tax office with you.
για απειλές.
→ Don't neglect your studies or I**'ll take away** your laptop.
για να μιλήσουμε για μελλοντικά γεγονότα.
→ His ordeal **will be** over soon.
για να προσφέρουμε να κάνουμε κάτι για κάποιον.
→ I**'ll fix** your printer for you.
για να ζητήσουμε από κάποιον να κάνει κάτι.
→ **Will** you **explain** to me how to use Twitter?

2.2 *Be going to*

Χρησιμοποιούμε *be going to*:
για μελλοντικά σχέδια.
→ He**'s going to pay** the phone bill today.
για προβλέψεις για το κοντινό μέλλον που στηρίζονται σε τωρινές καταστάσεις ή στοιχεία.
→ Look at the reviews! Her book **isn't going to be** a success.

Σημείωση: Κάποιες συνηθισμένες χρονικές εκφράσεις που χρησιμοποιούνται συχνά με τον Future Simple και το *be going to* είναι *this week/month/summer, tonight, this evening, tomorrow, tomorrow morning/afternoon/evening/night, next week/month/year, at the weekend, in March, in a few minutes/days/hours, on Thursday, on Wednesday morning* κλπ.
→ I'm going to change my password **in a few days**.

2.3 Future Continuous

Χρησιμοποιούμε Future Continuous:
για πράξεις που θα βρίσκονται σε εξέλιξη σε συγκεκριμένη χρονική στιγμή στο μέλλον.
→ I**'ll be posting** comments on my blog at seven o'clock tonight.
για σχέδια και πράγματα που έχουμε κανονίσει για το μέλλον.
→ We**'ll be discussing** the Industrial Revolution next month.

Σημείωση: Κάποιες συνηθισμένες χρονικές εκφράσεις που χρησιμοποιούνται συχνά με τον Future Continuous είναι *this time next week/month/summer, this time tomorrow morning/afternoon/night* κλπ.
→ **This time next week,** I'll be installing Skype on my PC.

2.4 Future Perfect Simple

Χρησιμοποιούμε Future Perfect Simple για να μιλήσουμε:
για κάτι που θα έχει ολοκληρωθεί ως ή πριν από μια συγκεκριμένη χρονική στιγμή στο μέλλον.
→ The cyborg anthropologist **will have finished** her talk by eight o'clock tonight.
για τη διάρκεια μιας πράξης ως κάποια χρονική στιγμή στο μέλλον.
→ By 2015, I**'ll have worked** as a literary critic for ten years.

Σημείωση: Κάποιες συνηθισμένες χρονικές εκφράσεις που χρησιμοποιούνται συχνά με το Future Perfect Simple είναι *by the end of the week/month/year, by this time tomorrow, by tomorrow evening/seven o'clock/2016* κλπ.
→ By 2050, our culture and values **will have changed**.

2 Grammar

2.5 Future Perfect Continuous

Χρησιμοποιούμε Future Perfect Continuous:
για να δείξουμε ότι κάτι θα συνεχίζεται ως ένα συγκεκριμένο γεγονός ή χρονική στιγμή στο μέλλον.
→ *I **will have been studying** for four years when I graduate from college.*
για πράξεις που θα βρίσκονται σε εξέλιξη στο μέλλον και θα επηρεάσουν μια άλλη πράξη.
→ *Her English will be up to scratch for the exam because she **will have been studying** for months.*

2.6 Shall

Χρησιμοποιούμε *shall* όταν θέλουμε να προτείνουμε ή να προσφέρουμε κάτι.
→ ***Shall I** send the text message to Sally?*
→ ***Shall we** reply to the emails right now?*
→ ***Shall I** pay the mobile phone bill online?*

2.7 Future in the Past

Χρησιμοποιούμε Future in the Past για να εκφράσουμε την ιδέα ότι στο παρελθόν σκεφτήκαμε πως κάτι θα συνέβαινε στο μέλλον.
Χρησιμοποιούμε *would* για να μιλήσουμε για προσφορές ή υποσχέσεις.
→ *John said he **would lend** me his smartphone.*
Χρησιμοποιούμε *was/were going to* για να μιλήσουμε για σχέδια.
→ *I knew Maria **was going to apply** for a student loan.*
Χρησιμοποιούμε *would* και *was/were going to* για να μιλήσουμε για προβλέψεις.
→ *I told you social media **would be** a double-edged sword.*
→ *I was sure that blog **wasn't going to have** many followers.*

2.8 Temporals

Χρησιμοποιούμε temporals όπως *when, before, after, until, once, by the time* κλπ για να μιλήσουμε για το μέλλοντα.
Σ' αυτή την περίπτωση, χρησιμοποιούμε present ή present perfect. Δε χρησιμοποιούμε future με temporals.
→ ***After** I **have uploaded** the photos, I'll send you a message.*
→ *I won't buy a webcam **until** I **read** some reviews.*

Όπως συμβαίνει με όλους του χρόνους του μέλλοντα, δεν μπορούμε να χρησιμοποιήσουμε Future in the Past με temporals. Στη θέση του Future in the Past, χρησιμοποιούμε Past Simple.
→ *I told Brian when he **decided** to start a blog that I would help him find a catchy name for it.*

Grammar Exercises

A Circle the correct words.

1 We **will have finished / finish** the meeting by three o'clock.
2 I think it **will rain / is raining** later.
3 We **have / are having** a get-together next Saturday.
4 The plane **departs / is departing** at 11 am tomorrow.
5 **Will / Shall** I pick you up after work?
6 By the end of the year, I **will have been living / am going to be living** here for ten months.
7 I don't remember her number. **I'm looking / I'm going to look** it up.
8 John **will / shall** call you later to check you are OK.

B Match.

1. Dad's thirsty.
2. It hasn't rained for days.
3. I just saw the weather forecast.
4. I moved here last week.
5. He's still doing his homework.
6. They've packed their suitcases.
7. This is a three-day trip.
8. I'm exhausted.

a. I'm going to go to bed.
b. He'll have been doing it for six hours soon.
c. I hope I'll have finished unpacking by tomorrow.
d. Apparently, it will rain all day tomorrow.
e. The plants are going to need some water.
f. On day two, we visit the Acropolis Museum.
g. They're leaving for Paris in the morning.
h. Shall I get him some water?

C Circle the correct words.

1. He said he would contact me when he **would arrive / arrived**.
2. Arthur promised that he **would keep / was keeping** in touch.
3. She left early because she **would meet / was meeting** a friend that afternoon.
4. It seemed that the party **was going to be / was being** a success.
5. I told Mary that when I **received / would receive** the package, I would let her know.
6. As soon as he **would call / called**, he would always ask how we all were.
7. After we ate out, we **would often watch / were often watching** a film.
8. The shop couldn't validate the purchase until she **would enter / entered** her PIN.

D Choose the correct answers.

1. I stayed late at work in ___ my colleague wanted help with his report.
   a until
   b case
   c soon as

2. I will have ___ the dishes soon enough.
   a finished
   b finishing
   c finish

3. Do you think the weather ___ be fine tomorrow?
   a is going
   b will
   c was

4. ___ the plane arrive at Heathrow or Gatwick?
   a Shall
   b Does
   c Is

5. What ___ you doing for your anniversary next weekend?
   a were
   b will
   c are

6. He promised he ___ phone if there was any more news.
   a will
   b would
   c was

7. We knew she ___ to become a star.
   a was going
   b would go
   c will go

8. ___ we all help prepare the food for the party?
   a Would
   b Are
   c Shall

27

2 Grammar

Exam Task

For questions 1-15, read the text below and think of the word which best fits the gap. Use only one word in each gap.

Smartphones

Some (1) _____ media researchers predict that soon most of us (2) _____ use smartphones to get online rather than laptops and tablets. In fact, most young people I know are already doing just that. They are no longer staring (3) _____ their computer screens in their rooms because Internet access is no longer confined (4) _____ a home connection. With Internet hot spots all over the place, the smartphone is the perfect means of surfing and (5) _____ with your friends and family. Smartphones are conveniently small to carry around and they offer a host (6) _____ apps for both entertainment and work. You can stay in (7) _____ and (8) _____ photos with friends and family. Aside (9) _____ this, you can also (10) _____ your horizons by visiting different websites.

Detractors say, however, that as soon (11) _____ people go home, they will always turn on the laptop and connect in the usual fashion. Not so, reply the researchers. By (12) _____ time next year, they believe smartphones will (13) _____ become the most popular means of getting online. The reason is that most people go online to connect with friends and family, and the smartphone is second to (14) _____ when it comes to doing this, whether you are out or at home. Whatever your point of (15) _____, smartphones are advancing and therefore promising much for the future.

3 Just for the Health of It!

page 31

3.1 monitor (v) /ˈmɒnɪtə/
check the progress of sb/sth • *The man with a head injury was monitored carefully overnight to make sure he was OK.* ❖ παρακολουθώ

Word Focus — page 32

3.2 amnesia (n) /æmˈniːzɪə/
a medical condition in which sb cannot remember things • *She has amnesia and cannot remember her name.* ❖ αμνησία

3.3 blunder (n) /ˈblʌndə/
a stupid or careless mistake • *Asking after her ex-husband was a bit of a blunder! You know she hates him.* ➢ blunder (v) ❖ γκάφα

3.4 neuron (n) /ˈnjʊərɒn/
a cell which is part of the nervous system • *Our brains consist of billions of neurons.* ❖ νευρώνας

3.5 spectrum (n) /ˈspektrəm/
a range • *People from across the social spectrum attend this university.* ❖ φάσμα

3.6 ravage (v) /ˈrævɪdʒ/
damage badly • *The fire ravaged the forest and not a single tree was left standing.* ❖ καταστρέφω

Reading — pages 32-33

3.7 anterograde amnesia (expr)
/ˈæntɪrəʊɡreɪd æmˈniːzɪə/
loss of memory after an event that caused amnesia • *After suffering a head injury, he got anterograde amnesia and can't remember anything from that day to today.*
❖ δευτεροπαθής ή εμπροσθόδρομη αμνησία

3.8 retrograde amnesia (expr)
/ˈretrəʊɡreɪd æmˈniːzɪə/
loss of memory before an event that caused amnesia • *The man with retrograde amnesia does not know his own name.* ❖ οπισθόδρομη αμνησία

3.9 recall (v) /rɪˈkɔːl/
remember • *He said he knew me but I could not recall ever having met him.* ❖ ανακαλώ

3.10 wipe out (phr v) /waɪp aʊt/
destroy • *He remembers nothing because the shock wiped out any memory of the accident.*
❖ εξαφανίζω, σβήνω

3.11 vivid (adj) /ˈvɪvɪd/
producing very clear images in the mind • *Grandma has vivid memories of her childhood as if it was only yesterday.* ➢ vividness (n)
❖ ζωηρός, ζωντανός

3.12 oblivious (adj) /əˈblɪvɪəs/
unaware • *Being deaf, he was oblivious to the sound of the doorbell.* ➢ oblivion (n)
❖ ανυποψίαστος, αδιάφορος

3.13 slip of the mind (expr) /slɪp əv ðə maɪnd/
sth you forget • *Because of a slip of the mind, she forgot to keep her dental appointment.*
❖ κάτι που ξεχνώ

3.14 accompany (v) /əˈkʌmpəni/
go/come with • *My headache was accompanied by a sore throat, so I knew it was flu.* ❖ συνοδεύω

3.15 bewilderment (n) /bɪˈwɪldəmənt/
confusion • *She felt terrible bewilderment when she could not remember her name.*
➢ bewildered (adj), bewildering (adj), bewilder (v) ❖ αμηχανία, σύγχυση

3.16 recollection (n) /rekəˈlekʃn/
memory of sth • *He has no recollection of the accident although he does remember the events leading up to it.* ➢ recollect (v)
❖ ανάμνηση

3.17 vast (adj) /vɑːst/
very large • *It would be impossible to count the vast number of hairs on one person's head.*
➢ vastness (n) ❖ τεράστιος

3.18 virus (n) /ˈvaɪrəs/
a microscopic living thing that causes disease • *There is a flu virus going around at the moment.* ❖ ιός

3.19 chunk (n) /tʃʌŋk/
a thick, solid piece of sth • *I ate a large chunk of cheese before lunch so I'm not very hungry now .* ❖ μεγάλο κομμάτι

3.20 literally (adv) /ˈlɪtərəli/
according to the original meaning of a word • *Literally millions of people watched the Olympic Games.* ➢ literal (adj) ❖ κυριολεκτικά

3.21 mixed blessing (expr) /mɪkst ˈblesɪŋ/
sth that has advantages and disadvantages • *Living here is a mixed blessing because although my friends live nearby, it is a noisy area.* ❖ ευχή και κατάρα

3.22 precise (adj) /prɪˈsaɪs/
exact • *The information she gave me was clear and precise.* ➢ precision (n), precisely (adj) ❖ ακριβής
✎ Opp: imprecise

3.23 insignificant (adj) /ɪnsɪɡˈnɪfɪkənt/
unimportant • *The price is insignificant; what matters is that you like the gift.* ➢ significance (n)
❖ ασήμαντος
✎ Opp: significant

3.24 **minor** (adj) /ˈmaɪnə/
small; less important • *It is hard to remember minor events because they tend not to make an impression on us.* ❖ ασήμαντος
✎ Opp: major

3.25 **task sb with sth** (expr) /tɑːsk ˈsʌmbədi wɪð ˈsʌmθɪŋ/
give sb the responsibility for doing sth • *I was tasked with writing up the minutes of our last meeting.* ❖ αναθέτω

Vocabulary   pages 34-35

3.26 **consult** (v) /kənˈsʌlt/
ask for expert advice • *He consulted a doctor about his constant headaches.* ➢ consultation (n), consultant (n) ❖ συμβουλεύομαι

3.27 **nurse** (v) /nɜːs/
care for a sick or injured person • *She nursed her brother when he had a high temperature.* ➢ nurse (n), nursing (n) ❖ φροντίζω

3.28 **practise** (v) /ˈpræk.tɪs/
work as a doctor, lawyer, etc. • *He wants to become a doctor and practise medicine in Africa.* ❖ ασκώ, εξασκώ (επάγγελμα)

3.29 **prescribe** (v) /prɪˈskraɪb/
(as a doctor) tell sb what medicine to take • *The doctor prescribed a course of antibiotics.* ➢ prescription (n) ❖ συνταγογράφω

3.30 **relieve** (v) /rɪˈliːv/
make pain or a bad feeling go away or become less • *Take an aspirin to relieve the pain.* ➢ relief (n), relieved (adj) ❖ ανακουφίζω

3.31 **respond** (v) /rɪˈspɒnd/
react positively • *The patient responded to the treatment and was allowed to leave the hospital.* ➢ response (n), responsive (adj) ❖ ανταποκρίνομαι

3.32 **sprain** (v) /spreɪn/
pull or twist • *I sprained my ankle and now I can't walk easily.* ➢ sprain (n) ❖ στραμπουλίζω

3.33 **emotional** (adj) /ɪˈməʊʃənl/
full of feeling • *She is very emotional and cries easily.* ➢ emotion (n) ❖ συναισθηματικός

3.34 **dehydrated** (adj) /ˌdiːhaɪˈdreɪtɪd/
having lost too much water from your body • *If you forget to drink water during the run, you risk getting dehydrated.* ➢ dehydrate (v), dehydration (n) ❖ αφυδατωμένος

3.35 **parched** (adj) /pɑːtʃt/
very dry • *It never rained in the desert and the soil was parched.* ❖ κατάξηρος

3.36 **muscular** (adj) /ˈmʌskjʊlə/
with strong, shapely muscles • *He works out every day to keep his body muscular.* ➢ muscle (n) ❖ μυώδης

3.37 **sane** (adj) /seɪn/
normal and reasonable • *The murderer was judged to be sane and fully aware of his actions.* ➢ sanity (n) ❖ λογικός, συνετός
✎ Opp: insane

3.38 **wholesome** (adj) /ˈhəʊlsəm/
good for your health • *We eat wholesome food like fruit, vegetables and nuts.* ❖ υγιεινός

3.39 **nutritious** (adj) /njuːˈtrɪʃəs/
full of substances that your body needs to be healthy or grow • *Children need nutritious food to help them grow.* ➢ nutrition (n) ❖ θρεπτικός

3.40 **beneficial** (adj) /ˌbenɪˈfɪʃl/
good or helpful • *Exercise and a good diet are beneficial to health.* ➢ benefit (v, n) ❖ ωφέλιμος

3.41 **delirium** (n) /dɪˈlɪriəm/
state of not being able to think or speak clearly, usually because of fever • *He was in a state of delirium when he ran into the road without looking.* ➢ delirious (adj) ❖ παραλήρημα

3.42 **hysteria** (n) /hɪˈstɪəriə/
violent and uncontrolled emotion • *She had a fit of hysteria and needed medication to calm down.* ➢ hysterical (adj) ❖ υστερία

3.43 **disorder** (n) /dɪsˈɔːdə/
a problem/illness of the mind or body • *He has a skin disorder which makes him excessively sensitive to the sun.* ❖ διαταραχή

3.44 **bony** (adj) /ˈbəʊni/
so thin that your bones show • *The bony model probably weighed about 48 kilos.* ➢ bone (n) ❖ κοκκαλιάρης

3.45 **anorexic** (adj) /ænəˈreksɪk/
suffering from a mental illness that makes sb stop eating • *She is anorexic so she finds it almost impossible to eat.* ➢ anorexia (n) ❖ ανορεξικός

3.46 **delicate** (adj) /ˈdelɪkət/
rather weak in health • *The delicate child could not go out in the cold without getting ill.* ❖ ευαίσθητος

3.47 **undernourished** (adj) /ˌʌndəˈnʌrɪʃt/
underfed • *The undernourished babies urgently needed food.* ❖ υποσιτιζόμενος

3.48 **forgetful** (adj) /fəˈgetfəl/
not able to remember things well • *He's forgetful so don't be surprised if he can't remember your name.* ➢ forget (v), forgetfulness (n) ❖ ξεχασιάρης

3.49 **contented** (adj) /kənˈtentɪd/
happy with life • *She felt contented just sitting in the garden and relaxing.* ➢ content (n) ❖ ευχαριστημένος, ικανοποιημένος

3.50 **scatty** (adj) /ˈskæti/
absent-minded and disorganised • *The scatty man was wearing one shoe and one sandal.* ❖ αφηρημένος

3.51 absent-minded (adj) /ˌæbsənt-ˈmaɪndɪd/
tending to forget things because you are thinking about sth else • *You're so absent-minded you forgot to meet me at the station again.* ❖ αφηρημένος

3.52 blood bank (n) /blʌd bæŋk/
a store of blood that can be used in hospitals • *She went to the blood bank to give blood.* ❖ τράπεζα αίματος

3.53 blood donor (n) /blʌd ˈdəʊnə/
sb who gives blood • *We need a blood donor to give blood to this patient.* ❖ αιμοδότης

3.54 intravenous (adj) /ˌɪntrəˈviːnəs/
through a vein • *An intravenous line was attached to his arm through which he was given medicine.* ➣ intravenously (adv) ❖ ενδοφλέβιος

3.55 blood pressure (n) /blʌd ˈpreʃə/
force with which blood flows around your body • *Low blood pressure can cause you to faint.* ❖ αρτηριακή πίεση

3.56 blood vessel (n) /blʌd ˈvesəl/
one of the tubes through which blood flows in your body • *Blood vessels are visible on the inside of your wrist.* ❖ αιμοφόρο αγγείο

3.57 blood transfusion (n) /blʌd trænsˈfjuːʒn/
putting blood from one person's body into the body of sb else as a medical treatment • *The patient had lost a lot of blood and needed a blood transfusion.* ❖ μετάγγιση αίματος

3.58 procedure (n) /prəˈsiːdʒə/
a way of doing sth • *The surgeon explained the procedure for the operation to the patient so that she knew what would happen.* ❖ διαδικασία

3.59 surgery (n) /ˈsɜːdʒəri/
an operation • *He needs heart surgery to unblock an artery.* ➣ surgeon (n), surgical (adj) ❖ χειρουργική επέμβαση

3.60 establish (v) /ɪsˈtæblɪʃ/
begin a relationship that will continue • *They have established a good relationship built on trust.* ➣ establishment (n), established (adj) ❖ καθιερώνω, τεκμηριώνω

3.61 donation (n) /dəʊˈneɪʃn/
the act of giving sth • *He makes a blood donation every three months at the blood bank.* ➣ donate (v), donor (n) ❖ δωρεά, αιμοδοσία

3.62 heal (v) /hiːl/
get better (of wound or cut) • *Your cut hand should heal in a couple of days.* ❖ επουλώνω, επουλώνομαι

3.63 recover (v) /rɪˈkʌvə/
get better from an illness • *It took her a long time to recover from pneumonia.* ➣ recovery (n) ❖ συνέρχομαι, αναρρώνω

3.64 injure (v) /ˈɪndʒə/
hurt • *Three people were injured when they slipped on ice.* ➣ injury (n), injured (adj) ❖ τραυματίζω

3.65 wound (v) /wuːnd/
injure sb, usually seriously, with a knife or gun • *The soldiers that were wounded were taken to hospital.* ➣ wound (n), wounded (adj) ❖ τραυματίζω

3.66 mortally (adv) /ˈmɔːtəli/
causing or resulting in death • *The man was mortally wounded in a fight and died an hour later.* ➣ mortal (adj), mortality (n) ❖ θανάσιμα

3.67 malaria (n) /məˈleərɪə/
a serious disease caused by the bite of a mosquito • *He got malaria and was very ill for weeks.* ❖ ελονοσία

3.68 swallow (v) /ˈswɒləʊ/
when sth goes from your mouth to your stomach • *Drink some water to help you swallow the pill.* ❖ καταπίνω

3.69 fever (n) /ˈfiːvə/
a high temperature • *If the thermometer reads more than 37°C, you have a fever.* ➣ feverish (adj) ❖ πυρετός

3.70 bark (n) /bɑːk/
the outside covering of a tree • *If you cut into the bark of this tree, it will drip resin.* ❖ φλοιός

3.71 miracle (n) /ˈmɪrəkl/
an event that is impossible according to the laws of nature • *It's a miracle that he wasn't injured in the crash.* ➣ miraculous (adj), miraculously (adv) ❖ θαύμα

3.72 tribe (n) /traɪb/
a group of people of the same race and with the same language and customs who live in a particular area • *I saw a documentary about a tribe who live in the Brazilian rainforest.* ➣ tribal (adj) ❖ φυλή

3.73 come down with (phr v) /kʌm daʊn wɪð/
get an illness • *I've come down with flu so I'll stay in bed.* ❖ αρρωσταίνω

3.74 fight off (phr v) /faɪt ɒf/
recover from an illness quickly • *She can always fight off a cold because she is so healthy.* ❖ καταπολεμώ

3.75 pass out (phr v) /pɑːs aʊt/
faint • *She passed out after standing in the sun for half an hour.* ❖ λιποθυμώ

3.76 pick up (phr v) /pɪk ʌp/
catch an illness from sb/sth • *He picked up a cold from somebody at work.* ❖ αρπάζω (ασθένεια)

3.77 take out (phr v) /teɪk aʊt/
remove sth • *The dentist took out her back tooth because it was rotten.* ❖ εξάγω, αφαιρώ

3.78 throw up (phr v) /θrəʊ ʌp/
vomit • *He threw up all over the carpet!* ❖ κάνω εμετό

3.79 **seasick** (adj) /ˈsiːˌsɪk/
nauseous from the movement of a boat • *I get seasick on boats, so I don't want to get the ferry to Crete.* ➢ seasickness (n) ❖ ναυτία

3.80 **wisdom tooth** (n) /ˈwɪsdəm tuːθ/
one of the large teeth at the back of your mouth • *His wisdom teeth began to show after he turned 18.* ❖ φρονιμίτης

3.81 **in agony** (expr) /ɪn ˈægəni/
in a lot of pain • *I was in agony when I broke my leg.* ❖ με φριχτούς πόνους

3.82 **bodily function** (expr) /ˈbɒdəli ˈfʌŋkʃn/
an organic process that takes place in the body • *Digestion is a bodily function.* ❖ σωματική λειτουργία

3.83 **failing eyesight** (expr) /ˈfeɪlɪŋ ˈaɪˌsaɪt/
gradual loss of the ability to see • *Because of her failing eyesight she can no longer read street signs at a distance.* ❖ μειωμένη όραση

3.84 **internal organ** (expr) /ɪnˈtɜːnəl ˈɔːgən/
a body part inside you • *He needs a donor for an internal organ, a heart in fact.* ❖ εσωτερικό όργανο

3.85 **terminal** (adj) /ˈtɜːmɪnəl/
fatal • *The doctor has given him three months to live because he has terminal cancer.* ❖ θανατηφόρος

3.86 **running sore** (n) /ˈrʌnɪŋ sɔː/
a sore area on the skin that has liquid coming out of it • *She had a running sore, so she went to the doctor.* ➢ sore (adj) ❖ πληγή, έλκος

3.87 **bruise** (n) /bruːz/
a blue, brown or purple mark on your skin that appears after you have fallen or been hit • *I got a nasty bruise on my knee where I hit it on the stool.* ➢ bruise (v) ❖ μελανιά

3.88 **gauze** (n) /gɔːz/
thin cotton cloth used for covering injuries like cuts and wounds • *The child had a gauze bandage around his hand.* ❖ γάζα

3.89 **fit** (n) /fɪt/
a short time when you cough, sneeze or laugh a lot in an uncontrollable way • *I get a sneezing fit whenever I sit in the garden.* ❖ επεισόδιο

3.90 **spasm** (n) /ˈspæzm/
uncontrollable tightening of your muscles • *The football player stopped running when he felt a spasm in his right thigh.* ❖ σπασμός

3.91 **imbalance** (n) /ɪmˈbæləns/
lack of balance • *Because of a chemical imbalance he takes these pills every day.* ❖ ανισορροπία
✎ Opp: balance

3.92 **inequality** (n) /ɪnɪˈkwɒləti/
lack of equality • *In some countries, inequality means that women are paid less for doing the same job a man does.* ❖ ανισότητα
✎ Opp: equality

3.93 **medication** (n) /medɪˈkeɪʃn/
medicine • *This flu medication must be taken twice a day.* ➢ medicate (v) ❖ φαρμακευτική αγωγή

3.94 **smashing** (adj) /ˈsmæʃɪŋ/
great • *That was a smashing meal. Is there any more food?* ❖ υπέροχος

3.95 **splitting headache** (adj) /ˈsplɪtɪŋ ˈhedeɪk/
a very bad headache • *He went to bed because he has a splitting headache.* ❖ έντονος πονοκέφαλος

3.96 **have a change of heart** (expr) /hæv ə tʃeɪndʒ ɒv hɑːt/
change your mind about sth • *She had a change of heart and decided to invite Bob after all.* ❖ αλλάζω γνώμη

3.97 **bite sb's head off** (expr) /baɪt ˈsʌmbədiz hed ɒf/
shout and get angry at sb • *Mum bit my head off when I asked her why she was angry.* ❖ φωνάζω σε κάποιο χωρίς λόγο

3.98 **get cold feet** (expr) /get kəʊld fiːt/
feel afraid to do sth at the last minute • *He didn't do the bungee jump because he got cold feet.* ❖ δειλιάζω

3.99 **be at each other's throats** (expr) /biː æt iːtʃ ˈʌðəz θrəʊts/
fight • *The sisters are at each other's throats again. They never stop fighting.* ❖ μαλώνω, τρώγομαι

3.100 **shout at the top of your lungs** (expr) /ʃaʊt æt ðə tɒp ɒv jɔː lʌŋz/
shout very loudly • *He shouted at the top of his lungs all through the football match.* ❖ φωνάζω όσο δυνατά μπορώ

3.101 **keep your chin up** (expr) /kiːp jɔː tʃɪn ʌp/
stay cheerful despite difficulties • *Keep your chin up; things could be worse.* ❖ κάνω κουράγιο

3.102 **turn a blind eye** (expr) /tɜːn ə blaɪnd aɪ/
deliberately ignore sth that you know should not be happening • *The teacher turned a blind eye to the students' bad behaviour on the last day of term.* ❖ κάνω τα στραβά μάτια

3.103 **be on the tip of your tongue** (expr) /biː ɒn ðə tɪp ɒv jɔː tʌŋ/
almost remember sth but not quite • *I know the word. It's on the tip of my tongue.* ❖ το 'χω στη γλώσσα μου, εδώ το έχω

Phrasal verbs

bring on	pick up
come down with	stem from
fight off	take out
get around	throw up
pass out	wipe out

Grammar   pages 36-37

3.104 dandruff (n) /ˈdændrʌf/
pieces of dead skin in your hair • *He uses a special shampoo to get rid of his dandruff.*
❖ πιτυρίδα

3.105 genetically modified (expr) /dʒəˈnetɪkli ˈmɒdɪfaɪd/
(food) that has had its DNA changed by genetic engineering • *Genetically modified food could harm your health.* ❖ γενετικά τροποποιημένα (τρόφιμα)

3.106 attention deficit disorder (ADD) (n) /əˈtenʃn ˈdefɪsɪt dɪsˈɔːdə/
a condition where sb cannot concentrate for long • *Her son has attention deficit disorder so he finds it hard to listen to a whole lesson.*
❖ σύνδρομο διάσπασης προσοχής

3.107 utterly (adv) /ˈʌtəli/
completely • *The film was utterly boring; don't go to see it.* ➢ utter (adj) ❖ εντελώς

3.108 stem from (phr v) /stem frɒm/
come from • *His back problem stems from an old football injury at school.*
❖ προέρχομαι από

3.109 soothing (adj) /ˈsuːðɪŋ/
calming; relaxing • *When she comes home from work, she likes to have a long, soothing bath.* ➢ soothe (v) ❖ καταπραϋντικός, χαλαρωτικός

3.110 gum (n) /gʌm/
pink flesh in your mouth that your teeth grow from • *She smiled so widely we could see her teeth and pink gums.* ❖ ούλο

Listening   page 38

3.111 plague (n) /pleɪg/
a disease that is usually fatal and spreads quickly to a large number of people • *The plague killed so many people in medieval times that they called it the Black Death.* ❖ πανούκλα

3.112 tooth decay (n) /tuːθ dɪˈkeɪ/
a chemical change that causes the slow destruction of the teeth • *He has terrible tooth decay because he eats sweets and does not brush his teeth.* ❖ τερηδόνα

3.113 sleep deprivation (n) /sliːp deprɪˈveɪʃn/
serious lack of sleep • *Sleep deprivation was a problem for the soldiers who had to guard the camp all night.* ❖ στέρηση ύπνου

3.114 lollipop (n) /ˈlɒlɪpɒp/
a hard sweet on a stick • *The child sucked the strawberry lollipop.* ❖ γλειφιτζούρι

3.115 bring on (phr v) /brɪŋ ɒn/
make sth unpleasant happen to sb • *Eating too much can bring on heart disease.*
❖ προκαλώ, επιφέρω

3.116 infectious (adj) /ɪnˈfekʃəs/
(disease) that can be passed easily from one person to another • *This flu is very infectious and everyone at work has got it.*
➢ infect (v), infection (n)
❖ μεταδοτικός, κολλητικός

3.117 medieval (adj) /ˌmediˈiːvl/
connected with the Middle Ages (about 1000AD to 1450AD) • *I'm interested in medieval history.* ❖ μεσαιωνικός

3.118 graveyard (n) /ˈgreɪvjɑːd/
an area of land, usually near a church, where people are buried • *We visited our grandparents' grave in the graveyard.* ❖ νεκροταφείο

3.119 conduct (v) /kənˈdʌkt/
do a particular activity like an experiment • *The scientists conducted a series of experiments.* ❖ διεξάγω, διενεργώ

3.120 sample (n) /ˈsɑːmpl/
a small quantity of sth that is examined in order to find out sth about the whole • *They examined a sample of the suspect's DNA.* ➢ sample (v) ❖ δείγμα

3.121 severe (adj) /səˈvɪə/
serious • *He has got severe symptoms so I recommend he goes to hospital.* ➢ severity (n)
❖ σοβαρός

3.122 rodent (n) /ˈrəʊdənt/
a small animal with sharp teeth, eg a rat, a mouse • *Rats and mice are common rodents.*
❖ τρωκτικό

3.123 contract (v) /kənˈtrækt/
get an illness • *You can contract this disease by drinking dirty water.* ❖ κολλάω (ασθένεια), προσβάλλομαι

3.124 flea (n) /fliː/
a jumping insect that bites people or animals to eat their blood • *This dog might have fleas because it keeps scratching.* ❖ ψύλλος

Speaking   page 39

3.125 conventional (adj) /kənˈvenʃənl/
traditional; used for a long time and considered normal • *I have great faith in conventional medicine.* ➢ convention (n) ❖ συμβατικός
✎ Opp: unconventional

3.126 alternative (adj) /ɔːlˈtɜːnətɪv/
not based on the usual western methods • *She is going to try some alternative treatments to get rid of the spots on her face.*
➢ alternative (n) ❖ εναλλακτικός

3.127 preventative measure (expr) /prɪˈventətɪv ˈmeʒə/
an action taken to stop sth happening • *A preventative measure against heartdisease is regular exercise.*
❖ προληπτικό μέτρο

3.128 **wellbeing** (n) /welˈbiːɪŋ/
general health • *Your parents care about your happiness and wellbeing.* ❖ ευημερία

3.129 **safeguard** (v) /ˈseɪfɡɑːd/
protect • *Take plenty of exercise to safeguard your health.* ❖ διαφυλάσσω, διασφαλίζω

3.130 **CPR** (abbr) /ˌsiː piː ˈɑː/
breathing air into sb's mouth and pressing on their chest to keep them alive • *The paramedic gave the child CPR and saved his life.* ❖ τεχνητή αναπνοή, καρδιοπνευμονική αναζωογόνηση (ΚΑΡΠΑ)
✎ CPR: cardiopulmonary resuscitation

3.131 **organic produce** (n) /ɔːˈɡænɪk ˈprɒdjuːs/
fruit, vegetables and other food grown or made without using artificial chemicals • *They sell organic produce at the local market.*
❖ προϊόντα βιολογικής καλλιέργειας

3.132 **paramedic** (n) /pærəˈmedɪk/
sb who is trained to give medical help • *The paramedic gave the injured man first aid in the ambulance.* ❖ μέλος παραϊατρικού προσωπικού

3.133 **dispense** (v) /dɪˈspens/
prepare medicines and give them to people • *A pharmacy dispenses medicines and gives advice about minor health problems.*
❖ παρασκευάζω και χορηγώ (φάρμακο)

3.134 **resuscitation** (n) /rɪsʌsɪˈteɪʃn/
breathing into the mouth of an unconscious person to help them breathe • *The man stopped breathing and needed resuscitation.*
➢ resuscitate (v) ❖ τεχνητή αναπνοή

3.135 **side-effect** (n) /saɪd-ɪˈfekt/
an undesirable effect that a drug has on your body as well as treating illness • *One side-effect of this medication is that it makes you feel sleepy.* ❖ παρενέργεια

3.136 **stretcher** (n) /ˈstretʃə/
canvas on poles used to carry an ill or injured person • *The injured player was carried off the field on a stretcher.* ❖ φορείο

3.137 **vaccination** (n) /væksɪˈneɪʃn/
the act of putting a substance into a person's body to prevent them from getting a disease • *Babies have their first vaccinations when they are three months old to protect them from serious diseases.* ➢ vaccinate (v) ❖ εμβολιασμός

Making you better

consult	prescribe
heal	recover
medication	relieve
monitor	resuscitation
nurse	surgery
paramedic	vaccination

Writing: an information sheet
pages 40-41

3.138 **succinct** (adj) /səkˈsɪŋkt/
using only a few words • *His explanation was short and succinct.* ➢ succinctly (adv)
❖ σύντομος, συνοπτικός

3.139 **heat stroke** (n) /hiːt strəʊk/
fever caused by very high temperatures • *The temperature was 45°C and some people suffered from heat stroke.* ❖ θερμοπληξία

3.140 **fibre** (n) /ˈfaɪbə/
thread that form materials such as cotton and linen • *In the summer, I wear clothes made from natural fibres.* ❖ ίνα

3.141 **hassle-free** (adj) /ˈhæsəl-friː/
with no problems • *We had a hassle-free journey as there was no traffic.* ❖ χωρίς ταλαιπωρία

3.142 **creepy-crawly** (n) /ˈkriːpi-ˈkrɔːli/
an insect, spider, worm, etc. • *There was a big creepy-crawly that looked like a beetle on the plant.* ❖ ζουζούνι

3.143 **mosquito** (n) /mɒsˈkiːtəʊ/
a small flying insect that sucks blood and may spread disease • *She got bitten by mosquitoes while she slept in the tent.* ❖ κουνούπι

3.144 **a pain in the neck** (expr) /ə peɪn ɪn ðə nek/
sth annoying • *Having so much homework is a pain in the neck.* ❖ βάσανο, κακός μπελάς

3.145 **insect repellent** (n) /ˈɪnsekt rɪˈpelənt/
a substance that keeps insects away • *We sprayed on insect repellent to stop being bitten by mosquitoes.* ❖ εντομοαπωθητικό

3.146 **get around** (phr v) /ɡet əˈraʊnd/
go from place to place • *She gets around the city on her bicycle.* ❖ κυκλοφορώ

3.147 **cope** (v) /kəʊp/
manage; deal with • *I've got too much work and I can't cope with everything.*
❖ αντεπεξέρχομαι, τα καταφέρνω

Disease carriers

creepy-crawly	mosquito
flea	rodent

Video 3: Paraguay Shaman
page 42

3.148 **shaman** (n) /ˈʃeɪmən/
a person in some religions and societies who can contact spirits and cure sick people • *The members of the tribe consulted the shaman when they got sick.* ❖ σαμάνος

3.149 **root** (n) /ruːt/
part of a plant which is under the ground • *The roots of this tree go deep into the ground.* ❖ ρίζα

3.150 **diabetes** (n) /daɪəˈbiːtiːz/
a condition when sb has too much sugar in their blood • *If you have diabetes, you must be very careful about your diet.* ➢ diabetic (adj, n) ❖ σακχαρώδης διαβήτης, ζάχαρο

3.151 **transmit** (v) /trænzˈmɪt/
pass sth from one person to another • *Flu can be transmitted through the air, when people sneeze, for example.* ❖ μεταδίδω

3.152 **chant** (n) /tʃɑːnt/
word(s) repeated over and over • *The children learnt the alphabet with an abc chant.* ➢ chant (v) ❖ επαναλαμβάνω ρυθμικά

3.153 **deforestation** (n) /diːfɒrɪsˈteɪʃn/
destruction of the forests • *The deforestation of this area means that many animal species have lost their homes.* ➢ deforest (v) ❖ αποψίλωση των δασών

3.154 **extensive** (adj) /ɪksˈtensɪv/
containing a lot of information and details • *He wrote an extensive report on the disease that was a thousand pages long.* ➢ extent (n) ❖ εκτενής

3.155 **healer** (n) /ˈhiːlə/
sb who can make sick people well • *The healer gave the sick man some herbs that would make him better.* ➢ heal (v) ❖ θεραπευτής

3.156 **potential** (adj) /pəˈtenʃl/
possible • *Deforestation of the Amazon is a potential disaster for the whole world.* ➢ potential (n) ❖ δυνητικός, πιθανός

3.157 **prayer** (n) /preə/
words spoken to a god • *He said a prayer to God to ask for good health.* ➢ pray (v) ❖ προσευχή

3.158 **urgent** (adj) /ˈɜːdʒənt/
needing to be done soon • *He needs urgent medical treatment as he seems to be having a heart attack.* ➢ urgency (n), urgently (adv) ❖ επείγων

Needing medical attention

amnesia	malaria
anorexic	plague
diabetes	running sore
disorder	side-effect
failing eyesight	sprain
fever	tooth decay
heat stroke	undernourished
hysteria	virus

Vocabulary Exercises

A Complete the phrasal verbs in these sentences.

1 He has _____ down with a bad cold.
2 I feel sick and I think I'm going to _____ up.
3 Do you think the dentist will have to _____ out my wisdom teeth?
4 Where did you _____ up that bad cough?
5 Did the shock _____ out his memory of the incident?
6 He managed to _____ off the flu, but his wife was ill for a long time.
7 I feel faint. I hope I don't _____ out.
8 The dust and air pollution _____ on an attack of asthma.

B Choose the correct answers.

1 He outlined the requirements of the report ___ in just a few minutes.
   a utterly   b succinctly   c literally

2 The tsunami ___ the coastline, leaving nothing standing.
   a ravaged   b wounded   c healed

3 I have a(n) ___ headache from looking at the screen for too long.
   a splitting   b vast   c infectious

4 Jane has ___ memories of the war, when she was just a child.
   a severe   b oblivious   c vivid

35

5 Many diseases can be ___ in saliva from one person to another.
  a depicted   b transmitted   c recalled

6 The patient ___ well to the treatment he received.
  a prescribed   b relieved   c responded

7 She suffers from ___ in new situations, so she takes medication to stay calm.
  a anxiety   b madness   c malaria

8 He gets more ___ as he grows older, so he keeps a diary to remind him of things he has done.
  a seasick   b forgetful   c emotional

C Match.

1 running   a crawly
2 creepy   b deprivation
3 preventative   c repellent
4 sleep   d function
5 mixed   e eyesight
6 blood   f measure
7 insect   g decay
8 failing   h blessing
9 bodily   i transfusion
10 tooth   j sore

D Choose the correct answers.

1 If something is **a pain in the neck**, it
  a is very annoying.   b hurts a lot.

2 People who **are always at each other's throats**
  a fight a lot.   b embrace a lot.

3 A **terminal** condition
  a can be cured.   b cannot be cured.

4 If you **get cold feet**, you will probably
  a refuse to do something.   b soon feel unwell.

5 A **hassle-free** holiday would have
  a no problems.   b many problems.

6 If you **keep your chin up**, you
  a stay cheerful.   b boast about yourself.

7 A **prayer** is something you say to
  a a healer.   b a god.

8 **Dandruff** is a condition that can be improved by
  a using medicated shampoo.
  b having a vaccination.

3 Grammar

3.1 Demonstrative Pronouns

Οι demonstrative pronouns (δεικτικές αντωνυμίες) είναι *this, that, these* και *those*. Τις χρησιμοποιούμε για να αναφερθούμε σε ένα ή περισσότερα πράγματα που βρίσκονται κοντά ή πιο μακριά.
→ Do you need **this**?
→ **Those** are better than **these**.

Χρησιμοποιούμε demonstrative pronouns για να αναφερθούμε και σε πρόσωπα.
→ Hi, **this** is Ken speaking. Is **that** Irene?

3.2 Reflexive Pronouns

Οι reflexive pronouns (αυτοπαθείς αντωνυμίες) αναφέρονται στο υποκείμενο μιας πρότασης. Χρησιμοποιούνται:
για να δώσουμε έμφαση στο υποκείμενο (subject).
→ My mother **herself** realised she was dehydrated and called the doctor.
όταν το υποκείμενο (subject) και το αντικείμενο (object) είναι ίδια.
→ I cut **myself** while shaving.
μετά από πρόθεση όταν το υποκείμενο και το αντικείμενο ταυτίζονται.
→ Frank is proud of **himself** because he has been exercising regularly.

3.3 Indefinite Pronouns

Υπάρχουν δύο είδη indefinite pronouns (αόριστες αντωνυμίες). Η πρώτη κατηγορία περιλαμβάνει αντωνυμίες που αναφέρονται σε αόριστα ουσιαστικά (non-specific nouns). Τέτοιες αντωνυμίες είναι οι: *anybody, anyone, anything, everyone, everybody, everything, nobody, no one, none, nothing, somebody, someone, something*.
→ Simon remembers **everyone** from school but **no one** from the neighbourhood.
→ I haven't talked to **anyone** about the accident.

Η δεύτερη κατηγορία περιλαμβάνει αντωνυμίες που αναφέρονται σε συγκεκριμένο ουσιαστικό (specific noun), του οποίου το νόημα είναι εύκολα κατανοητό είτε γιατί είχε αναφερθεί προηγουμένα είτε γιατί το κάνουν σαφές οι λέξεις που ακολουθούν την αόριστη αντωνυμία. Αυτές οι αντωνυμίες είναι *all, any, each, few, neither, some, another, both, either, many, one, several*.
→ **Many** people suffer from sleep deprivation but **few** consult a doctor about it.

3.4 Reciprocal Pronouns

Οι reciprocal pronouns (αλληλοπαθείς αντωνυμίες) αναφέρονται σε ουσιαστικά πληθυντικού αριθμού ή σε δύο ή περισσότερα ουσιαστικά. Χρησιμοποιούμε reciprocal pronouns όταν μιλάμε για μια αμοιβαία πράξη ή ένα αμοιβαίο αίσθημα.
→ They sprayed insect repellent on **each other**.
Οι reciprocal pronouns έχουν και κτητικό τύπο.
→ My parents often talked about **one another's** childhood memories.

3.5 Adverbs και Adverb Phrases

Ένα adverb (επίρρημα) μπορεί να είναι μια μόνο λέξη, ή φράση ή πρόταση.
→ Tourists use public transport **often**.
→ Tourists use public transport **with ease**.
→ Tourists use public transport **when they know their destination**.
→ Tourists use public transport **to save money on fares**.

3.6 Adverb Forms

Τα περισσότερα μονολεκτικά επιρρήματα έχουν την κατάληξη *-ly*, που συνήθως δηλώνει τροπικό επίρρημα. Άλλα μονολεκτικά επιρρήματα (τόπου, χρόνου κλπ) δεν έχουν κατάληξη *-ly*, πχ: *always, soon, today, ever, yet, away, here, so, too*.
→ I'll leave the newspaper **here** for Martha.
→ He has **always** been absent-minded.

3 Grammar

Ορισμένα adverbs έχουν δύο τύπους, πχ: *wide/widely, hard/hardly, high/highly, slow/slowly, late/lately, close/closely*. Σε αυτές τις περιπτώσεις η σημασία τους είναι διαφορετική.
→ *Vera tried **hard** not to throw up on the ship.*
→ *He **hardly** drinks any water, even when it's hot.*

3.7 Intensifying Adverbs

Χρησιμοποιούμε intensifying adverbs (επιρρήματα διαβάθμισης):
για να προσδιορίσουμε επίθετα.
→ *Visiting your dentist is **absolutely necessary**.*
για να προσδιορίσουμε άλλα επιρρήματα.
→ *He completed the report on the accident **incredibly fast**.*

Grammar Exercises

A Choose the correct answers.

1 The paramedic ___ said that first aid had saved your life.
   a himself   b itself   c yourself

2 ___ of these pills are out of date.
   a Any   b Some   c Something

3 The twins really love ___ other.
   a one   b each   c all

4 ___ who need eye surgery can consult the specialist.
   a Someone   b These   c Those

5 Some foods are beneficial, but ___ should be eaten in moderation.
   a all   b any   c anything

6 I need some vitamins. ___ look cheaper than those over there.
   a Those   b These   c This

7 They often help one ___ to write assignments.
   a each   b other   c another

8 Are you enjoying ___, children?
   a yourself   b yourselves   c themselves

B Complete the sentences with the words below.

| anything | herself | much | one's | others | that | this | those |

1 Stress has a negative effect on _____ health.
2 Not _____ is known about the benefits of antibiotics.
3 _____ you can do to help will be appreciated.
4 _____ who talked to the shaman felt better afterwards.
5 She often asked _____ how she could relieve stress.
6 Some people listen to music to relax while _____ take up a sport.
7 _____ dental care leaflet looks informative, whereas that one seems too complicated.
8 'My son is studying medicine.' '_____ is interesting.'

C Circle the correct words.

1. The dentist will see you **in / when** ten minutes.
2. I will give you the injection **to / when** you are ready.
3. **Oddly / Odd** enough, he wasn't worried about having surgery.
4. The nurse will see you **now / to** monitor your progress.
5. He arrived **late / lately** for the meeting.
6. She has been improving **slow / slowly**.
7. He was **wide / widely** awake when the earthquake struck.
8. I only go to the doctor **when it absolutely / when absolutely** necessary.
9. **Strange / Strangely**, he refused to consult another doctor.
10. Please tell the dentist to stop the procedure if at any time you feel **uncomfortable / uncomfortably**.

Exam Task

For questions 1-10, read the text below. Use the word at the end of some of the lines to form a word that fits the gap in the same line.

Alternative therapies

A number of people turn to alternative medicine when the effect of mainstream treatments appears to be (1) _____ or has no results. Some choose homeopathy and others opt for hypnotherapy or faith healing. They hope to cure (2) _____ diseases or alleviate the pain of (3) _____ with methods which are not approved by the scientific community. So why do people turn their backs on mainstream medicine that is proven to be (4) _____ and scientifically sound? Perhaps it is (5) _____ caused by cold, white-coated doctors who deal with each 'case' before moving swiftly on to the next. Modern medics are often in a hurry and many seem (6) _____ to their patients' need for compassion and the personal touch. If patients do not understand their treatments or feel cut off from having any say in the procedures that are to be carried out, they are likely to suffer from (7) _____. Should doctors ignore this, a patient may well seek an alternative opinion. This is where alternative therapies are a popular option. Homeopaths, hypnotherapists and faith healers usually give each patient all the time they desire because they are private consultants. They are paid to listen. Talking to a (8) _____ could have a placebo effect, which is why alternative therapies are sought after. But people should beware of (9) _____ prescribed by someone who is not a qualified doctor. Some alternative therapists are (10) _____ unscrupulous, so background checks should be carried out before consultations take place.

SIGNIFICANCE

INFECTION
INJURE

PRECISION
BEWILDER

OBLIVION

ANXIOUS

HEAL

MEDICATE
UTTER

4 Lights, Camera, Action!

Word Focus — page 44

4.1 film buff (n) /fɪlm bʌf/
sb who is very interested in cinema • *Film buffs try to see every new movie that comes out.* ❖ λάτρης ταινιών

4.2 footage (n) /ˈfʊtɪdʒ/
film showing a particular event • *We saw footage of the 1969 Moon landing.* ❖ πλάνα αρχείου

4.3 inundate (v) /ˈɪnʌndeɪt/
give or send sb more things than they can deal with • *The celebrity was inundated with questions about his private life.* ❖ κατακλύζω

4.4 unravel (v) /ʌnˈrævl/
unfold • *The story slowly unravels during this film.* ❖ ξετυλίγω

4.5 pterosaur (n) /ˈterəsɔːr/
an extinct reptile that could fly • *We saw the bones of a pterosaur at the natural history museum.* ❖ πτερόσαυρος

Reading — pages 44-45

4.6 still (n) /stɪl/
a photograph from a film • *Look at these stills from the film.* ❖ στιγμιότυπο, καρέ

4.7 soundtrack (n) /ˈsaʊndtræk/
music for a film • *The soundtrack for many films is available on CD.* ❖ μουσική ταινίας

4.8 taste (n) /teɪst/
the kind of things that sb likes • *She has very bad taste in films – she only watches romantic comedies.* ➢ tasteful (adj) ❖ γούστο

4.9 blockbuster (n) /ˈblɒkbʌstə/
a successful film • *The blockbuster film The Hobbit was amazing.* ❖ μπλοκμπάστερ, επιτυχία (κινηματογραφική)

4.10 sugary-sweet (adj) /ˈʃʊɡəri-swiːt/
too nice and therefore insincere • *The sugary-sweet film ended with everyone living happily ever after.* ❖ πολύ ιδεαλιστικός

4.11 exhilarating (adj) /ɪɡˈzɪləreɪtɪŋ/
making you excited, happy and full of energy • *He felt great after an exhilarating run.* ➢ exhilarate (v), exhilaration (n) ❖ απολαυστικός, ευφρόσυνος

4.12 director (n) /daɪˈrektə/
a person in charge of how a film is made • *Francis Ford Coppola was the director of the three Godfather films.* ➢ direct (v) ❖ σκηνοθέτης

4.13 contributor (n) /kənˈtrɪbjʊtə/
sb who makes videos that are then posted online • *YouTube contributors post some entertaining videos.* ➢ contribute (v) ❖ συνεργάτης, χρήστης

4.14 submit (v) /sʌbˈmɪt/
give a form, article of other piece of writing to sb so they can approve or accept it • *He submitted his report to the committee.* ➢ submission (n) ❖ παραδίδω, υποβάλλω

4.15 make up (phr v) /meɪk ʌp/
form • *This exhibition is made up of photos from all over the world.* ❖ αποτελώ

4.16 shoot (v) /ʃuːt/
film • *They are shooting the car chase scenes for the film at the moment.* ➢ shot (n) ❖ γυρίζω (ταινία κλπ)

4.17 sift through (phr v) /sɪft θruː/
look through sth carefully • *I sifted through her papers to find her birth certificate.* ❖ ψάχνω

4.18 paste together (expr) /peɪst təˈɡeðə/
join • *Let's paste together these funny cat videos and post them online.* ❖ κολλώ

4.19 feature-length (adj) /ˈfiːtʃə-leŋθ/
as long as a film, usually 90 minutes approximately • *The documentary was as long as a feature-length film.* ❖ κανονικού μήκους ταινία

4.20 heart-warming (adj) /ˈhɑːt-ˈwɑːmɪŋ/
touching in a happy way • *She enjoyed the heart-warming film about a rescue dog that found a home.* ❖ συγκινητικός

4.21 deny (v) /dɪˈnaɪ/
refuse to give sb sth • *His parents denied him the chance to join the basketball team because they insisted he focus on his studies.* ➢ denial (n) ❖ στερώ

4.22 veteran (n) /ˈvetərən/
sb who has been a soldier in a war • *My great-grandfather was a veteran of the Second World War.* ❖ βετεράνος

4.23 desperate (adj) /ˈdesprət/
in a bad situation and willing to do anything • *I was desperate to get my injured dog to the vet.* ➢ desperation (n), desperately (adv) ❖ απελπισμένος

4.24 application (n) /æplɪˈkeɪʃn/
form you fill in to apply for sth • *He submitted an application to the adult education centre to do a course in German.* ➢ apply (v), applicant (n) ❖ αίτηση

4.25 fierce opposition (expr) /fɪəs ɒpəˈsɪʃn/
strong resistance • *The mayor faced fierce*

4.26 **cutting-edge** (adj) /ˈkʌtɪŋ ˌedʒ/
opposition from the locals who did not want a car park to be built in town. ❖ έντονη αντίθεση

4.26 **cutting-edge** (adj) /ˈkʌtɪŋ ˌedʒ/
the newest; the most advanced • *This smartphone features some cutting-edge technology.* ❖ πρωτοποριακός

4.27 **dominant** (adj) /ˈdɒmɪnənt/
the most powerful and important • *Humans are the most dominant species on Earth.*
➢ dominate (v), dominance (n) ❖ κυρίαρχος

4.28 **fall to** (phr v) /fɔːl tuː/
be the responsibility of • *It fell to me to give Mary the bad news because nobody else had the strength to do it.* ❖ πέφτει σε (κάποιον να)

4.29 **reptile** (n) /ˈreptaɪl/
a cold-blooded animal like a snake • *Crocodiles are extremely dangerous reptiles.* ❖ ερπετό

4.30 **defy** (v) /dɪˈfaɪ/
not happen according to what you would expect • *His ability to stay underwater for so long defies belief.* ➢ defiance (n)
❖ είμαι απερίγραπτος/απίστευτος

4.31 **gravity** (n) /ˈɡrævɪti/
force that makes things fall to the ground
• *Gravity was the force that the first plane designers had to contend with.* ❖ βαρύτητα

4.32 **state-of-the-art** (adj) /steɪt-əv-ðiː-ˈɑːt/
the most modern and developed • *The new smartphone uses state-of-the-art technology.*
❖ τελευταίας τεχνολογίας

4.33 **capture** (v) /ˈkæptʃə/
express successfully • *Your book captures the atmosphere of the 1950s perfectly.*
❖ εκφράζω, απαθανατίζω

4.34 **electrifying** (adj) /ɪˈlektrɪfaɪɪŋ/
very exciting • *He gave an electrifying performance and the audience loved him.*
➢ electrify (v) ❖ συγκλονιστικός, συναρπαστικός

4.35 **immersed** (adj) /ɪˈmɜːsd/
become completely involved in an activity
• *He was so immersed in the video game he didn't hear the phone.* ❖ βυθισμένος

4.36 **ecstatic** (adj) /ɪkˈstætɪk/
very happy and enthusiastic • *I was ecstatic when I heard I had won first prize.*
➢ ecstasy (n) ❖ εκστασιασμένος

4.37 **heart-rending** (adj) /ˈhɑːt-ˌrendɪŋ/
touching in a very sad way • *The heart-rending film about the death of a man with AIDS made me cry.* ❖ σπαραχτικός

4.38 **tender age** (expr) /ˈtendə eɪdʒ/
young and innocent age • *He wrote his first book at the tender age of 12.* ❖ τρυφερή ηλικία

4.39 **flee** (v) /fliː/
run away from • *When he realised he would be prosecuted, the government minister fled the country.* ❖ το σκάω

4.40 **daring** (adj) /ˈdeərɪŋ/
willing to do dangerous things • *This book is about a daring escape from prison.*
➢ dare (v, n) ❖ τολμηρός

4.41 **marry off** (phr v) /ˈmæri ɒf/
find a husband or wife for sb • *She was married off to a rich man because her family needed money.* ❖ με παντρεύουν

4.42 **track down** (phr v) /træk daʊn/
find • *She tracked down her relatives in the USA through Facebook.* ❖ εντοπίζω

4.43 **catwalk** (n) /ˈkætwɔːk/
the long structure where models walk in fashion shows • *The model walked down the catwalk in a beautiful dress.* ❖ πασαρέλα

4.44 **enlist** (v) /ɪnˈlɪst/
persuade sb to help you to do sth • *He enlisted the help of a private detective to find the stolen painting.* ❖ επιστρατεύω

4.45 **illiterate** (adj) /ɪˈlɪtərət/
unable to read or write • *The illiterate man asked me to tell him what was written on the form.* ➢ illiteracy (n) ❖ αναλφάβητος, αγράμματος
✎ Opp: literate

4.46 **portray** (v) /pɔːˈtreɪ/
represent • *He portrays a spy in this film.*
➢ portrayal (n) ❖ απεικονίζω

4.47 **struggle** (n) /ˈstrʌɡl/
a period of time when sb tries to deal with a difficult problem • *It was a struggle to get into college but he managed it.* ➢ struggle (v)
❖ αγώνας

4.48 **faint-hearted** (adj) /ˈfeɪnt-ˌhɑːtɪd/
scared of anything that is not safe • *This scary rollercoaster isn't for the faint-hearted.*
❖ δειλός

Vocabulary pages 46-47

4.49 **aisle** (n) /aɪl/
a narrow gap between seats in a cinema or theatre • *We walked down the aisle to the front seats.* ❖ στενός διάδρομος (μεταξύ σειρών καθισμάτων κινηματογράφου, θεάτρου κλπ)

4.50 **backstage** (n) /ˈbæksteɪdʒ/
behind the stage • *The actors waited quietly backstage for their cue to go on.*
❖ παρασκήνια

4.51 **foyer** (n) /ˈfɔɪə/
the entrance area of a cinema, theatre, etc.
• *Let's meet in the cinema foyer, where we can get something to drink.* ❖ φουαγιέ

4.52 **interval** (n) /ˈɪntəvl/
a break in the middle of film or play • *We bought popcorn and lemonade during the interval.* ❖ διάλειμμα

4.53 **row** (n) /rəʊ/
a line of seats • *Our seats are in row 14.* ❖ σειρά

4.54 **set** (n) /set/
scenery for a play • *The set for the play was an ordinary living room.* ❖ σκηνικά

4.55 **usher** (n) /'ʌʃə/
sb who shows you to your seat • *The usher showed us our seats.* ❖ ταξιθέτης θεάτρου

4.56 **wings** (pl n) /wɪŋz/
the side of a stage where actors are hidden from the audience • *The dancers who were on next waited in the wings.* ❖ παρασκήνια

4.57 **minimalist** (adj) /'mɪnɪməlɪst/
using only a very few simple ideas or elements • *They decorated their home in a minimalist style.* ➣ minimalism (n) ❖ μινιμαλιστικός

4.58 **chick flick** (n) /tʃɪk flɪk/
a film made especially for women • *My brother hates watching chick flicks. He thinks they're stupid.* ❖ ταινία για/που έχει απήχηση σε γυναίκες

4.59 **tear-jerker** (n) /'tɪə-ˌdʒɜːkə/
a film that makes you cry • *Steel Magnolias is a tear-jerker of a film and it always makes me cry.* ❖ δακρύβρεκτο μελό

4.60 **woe** (n) /wəʊ/
great sadness • *I didn't enjoy this tale of woe because I can't stand sad stories.* ❖ λύπη, συμφορά, βάσανο

4.61 **exploitable** (adj) /ɪksˈplɔɪtəbl/
used to gain an advantage for yourself • *Canada is a huge country with many exploitable resources.* ➣ exploit (v, n), exploitation (n) ❖ εκμεταλλεύσιμος

4.62 **tug at sb's heartstrings** (expr) /tʌg ət ˈsʌmbədiz ˈhɑːtstrɪŋz/
cause sb to feel strong love or pity • *The final scene of the film tugs at your heartstrings. It's very moving.* ❖ αγγίζω τις ευαίσθητες χορδές κάποιου, συγκινώ

4.63 **underdog** (n) /'ʌndədɒg/
sb who is least likely to succeed • *The crowd cheered the underdog, who had the lowest score.* ❖ αουτσάιντερ

4.64 **chic** (adj) /ʃiːk/
elegant; fashionable • *She's very chic and dresses beautifully.* ➣ chic (n) ❖ σικ, κομψός

4.65 **allure** (n) /əˈljʊə/
attraction • *The allure of working in films brings many hopeful actors to Hollywood.* ➣ alluring (adj) ❖ θέλγητρο, γοητεία

4.66 **reveal** (v) /rɪˈviːl/
make people aware of sth • *He revealed that he was a government spy.* ➣ revelation (n) ❖ αποκαλύπτω

4.67 **release** (v) /rɪˈliːs/
make music, a film, etc. available for people to buy or see • *When will the next Jason Bourne film be released?* ➣ release (n) ❖ κυκλοφορώ

4.68 **rehearse** (v) /rɪˈhɜːs/
practise before a show • *The actors rehearsed the scene before it was shot.* ➣ rehearsal (n) ❖ κάνω πρόβες

4.69 **heartthrob** (n) /ˈhɑːtθrɒb/
an attractive man that women find very attractive • *I don't know why, but some teenage girls think Justin Bieber is a real heartthrob.* ❖ κούκλος

4.70 **compile** (v) /kəmˈpaɪl/
collect and put together • *The group has compiled a list of their best songs on this album.* ➣ compilation (n) ❖ συλλέγω

4.71 **rank** (v) /ræŋk/
put in order of importance • *Which film is ranked number 1 at the moment?* ➣ rank (n) ❖ κατατάσσω (βαθμολογικά)

4.72 **animate** (v) /ˈænɪmeɪt/
bring to life in cartoon form • *Walt Disney animated the story of Snow White.* ➣ animation (n) ❖ δημιουργώ κινούμενα σχέδια

4.73 **crucial** (adj) /ˈkruːʃl/
very important • *Comedy has always played a crucial role in theatre.* ❖ ζωτικός, αποφασιστικός, κρίσιμος

4.74 **deem** (v) /diːm/
consider • *An Oscar is deemed to be an important award in the film industry.* ❖ θεωρώ

4.75 **dressing room** (n) /ˈdresɪŋ ruːm/
a room where actors put on clothes and make-up before a play • *The actor changed into his costume in his dressing room.* ❖ καμαρίνι

4.76 **female lead** (n) /ˈfiːmeɪl liːd/
the main role for a woman • *Meryl Streep played the female lead in the film* The Iron Lady. ❖ κύριος γυναικείος ρόλος

4.77 **title role** (n) /ˈtaɪtl rəʊl/
the role of the character whose name is in the title of a film or play • *Lambros Kostantaras played the title role in many Finos Films.* ❖ κύριος ρόλος

4.78 **stage fright** (n) /steɪdʒ fraɪt/
nervousness before performing in front of an audience • *He got stage fright and refused to perform.* ❖ τρακ

4.79 **dress rehearsal** (n) /dres rɪˈhɜːsl/
final practice before the first performance where actors wear their costumes • *In the dress rehearsal, a few changes to the costumes were made.* ❖ πρόβα τζενεράλε

4.80 **cast** (n) /kɑːst/
people who act in a play or film • *The Skyfall cast includes Daniel Craig as Bond and Javier Bardem as Silva.* ➣ cast (v) ❖ όλοι οι ηθοποιοί που εμφανίζονται σε μια ταινία, θίασος

4.81 **opening night** (n) /ˈəʊpənɪŋ naɪt/
the first public performance of a play or show • *The actors felt nervous on opening night and hoped the play would be a success.* ❖ πρεμιέρα

4.82 **standing ovation** (n) /ˈstændɪŋ əʊˈveɪʃn/
when the audience stand up and clap in appreciation • *The audience were so impressed that they gave the orchestra a standing ovation.*
❖ ενθουσιώδεις επευφημίες, με το κοινό να στέκεται όρθιο

4.83 **showbiz** (n) /ˈʃəʊbɪz/
the business of entertainment • *He enjoys being in showbiz as he adores all the attention he gets.* ❖ στη σόουμπιζ

4.84 **flamboyantly** (adv) /flæmˈbɔɪəntli/
noticeably loud and stylish • *He dresses flamboyantly in silk shirts and colourful ties.*
➣ flamboyance (n), flamboyant (adj)
❖ επιδεικτικά

4.85 **in character** (expr) /ɪn ˈkærɪktə/
in the role an actor is playing • *He tried to stay in character off the set so he could get used to the role.* ❖ στο ρόλο που υποδύομαι

4.86 **crew** (n) /kruː/
a group of people with special skills who work together • *The crew prepared the set for the filming of the indoor scenes.*
❖ (κινηματογραφικό) συνεργείο

4.87 **extra** (n) /ˈekstrə/
an actor with a small role in a film • *There were two extras in the café scene who sat at a table and pretended to talk to each other.*
❖ κομπάρσος

4.88 **to the accompaniment of** (expr)
/tʊ ðə əˈkʌmpənɪmənt ɒv/
happening together with • *The bride walked down the aisle to the accompaniment of music.*
❖ με τη συνοδεία

4.89 **wild applause** (expr) /waɪld əˈplɔːz/
loud clapping and cheering • *U2 came out on stage to wild applause from the crowd.*
❖ ενθουσιώδη χειροκροτήματα

4.90 **at a moment's notice** (expr)
/æt ə ˈməʊmənts ˈnəʊtɪs/
with very little warning • *She was fired at a moment's notice and left the office the same day.* ❖ χωρίς ειδοποίηση

4.91 **understudy** (n) /ˈʌndəstʌdi/
an actor who learns a part in a play so that they can take over if the usual actor is ill
• *The actor had the flu, so the understudy took her place in the play that night.*
❖ αντικαταστάτης ηθοποιού

Jobs in the film and theatre industry
cast editor usher
crew extra
director understudy

Grammar pages 48-49

4.92 **enviously** (adv) /ˈenvɪəsli/
wanting sth that sb else has • *She looked enviously at her sister's new shoes and wished they were hers.* ➣ envy (v, n), envious (adj) ❖ φθονερά

4.93 **inhabit** (v) /ɪnˈhæbɪt/
live in a place • *The desert is inhabited by some strange animals.* ➣ inhabitant (n) ❖ κατοικώ

4.94 **strive** (v) /straɪv/
try hard • *He is striving to become a musician and practises the guitar every day.* ❖ αγωνίζομαι

4.95 **audition** (v) /ɔːˈdɪʃn/
take part in a short performance to see if you can be chosen for sth • *I auditioned for a role in the school play.* ➣ audition (n) ❖ κάνω δοκιμαστικό

4.96 **publicity** (n) /pʌbˈlɪsəti/
attracting the public's attention • *The film got a lot of publicity with its popular trailer on YouTube.* ❖ δημοσιότητα

4.97 **pull out** (phr v) /pʊl aʊt/
withdraw from an agreement • *The actor had to pull out of the play because he broke his leg.*
❖ αποσύρομαι από

4.98 **stand-up comedy** (n) /stænd-ʌp ˈkɒmədi/
a performance involving one person telling jokes • *I don't like stand-up comedy because I don't think it's very funny.*
❖ όρθια κωμωδία (είδος κωμωδίας όπου ο καλλιτέχνης απευθύνεται στο κοινό)

4.99 **premiere** (n) /ˈpremɪeə/
first performance of a play or film • *The premiere was a success and the audience loved the film.* ❖ πρεμιέρα

4.100 **leading man** (n) /ˈliːdɪŋ mæn/
an actor with the main male part in a film or play • *The leading man in the film is very good-looking.* ❖ πρωταγωνιστής
✎ Also: leading lady

4.101 **thespian** (n) /ˈθespiən/
an actor • *Most people agree that John Gielgud was one of the greatest thespians of his generation.* ❖ ηθοποιός

4.102 **break a leg** (expr) /breɪk ə leg/
used to wish a sb good luck • *'Break a leg!' he said to the actor.* ❖ καλή τύχη/επιτυχία

4.103 **drama queen** (n) /ˈdrɑːmə kwiːn/
sb who reacts in a melodramatic way to situations • *He's such a drama queen! He makes a fuss about the slightest thing.* ❖ μελοδραματικός

Phrasal verbs
fall to pull out
make up sift through
paste together track down

Listening   page 50

4.104 frustrated (adj) /frʌˈstreɪtɪd/
annoyed because you cannot do sth • *She was frustrated because she could not get a role in a film.* ➢ frustrate (v), frustration (n), frustrating (adj) ❖ απογοητευμένος

4.105 regretful (adj) /rɪˈgretfəl/
sorry you did not do sth • *She felt regretful that she had never pursued a career in politics.* ➢ regret (v, n) ❖ περίλυπος, μετανιωμένος

4.106 editor (n) /ˈedɪtə/
a person who chooses what goes in the final version of a film • *The film editor put the scenes together perfectly.* ➢ edit (v)
❖ υπεύθυνος για το μοντάζ μιας ταινίας

4.107 box office (n) /bɒks ˈɒfɪs/
the place where tickets are sold for a show, play or film • *I collected the tickets we had ordered online at the theatre box office.* ❖ εκδοτήριο εισιτηρίων για το σινεμά, θέατρο κλπ

4.108 reluctance (n) /rɪˈlʌktəns/
unwillingness • *His reluctance to sing meant that he did not get a part in the musical.*
➢ reluctant (adj) ❖ απροθυμία

Adjectives of feeling
desperate
ecstatic
electrifying
exhilarating
faint-hearted
frustrated
heart-rending
heart-warming
regretful

Speaking   page 51

4.109 controversial (adj) /kɒntrəˈvɜːʃl/
causing disagreement • *The controversial singer Lady Gaga has gained publicity by shocking people.* ➢ controversy (n)
❖ αμφιλεγόμενος

4.110 contempt of court (expr) /kənˈtempt əv kɔːt/
deliberate disregard for the regulations of a court • *The judge threatened to punish her for contempt of court.* ❖ ασέβεια προς το δικαστήριο

4.111 star-studded (adj) /ˈstɑː-stʌdɪd/
with many famous performers • *The film has a star-studded cast of the most well-known names in Hollywood.* ❖ με διασημότητες

4.112 twist (n) /twɪst/
an unexpected event in a story • *The twist at the end of the book really surprised me.*
➢ twist (v) ❖ μια τροπή στην πλοκή (έργου, ιστορίας κλπ.)

Writing: a review   pages 52-53

4.113 rave (about) (v) /reɪv əˈbaʊt/
write about sb/sth very enthusiastically
• *He didn't just like the film; he raved about it.* sentence ❖ εγκωμιάζω, παραληρώ

4.114 visual (adj) /ˈvɪʒuəl/
which can be seen • *Do you have a visual record of the performance on your camcorder?*
➢ vision (n) ❖ οπτικός

4.115 evil-doer (n) /ˈiːvl-ˌduə/
a bad person • *Javier Bardem pays the evil-doer in the Bond film Skyfall.* ❖ ο κακός

4.116 sequence (n) /ˈsiːkwəns/
a part of a film that deals with a single subject or action • *'The next sequence will be filmed on location in Italy,' said the director.*
❖ σκηνή, κομμάτι

4.117 project (v) /prɒˈdʒekt/
show on a screen • *The film was much more impressive when it was projected onto the big screen.* ➢ projection (n) ❖ προβάλλω

4.118 riot (n) /ˈraɪət/
a lot of different types of the same thing • *The flowers in the garden are a riot of colour.*
❖ πανδαισία, ποικιλία

4.119 all rolled into one (expr) /ɔːl rəʊld ˈɪntu wʌn/
If sb/sth is a number of things all rolled into one, they include all those things. • *Emma is a mother, a wife, a businesswoman a cook, a nurse and a friend all rolled into one.*
❖ όλα (αυτά) μαζί/σε ένα

4.120 feast for the eyes (expr) /fiːst fɔː ðə aɪz/
sth lovely to look at • *The beautiful shots of the coral reefs were a feast for the eyes.*
❖ χάρμα οφθαλμών

4.121 let-down (n) /ˈlet-daʊn/
a disappointment • *The film was a let-down; I expected it to be better.* ➢ let down (phr v)
❖ απογοήτευση

4.122 dated (adj) /ˈdeɪtɪd/
old-fashioned • *The clothes she wore were dated and didn't suit her.* ➢ date (n, v)
❖ ξεπερασμένος, παλιομοδίτικος

4.123 miss the mark (expr) /mɪs ðə mɑːk/
fail to have the desired effect • *He tried to tell a funny story, but it missed the mark and no one laughed.* ❖ αποτυγχάνω, δεν τα καταφέρνω

4.124 hands down (expr) /hændz daʊn/
easily • *I beat him hands down at tennis 6–0, 6–1.* ❖ εύκολα

Video 4: Skin Mask page 54

4.125 **skin tone** (n) /skɪn təʊn/
colour of your skin • *You need a light beige foundation for your skin tone.*
❖ τόνος/απόχρωση του δέρματος

4.126 **eyebrow** (n) /ˈaɪbraʊ/
a line of hair above your eye • *She raised her eyebrows in surprise.* ❖ φρύδι

4.127 **lashes** (pl n) /ˈlæʃɪz/
hair around your eyes • *She applied mascara to her lashes.* ❖ βλεφαρίδες

4.128 **fundamental** (adj) /ˌfʌndəˈmentl/
basic; most important • *There's a fundamental difference in their attitudes, so they often disagree.* ➣ fundamentally (adv)
❖ θεμελιώδης, βασικός

4.129 **motionless** (adj) /ˈməʊʃnləs/
not moving • *He sat motionless in the chair as the barber shaved his beard.* ➣ motion (n)
❖ ακίνητος

4.130 **mould** (n) /moʊld/
a container in which you pour a liquid so that, when it becomes solid, it has the shape of the container • *We poured the cake mixture into the mould and then put it in the oven.*
➣ mould (v) ❖ καλούπι

4.131 **shade** (n) /ʃeɪd/
a particular type of a colour, eg dark or light
• *Her hair is a light shade of brown.*
❖ απόχρωση

4.132 **layer** (n) /ˈleɪə/
a quantity of sth on top of another quantity
• *You need another layer of paint on the wall.*
➣ layer (v) ❖ στρώση

4.133 **wrap** (v) /ræp/
cover completely with sth • *I wrapped her present in gold paper.* ❖ τυλίγω

4.134 **solid** (adj) /ˈsɒlɪd/
hard • *The cement takes a day to become solid, so don't walk on it.* ❖ στερεός

4.135 **combination** (n) /kɒmbɪˈneɪʃn/
a mixture • *A combination of comedy and touching family moments makes this film very enjoyable.* ➣ combine (v) ❖ συνδυασμός

Vocabulary Exercises

A Complete the table.

Nouns	Adjectives	Nouns	Adjectives
vision	1	controversy	7
regret	2	dare	8
desperation	3	motion	9
illiteracy	4	exploitation	10
exhilaration	5	dominance	11
ecstasy	6	frustration	12

B Circle the odd one out.

1 cast   extra   stage
2 plot   row   aisle
3 usher   aisle   row
4 eyebrows   lashes   heartstrings
5 director   film buff   editor
6 foyer   backstage   wings
7 box office   female lead   title role
8 cutting-edge   sugary-sweet   state-of-the-art

C Match the words and make compound nouns.

1 sound   buff   _____
2 film   buster   _____
3 stage   tone   _____
4 block   study   _____
5 dress   walk   _____
6 heart   fright   _____
7 skin   flick   _____
8 cat   rehearsal   _____
9 under   throb   _____
10 chick   track   _____

D Circle the correct words.

1 Flying seems to defy / deny the laws of gravity.
2 Did you release / submit your homework to the teacher?
3 The actors must rehearse / shoot before we start filming.
4 The album was enlisted / ranked number one this week and is at the top of the charts.
5 Tom Hanks captures / portrays an astronaut in the film *Apollo 13*.
6 The story slowly compiles / unravels as the book develops.
7 The man was terrified so he fled / strove to the nearest police station.
8 This album is deemed / revealed to contain the singer's best material yet.

4 Grammar

4.1 Gerunds

Για να σχηματίσουμε gerund (γερούνδιο) προσθέτουμε την κατάληξη -ing σε ένα ρήμα. Χρησιμοποιούμε το gerund:
σαν ουσιαστικό.
→ **Acting** is not for everyone.
μετά από πρόθεση.
→ Pete was blamed **for losing** the tickets.
μετά από το ρήμα go όταν μιλάμε για δραστηριότητες.
→ We **go shopping** for books once a month.

Χρησιμοποιούμε επίσης gerund μετά από κάποια ρήματα και φράσεις:
admit, avoid, be used to, can't help, can't stand, deny, dislike, (don't) mind, enjoy, fancy, feel like, finish, forgive, hate, have difficulty, imagine, involve, it's no good, it's no use, it's (not) worth, keep, like, love, miss, practise, prefer, prevent, regret, risk, spend time, suggest.
→ **It's not worth getting** a 3D TV.
→ Hans **likes doing** dangerous stunts.

4.2 Infinitives

	Active / Ενεργητική	Passive / Παθητική
Present (Παρόν)	(to) offer	(to) be offered
Perfect (Παρελθόν)	(to) have offered	(to) have been offered

→ They will **hire** a production company.
→ A production company will **be hired**.

4.3 Full Infinitives

Σχηματίζουμε full infinitives με *to* και το ρήμα. Χρησιμοποιούμε full infinitives:
για να εξηγήσουμε το σκοπό μιας πράξης.
→ Melissa went backstage **to find** the director.
μετά από επίθετα όπως *afraid, scared, happy, glad, pleased, sad* κλπ.
→ I was **glad to be given** an invitation to the opening night.
μετά από τις λέξεις *too* και *enough*.
→ I was **too** nervous **to go** on stage.
→ The film wasn't good **enough to receive** an Academy Award.

Χρησιμοποιούμε επίσης full infinitives μετά από συγκεκριμένα ρήματα και φράσεις:
afford, agree, allow, appear, ask, begin, choose, decide, expect, fail, forget, hope, invite, learn, manage, need, offer, persuade, plan, prepare, pretend, promise, refuse, seem, start, want, would like.
→ He **decided to find** work as a cameraman.
→ She **has arranged to interview** Waris Darie, the famous fashion model.

4.4 Bare Infinitives

Χρησιμοποιούμε bare infinitives (απαρέμφατα χωρίς *to*) μετά από:
modal verbs.
→ We **should buy** tickets for the rock musical.
had better για να δώσουμε συμβουλή.
→ You **had better come** early for the dress rehearsal.
would rather για να εκφράσουμε προτίμηση.
→ I **would rather go** to the theatre than the cinema.

Σημείωση:
1. Χρησιμοποιούμε *let* + αντικείμενο + bare infinitive για να δώσουμε την άδειά μας σε κάποιον να κάνει κάτι. Χρησιμοποιείται μόνο στην ενεργητική φωνή. Στην παθητική μπορούμε να χρησιμοποιήσουμε *be allowed to*.
    → My parents **didn't let** me **watch** violent films.
    → I **wasn't allowed to watch** violent films.

4 Grammar

2. Χρησιμοποιούμε *make* + αντικείμενο + bare infinitive για να πούμε πως κάποιος αναγκάζεται να κάνει κάτι. Στην παθητική (passive voice) χρησιμοποιούμε full infinitive.
   → *The voice coach **made** them **repeat** their lines over and over.*
   → *They **were made to repeat** their lines over and over by the voice coach.*

4.5 Gerund ή Infinitive?

Ορισμένα ρήματα ακολουθούνται από gerund ή *to* + infinitive χωρίς να αλλάζει η σημασία τους. Τέτοια ρήματα είναι *begin, bother, continue, hate, like, love* και *start*.
→ *Otto **likes collecting / to collect** photographs from old films.*

Υπάρχουν άλλα ρήματα που ακολουθούνται από gerund ή *to* + infinitive, αλλά αλλάζει η σημασία τους. Τα πιο συνηθισμένα από αυτά είναι *forget, go on, regret, remember, stop* και *try*.
→ *I **regret watching** the historical drama. It wasn't realistic.* (Το είδα αλλά το έχω μετανιώσει.)
→ *We **regret to announce** that tonight's performance is cancelled.* (Λυπάμαι που πρέπει να ανακοινώσω κάτι δυσάρεστο.)
→ *I **remember seeing** Michael Jackson in concert.* ('Εχω ανάμνηση, θυμάμαι που τον είδα.)
→ *I **remembered to pick up** the theatre tickets.* (Πρώτα το θυμήθηκα, και στη συνέχεια τα αγόρασα.)
→ *We **stopped collecting** videos years ago.* (Δεν το κάνουμε πια.)
→ *We **stopped to buy** the book To Kill a Mockingbird.* (Σταματήσαμε αυτό που κάναμε ώστε να αγοράσουμε το βιβλίο.)

4.6 Discourse Markers

Οι discourse markers δίνουν συνοχή σε ένα γραπτό ή σε μια ομιλία και μερικές φορές δηλώνουν τη στάση ή τη διάθεση του συγγραφέα ή του ομιλητή. Επίσης, χρησιμοποιούμε discourse markers για να προσθέσουμε πληροφορίες, για να περιγράψουμε μια σειρά από γεγονότα, για να περιγράψουμε κάτι, για να μιλήσουμε για αιτία και αποτέλεσμα, για να συγκρίνουμε, για να προσδιορίσουμε, για να εκφράσουμε αντίθεση, για να δώσουμε έμφαση, για να επαναλαβάνουμε κάτι, για να γενικεύσουμε, για να δώσουμε την άδειά μας σε κάποιον κλπ.
→ *It was a foreign film. **What is more**, it was shot on location.* (πρόσθεση)
→ *She was a child star with various professional commitments. **As a result**, she had no time to play with other children.* (αποτέλεσμα)
→ *The film didn't get rave reviews. **On the other hand**, film critics aren't always right.* (αντίθεση)
→ *'May I ask for his autograph?' **'Go right ahead**, he won't mind.'* (δίνω την άδεια)

Grammar Exercises

A Complete the sentences with the gerund, bare infinitive or full infinitive of the verbs below.

| admit | audition | dance | have | improve | publish | sing | track |

1 You should focus on _____ your singing if you want to be a pop star.
2 We had problems _____ down our relatives online.
3 She isn't confident enough _____ for a title role in this play.
4 I hate _____ it, but I am a terrible actor.
5 If you can't _____, you should learn. It's good physical exercise.
6 Since I was a child, _____ has been my passion, which is why I went to the ballet school.
7 Imagine _____ a novel at the tender age of 14!
8 If you want to learn to speak Mandarin, why not _____ some private tuition?

B Complete the sentences with your own ideas. Use the gerund, full infinitive or bare infinitive.

1 When I was a young child, I remember _____.
2 I want to study _____.
3 During an exam, there is no time _____.
4 Since I was little, _____.
5 I can't _____.
6 In my studies, I focus on _____.
7 Parents should let a child _____.
8 Imagine _____.

C Complete the sentences with one word in each gap.

1 I bought the book you recommended. By the _____, did you finish the one I lent you?
2 You must come to the party. After _____, it's your success we're celebrating.
3 I loved the first Harry Potter book. All _____ all, the entire series is exceptional.
4 'She isn't really quitting the music industry, is she?' 'As a _____ of fact, she is.'
5 I don't want to see a flick tonight. _____ honestly, I'm bored of the cinema.
6 Dave never learns his lines. _____ you, neither do I.
7 'Janice got the role you wanted.' '_____ you can't be serious!'
8 My cousin is an ornithologist; _____ is, he studies birds.

4 Grammar

Exam Task

For questions 1-6, complete the second sentence so that it has a similar meaning to the first sentence, using the word given. Do not change the word given. You must use between three and six words, including the word given.

1 This book contains poems by women poets of the twentieth century.
   UP
   This book _____ of poems by women poets of the twentieth century.

2 Bill had to edit the film because he was the only one who knew how.
   FELL
   Because he was the only one who knew how, editing _____ Bill.

3 She was forced to marry a rich businessman.
   OFF
   She was _____ a rich businessman.

4 He used to be a heart surgeon but he retired ten years ago.
   BY
   He was _____ but he retired ten years ago.

5 We were told to leave our desks immediately.
   NOTICE
   We were told _____ to leave our desks.

6 The model was forced to withdraw from the fashion show due to ill health.
   PULL
   The model had _____ the fashion show due to ill health.

5 Eat Up!

page 57

5.1 **eat up** (phr v) /iːt ʌp/
eat all of sth • *Mum told us to eat up our vegetables.* ❖ τα τρώγω όλα

Word Focus page 58

5.2 **condiment** (n) /ˈkɒndɪmənt/
a substance added to food for flavour eg salt, ketchup • *The child's favourite condiments are mustard and ketchup.* ❖ καρύκευμα, σάλτσα

5.3 **stunt** (v) /stʌnt/
prevent from growing or developing properly • *A lack of food stunted the child's growth.* ❖ εμποδίζω την ανάπτυξη

5.4 **fatty acid** (n) /ˈfæti ˈæsɪd/
an acid that the cells in your body need to function properly • *Olive oil is rich in unsaturated fatty acids.* ❖ λιπαρό οξύ

5.5 **cognition** (n) /kɒgˈnɪʃn/
the process by which knowledge and understanding are developed in the brain • *The child psychologist set the child some puzzles to study his cognition.* ❖ νόηση

5.6 **craving** (n) /ˈkreɪvɪŋ/
a strong desire for sth, usually food • *She has to resist a craving for chocolate if she wants to lose weight.* ➢ crave (v) ❖ λαχτάρα, επιθυμία

5.7 **pig out** (phr v) /pɪg aʊt/
eat to excess • *I pigged out at supper and now I'm really full.* ❖ παρατρώγω

5.8 **obesity** (n) /əʊˈbiːsɪti/
the condition of being very overweight • *Obesity is a serious problem in the Western world, where people eat too much.* ➢ obese (adj) ❖ παχυσαρκία

Reading pages 58-59

5.9 **savoury** (adj) /ˈseɪvəri/
salty • *The best savoury dish you served was the pizza.* ❖ αλμυρός, πικάντικος ✎ Opp: sweet

5.10 **peckish** (adj) /ˈpekɪʃ/
a little hungry • *If you're peckish, why not have a banana?* ➢ peck (v) ❖ πεινασμένος

5.11 **cut down on** (phr v) /kʌt daʊn ɒn/
reduce • *He cut down on sweets and lost a kilo.* ❖ περιορίζω, ελαττώνω

5.12 **processed food** (n) /ˈprəʊsest fuːd/
prepared food, often in tins or packets • *These processed foods are easy to prepare in the microwave but not that good for you.* ❖ επεξεργασμένα τρόφιμα

5.13 **pile on** (phr v) /paɪl ɒn/
put on a lot of (weight) • *She piled on 15 kilos when she was pregnant.* ❖ παίρνω βάρος

5.14 **pound** (n) /paʊnd/
a measurement of weight (1 kilo = 2.2 pounds) • *It took me six months to lose 20 pounds.* ❖ λίβρα

5.15 **lace with** (phr v) /leɪs wɪð/
add an ingredient to a drink or dish to enhance its flavour or strength • *The dessert was laced with an orange liqueur and smelled wonderful.* ❖ προσθέτω (οινοπνευματώδες ποτό) σε ποτό/φαγητό

5.16 **play havoc** (expr) /pleɪ ˈhævək/
create a very confusing and possibly dangerous situation • *The medicine she was allergic to played havoc with her health.* ❖ προκαλώ όλεθρο

5.17 **navigate** (v) /ˈnævɪgeɪt/
find your position and the direction you need to go in • *We navigated through the busy streets using a map.* ➢ navigator (n), navigation (n) ❖ πλοηγώ, οδηγώ

5.18 **maze** (n) /meɪz/
a complex system of paths • *We got lost in the maze and couldn't find the way out.* ❖ λαβύρινθος

5.19 **swap** (v) /swɒp/
change one thing for another • *I swapped biscuits for fruit and feel much better.* ❖ ανταλάσσω

5.20 **flaxseed** (n) /ˈflæksiːd/
the seed of a Mediterranean plant with small blue flowers • *You can use flaxseed oil to dress salads.* ❖ λιναρόσπορος

5.21 **antioxidant** (n) /æntiˈɒksɪdənt/
substance which inhibits oxidation • *Berries are rich in antioxidants so add them to your diet.* ❖ αντιοξειδωτικό

5.22 **consumption** (n) /kənˈsʌmpʃn/
eating or drinking sth • *Your consumption of coffee is excessive, which is why you cannot sleep.* ➢ consume (v), consumer (n) ❖ κατανάλωση

5.23 **counterpart** (n) /ˈkaʊntəpɑːt/
sb/sth that has the same job or function as sth/sb else in a different organisation or place • *The head of the accounts department spoke to his counterpart in the US office to discuss finance.* ❖ ομόλογος, αντίστοιχος

5.24 **fizzy** (adj) /ˈfɪzi/
with bubbles • *I'll have a fizzy lemonade, please.* ➢ fizz (v, n) ❖ ανθρακούχος

5.25 quench one's thirst (expr) /kwentʃ wʌnz θɜːst/
drink so one is no longer thirsty • *This mineral water really quenches your thirst.* ❖ ξεδιψώ

5.26 run the risk (expr) /rʌn ðə rɪsk/
do sth that could harm you • *You run the risk of getting sick if you don't eat well or exercise.* ❖ διατρέχω τον κίνδυνο

5.27 sufficient (adj) /sə'fɪʃənt/
enough • *There is sufficient calcium in a glass of milk for your daily needs.* ➣ sufficiently (adv), suffice (v) ❖ αρκετός
Opp: insufficient

5.28 chew (v) /tʃuː/
bite food into small pieces so it is easier to swallow • *Chew your food properly before you swallow it.* ❖ μασάω

5.29 shed (v) /ʃed/
lose • *I shed six kilos when I went on a diet.* ❖ χάνω, αποβάλλω

5.30 banish (v) /'bænɪʃ/
get rid of • *You should banish thoughts of treats during this strict diet.* ➣ banishment (n) ❖ διώχνω

5.31 exposure (n) /ɪks'pəʊʒə/
having no protection from sth harmful • *Too much exposure to the sun is bad for your skin.* ➣ expose (v) ❖ έκθεση

5.32 habituation (n) /hæbɪtuː'eɪʃn/
the act or process of becoming used to sth • *She studies the habituation of teenagers to violence.* ➣ habituate (v), habituated (adj) ❖ εθισμός, συνήθεια

5.33 deter (v) /dɪ'tɜː/
make sb not want to do sth • *The fear of being caught by their mum deterred the boys from stealing biscuits.* ➣ deterrent (n) ❖ αποτρέπω

5.34 urge (n) /ɜːdʒ/
a strong desire to do sth • *He had an urge to drink coffee as he walked past the coffee shop.* ➣ urge (v) ❖ επιθυμία

Vocabulary pages 60-61

5.35 cuisine (n) /kwɪ'ziːn/
a style of cooking • *French cuisine is famous for its rich sauces.* ❖ κουζίνα (ελληνική, κινέζικη, κλπ)

5.36 culinary (adj) /'kʌlɪnəri/
to do with cooking • *He is interested in doing a culinary course as he wants to be a chef.* ❖ γαστρονομικός

5.37 simmer (v) /'sɪmə/
boil gently • *I'll simmer the potatoes in water for 10 minutes until they are soft.* ❖ σιγοβράζω

5.38 chop (v) /tʃɒp/
cut into pieces • *He chopped the onion into small pieces.* ➣ chop (n) ❖ κόβω, ψιλοκόβω

5.39 grate (v) /greɪt/
cut into very small pieces using a tool with a rough surface • *I'll grate some carrots for the salad.* ➣ grater (n) ❖ τρίβω (τυρί, ντομάτα, κλπ)

5.40 blend (v) /blend/
mix together substances to form a single smooth substance • *The chef blended the onion and potato to make soup.* ➣ blender (n) ❖ αναμειγνύω

5.41 whet one's appetite (expr) /wet wʌnz 'æpɪtaɪt/
increase one's appetite • *The smell of freshly cooked bread always whets my appetite.* ❖ ανοίγει την όρεξη

5.42 sip (v) /sɪp/
drink slowly by taking small mouthfuls • *She sipped her hot tea.* ➣ sip (n) ❖ σιγοπίνω

5.43 nibble (v) /'nɪbl/
eat small amounts by taking very small bites • *The mouse nibbled the piece of cheese.* ➣ nibble (n) ❖ τσιμπώ

5.44 munch (v) /mʌntʃ/
eat/chew noisily • *He munched his apple.* ❖ κριτσανίζω, μασουλώ

5.45 gobble (v) /'gɒbl/
eat quickly and greedily • *The boy was so hungry he gobbled his supper in two minutes.* ❖ καταβροχθίζω

5.46 sour (adj) /'saʊə/
with an acid taste like lemon or vinegar • *He made a face when he tasted the sour sauce.* ➣ sourness (n) ❖ ξινός

5.47 tart (adj) /tɑːt/
sharp or acid in taste • *The berries were not ripe, so they tasted quite tart.* ➣ tartness (n) ❖ στυφός

5.48 acidic (adj) /æ'sɪdɪk/
sharp-tasting or sour • *I don't add vinegar to my salads because acidic food makes my stomach ache.* ➣ acidity (n), acid (n) ❖ όξινος

5.49 ravenous (adj) /'rævənəs/
very hungry • *He hadn't eaten all day, so he was ravenous.* ❖ πολύ πεινασμένος

5.50 famished (adj) /'fæmɪʃt/
very hungry • *I'm famished. Let's eat.* ❖ πολύ πεινασμένος

5.51 feast (n) /fiːst/
a large special meal • *The wedding feast finished with profiteroles for dessert.* ➣ feast (v) ❖ φαγοπότι, τσιμπούσι

5.52 banquet (n) /'bæŋkwɪt/
a special formal meal • *Delicious food was served at the banquet held for the king and queen.* ❖ συμπόσιο

5.53 spread (n) /spred/
a large meal with many different dishes • *What a spread! Look at all this delicious food!* ❖ πλούσιο τραπέζι

5.54 **poach** (v) /pəʊtʃ/
cook in boiling water (usually eggs) • *He cracked the egg, dropped it in boiling water and poached it.* ➢ poached (adj) ❖ βράζω, ποσάρω

5.55 **blanch** (v) /blɑːntʃ/
cook quickly in boiling water • *Blanch the spinach for thirty seconds in boiling water.* ➢ blanched (adj) ❖ ζεματίζω

5.56 **stale** (adj) /steɪl/
not fresh • *This bread is dry and stale so don't eat it.* ➢ staleness (n) ❖ μπαγιάτικος
✎ Opp: fresh

5.57 **mouldy** (adj) /ˈməʊldi/
old and covered in a blue or green substance that grows on old food • *I'm not eating this mouldy cheese!* ➢ mould (n) ❖ μουχλιασμένος

5.58 **off** (adj) /ɒf/
no longer fresh • *The milk must be off because it smells awful.* ❖ χαλασμένος

5.59 **bland** (adj) /blænd/
without much flavour • *If the dish is too bland, you can add some spices.* ➢ blandness (n) ❖ άνοστος

5.60 **scrumptious** (adj) /ˈskrʌmʃəs/
really delicious • *May I have another of those scrumptious cupcakes?* ❖ πεντανόστιμος

5.61 **appetising** (adj) /ˈæpɪtaɪzɪŋ/
looking and smelling delicious • *The pies in this bakery look very appetising.* ➢ appetite (n) ❖ νόστιμος, δελεαστικός

5.62 **portion** (n) /ˈpɔːʃn/
an amount of food for one person • *I had a large portion of soup as it was so good.* ❖ μερίδα

5.63 **helping** (n) /ˈhelpɪŋ/
an amount of food served to a person at a meal • *Would you like another helping of mashed potato?* ❖ μερίδα

5.64 **serving** (n) /ˈsɜːvɪŋ/
an amount of food for one person • *I helped myself to a serving of lasagne.* ➢ serve (v) ❖ μερίδα

5.65 **platter** (n) /ˈplætə/
a large serving dish • *There was a variety of shellfish arranged on the platter.* ❖ πιατέλα

5.66 **dishcloth** (n) /ˈdɪʃklɒθ/
a towel you dry dishes with • *I use this cotton dishcloth to dry the plates.* ❖ πετσέτα κουζίνας

5.67 **napkin** (n) /ˈnæpkɪn/
a piece of material or paper you use to wipe your hands and mouth when you eat • *Don't forget to put napkins out when you lay the table.* ❖ πετσέτα, χαρτοπετσέτα

5.68 **cultivate** (v) /ˈkʌltɪveɪt/
grow • *Olives have been cultivated in Greece from ancient times.* ➢ cultivation (n) ❖ καλλιεργώ

5.69 **harvest** (v) /ˈhɑːvɪst/
cut or collect a crop • *The apples will be harvested in October, when they are ripe.* ➢ harvest (n) ❖ θερίζω, μαζεύω τη σοδειά

5.70 **covering** (n) /ˈkʌvərɪŋ/
sth that covers sth else • *There is a covering of snow on the ground this morning.* ➢ cover (v, n) ❖ επίστρωση

5.71 **topping** (n) /ˈtɒpɪŋ/
sth you put on top of food to make it taste better • *The pizza toppings are cheese, tomato and ham.* ➢ top (v, n) ❖ επικάλυψη

5.72 **stable** (adj) /ˈsteɪbl/
unlikely to change • *His health is stable now so he is out of danger.* ➢ stability (n) ❖ σταθερός

5.73 **staple** (adj) /ˈsteɪpl/
Staple food is food that forms the basic part of your diet. • *Bread is a staple food in European cuisine.* ❖ βασικό είδος διατροφής

5.74 **eatable** (adj) /ˈiːtəbl/
tasty to eat • *This banana is very ripe but it's still eatable.* ➢ eat (v) ❖ φαγώσιμος

5.75 **edible** (adj) /ˈedɪbl/
safe to eat • *Potato leaves are not edible and will make you sick if you eat them.* ❖ φαγώσιμος
✎ Opp: inedible

5.76 **flavouring** (n) /ˈfleɪvərɪŋ/
a substance added to food to give it a particular flavour • *Add a flavouring like vanilla essence to the cake mixture.* ➢ flavour (n, v) ❖ αρωματικό, καρύκευμα

5.77 **dissolve** (v) /dɪˈsɒlv/
mix with liquid and become part of it • *The salt dissolved quickly in the boiling water.* ❖ διαλύω

5.78 **extract** (v) /ˈekstrækt/
remove • *Oil is extracted from rose petals to use for perfume.* ➢ extract (n) ❖ βγάζω, εκθλίβω

5.79 **ethnic** (adj) /ˈeθnɪk/
from faraway or exotic countries • *I buy ethnic food from this international supermarket.* ➢ ethnicity (n) ❖ εθνικός, έθνικ

5.80 **per capita** (adv) /pə ˈkæpɪtə/
for each person • *What is the average income per capita in this country?* ❖ κατά κεφαλήν

5.81 **leftovers** (pl n) /ˈleftˌəʊvəz/
food not eaten by the end of a meal • *There are some leftovers in the pot which we can heat up and eat tomorrow.* ❖ περισσεύματα

5.82 **scraps** (pl n) /skræps/
food left on sb's plate • *Mum gave the chicken scraps from our plates to the cat.* ❖ αποφάγια, αποκόμματα

5.83 **beverage** (n) /ˈbevərɪdʒ/
a drink • *She often has a hot beverage like tea or coffee in the morning.* ❖ ρόφημα

5.84 **soft drink** (n) /sɒft drɪŋk/
a drink that has no alcohol • *They serve soft drinks here, so would you like an orangeade?* ❖ αναψυκτικό

5.85 **sharp** (adj) /ʃɑːp/
with a taste like lemon • *This juice is so sharp I'll have to add some sugar.* ➢ sharpness (n) ❖ ξυνός

5.86 **beat** (v) /biːt/
mix with circular motions, often with a fork • *I beat the egg whites to make meringue.* ❖ κτυπώ

5.87 **crack** (v) /kræk/
break • *She cracked two eggs into a bowl and threw away the shells.* ➢ crack (n) ❖ σπάζω

5.88 **vigorously** (adv) /ˈvɪɡərəsli/
with energy • *Beat the milk vigorously to make it frothy for your latte.* ➢ vigorous (adj) ❖ δυνατά, έντονα, δυναμικά

5.89 **pack away** (phr v) /pæk əˈweɪ/
eat a lot of food • *He can pack away two steaks in one meal.* ❖ καταναλώνω μεγάλες ποσότητες

5.90 **dine out** (phr v) /daɪn aʊt/
eat at a restaurant • *Let's dine out at a Chinese restaurant tonight.* ❖ δειπνώ, τρώγω έξω

5.91 **live on** (phr v) /lɪv ɒn/
eat a particular type of food to live • *The students lived on sandwiches because they didn't know how to cook.* ❖ ζω με

5.92 **pick at** (phr v) /pɪk æt/
eat only a little because you do not feel hungry or you do not like the food • *The little boy picked at his vegetables because he didn't want to eat them.* ❖ τσιμπολογώ ανόρεχτα

5.93 **polish off** (phr v) /ˈpɒlɪʃ ɒf/
finish all of a particular dish or portion of food • *We polished off a whole chicken for lunch.* ❖ τελειώνω

5.94 **tuck in** (phr v) /tʌk ɪn/
start eating enthusiastically • *Supper is served. Tuck in everyone.* ❖ ξεκινώ να τρώγω με λαχτάρα

5.95 **warm up** (phr v) /wɔːm ʌp/
heat food that has already been cooked • *He warmed up yesterday's leftovers in the microwave.* ❖ ζεσταίνω

5.96 **whip up** (phr v) /wɪp ʌp/
prepare a meal very quickly • *I whipped up an omelette for supper.* ❖ μαγειρεύω κάτι στα γρήγορα

5.97 **wake up and smell the coffee** (expr) /weɪk ʌp ænd smel ðə ˈkɒfi/
used to tell sb to become aware of what is happening • *Wake up and smell the coffee. He simply doesn't like you!* ❖ συνειδητοποιώ

5.98 **brew** (v) /bruː/
prepare a hot beverage • *I'll brew some coffee for breakfast.* ❖ βράζω, ψήνω (καφέ, κλπ)

5.99 **have one's cake and eat it too** (expr) /hæv wʌnz keɪk ænd iːt ɪt tuː/
have the advantages of sth without its disadvantages • *He wanted to have his cake and eat it too – to be independent and live with his parents for free.* ❖ θέλω και την πίτα ολόκληρη και το σκύλο χορτάτο

5.100 **the best thing since sliced bread** (expr) /ðə best θɪŋ sɪns slaɪst bred/
used to say that sth new is very good • *They think Mary is wonderful; in fact, they think she's the best thing since sliced bread.* ❖ ότι καλύτερο

5.101 **spiced** (adj) /spaɪst/
with spices • *This spiced sauce is delicious; it's got cinnamon and paprika.* ➢ spice (n) ❖ πικάντικος

5.102 **diced** (adj) /daɪst/
cut into cubes • *The cheese must be diced before you put it in the salad.* ➢ dice (v) ❖ κομμένος σε κύβους

5.103 **there's no use crying over spilt milk** (expr) /ðeəz nəʊ juːs ˈkraɪɪŋ ˈəʊvə spɪlt mɪlk/
used to say it is not worth feeling sorry about an earlier mistake that you cannot change • *You've burnt the dinner, but there's no use crying over spilt milk. We'll just order a pizza.* ❖ ότι έγινε έγινε

5.104 **spoilt** (adj) /spɔɪlt/
bad, so it cannot be eaten • *I didn't put the yoghurt in the fridge and now it's spoilt.* ➢ spoil (v) ❖ χαλασμένος

5.105 **split** (adj) /splɪt/
divided • *This chocolate bar split in two is a big enough snack for both of us.* ❖ χωρισμένος, μοιρασμένος στα δύο

5.106 **have egg on one's face** (expr) /hæv eg ɒn wʌnz feɪs/
look foolish • *He made a stupid mistake. Now he has egg on his face.* ❖ ρεζιλεύομαι

5.107 **you are toast** (expr) /juː ɑː təʊst/
you are in trouble • *If you break my bike, you're toast.* ❖ έχεις μπελάδες, την έβαψες

5.108 **roast** (n) /rəʊst/
meat cooked in the oven • *We had roast for Sunday lunch.* ❖ ψητό κρέας

5.109 **oats** (pl n) /əʊts/
grain used for making cereal or porridge • *Oats for breakfast give you a good start to the day.* ❖ βρώμη

5.110 **full of beans** (expr) /fʊl ɒv biːnz/
energetic • *Jack is full of beans and is running around the garden.* ❖ ζωηρός

5.111 **raisin** (n) /ˈreɪzən/
a dried red grape • *There are raisins in this fruit cake.* ❖ σταφίδα

5.112 **a hot potato** (expr) /ə hɒt pəˈteɪtəʊ/
a problem nobody wants to deal with • *The economic crisis is a hot potato that no politician wants to be responsible for.*
❖ ακανθώδες πρόβλημα

5.113 **sizzling** (adj) /ˈsɪzlɪŋ/
very hot • *She served sizzling burgers straight off the barbecue.* ➢ sizzle (v) ❖ καυτός

5.114 **skim** (v) /skɪm/
remove sth from the surface of a liquid • *He skimmed the froth off the water that the beans were boiling in.* ➢ skimmed (adj)
❖ ξαφρίζω

5.115 **nutrient** (n) /ˈnjuːtrɪənt/
a substance that helps things grow • *There are many nutrients in fruit so always include them in your diet.* ➢ nutrition (n), nutritious (adj)
❖ θρεπτική ουσία

5.116 **supplement** (n) /ˈsʌplɪmənt/
a substance added to sb's diet to improve it • *She takes a vitamin supplement every morning.* ➢ supplement (v) ❖ συμπλήρωμα

5.117 **digest** (v) /daɪˈdʒest/
change food you have eaten into substances that your body can use • *Fatty foods can be hard to digest.* ➢ digestion (n) ❖ χωνεύω

5.118 **disgraceful** (adj) /dɪsˈɡreɪsfl/
unacceptable; that people should feel ashamed about • *Your behaviour last night was disgraceful and you must apologise.*
➢ disgrace (n, v) ❖ απαράδεκτος, αισχρός

5.119 **grain** (n) /ɡreɪn/
the seed of a plant such as wheat or rice • *Her diet is rich in grains, and she eats lots of bread and rice.* ❖ δημητριακά, σιτηρά

Verbs for preparing food

beat	grate
blanch	poach
blend	simmer
chop	skim
crack	

Grammar   pages 62-63

5.120 **look down on** (phr v) /lʊk daʊn ɒn/
think that you are better than ab else • *He looks down on people who are not as clever as he is.* ❖ έχω άσχημη γνώμη για, περιφρονώ

5.121 **pull through** (phr v) /pʊl θruː/
recover from a very serious illness or injury • *She got pneumonia, but she pulled through.*
❖ αναρρώνω

5.122 **take after** (phr v) /teɪk ˈɑːftə/
look or behave like an older relative • *He takes after his grandfather in looks and personality.*
❖ μοιάζω

5.123 **clean sth out** (phr v) /kliːn ˈsʌmθɪŋ aʊt/
clean sth thoroughly • *I clean the cupboards out every spring.* ❖ καθαρίζω

5.124 **put up with** (phr v) /pʊt ʌp wɪð/
tolerate • *How can you put up with the noise from next door?* ❖ ανέχομαι

5.125 **renovate** (v) /ˈrenəʊveɪt/
repair an old building or furniture so that it is in good condition • *The old house needed renovating to modernise it.* ➢ renovation (n)
❖ ανακαινίζω

5.126 **gulp** (v) /ɡʌlp/
drink very quickly • *She gulped her coffee and left quickly so as not to miss her train.* ➢ gulp (n)
❖ καταπίνω βιαστικά

5.127 **mussel** (n) /ˈmʌsəl/
a shellfish with a purple/black shell • *We ate mussels in a red sauce for the main course.* ❖ μύδι

5.128 **incident** (n) /ˈɪnsɪdənt/
an event, often bad • *There was an incident in town today when two people got into a fist fight.* ❖ περιστατικό

Listening   page 64

5.129 **cuttlefish** (n) /ˈkʌtlfɪʃ/
a sea animal with a soft body and a hard shell inside it • *I ordered fried cuttlefish at the Greek restaurant.* ❖ σουπιά

5.130 **go off** (phr v) /ɡəʊ ɒf/
become bad to eat • *This fish has gone off so don't eat it.* ❖ χαλάω (για τρόφιμα)

5.131 **peak condition** (phr) /piːk kənˈdɪʃn/
the best physical state • *The athlete is in peak condition and hopes to win a gold medal.*
❖ άριστη φόρμα

5.132 **cut out** (phr v) /kʌt aʊt/
omit; remove • *If you want to lose weight, cut out sugar from your diet.* ❖ αφαιρώ, βγάζω

5.133 **chickpea** (n) /ˈtʃɪk piː/
a round seed that looks like a brown pea, and that is eaten as a vegetable • *Soak the chickpeas overnight in cold water before you boil them.* ❖ ρεβίθι

5.134 **pulses** (pl n) /pʌlsɪz/
the seeds of plants such as peas, chickpeas and lentils • *Pulses are rich in protein.* ❖ όσπρια

Hunger and thirst

consume	peckish
craving	quench one's thirst
famished	ravenous
gobble	sip
munch	starving
nibble	whet one's appetite

Speaking page 65

5.135 eat on the hoof (expr) /iːt ɒn ðə huːf/
eat quickly while you are doing sth else • *I usually eat on the hoof while I work at my desk.* ❖ τρώω στα γρήγορα, τρώω στα όρθια

5.136 battery hen (n) /ˈbætəri hen/
hen kept in a cage • *The battery hens on the farm were a sorry sight in their small cages.* ❖ κότα εντατικής κτηνοτροφίας

5.137 free range (adj) /friː reɪndʒ/
(for a farm animal) able to move around • *Free range chicken is more expensive but at least the hens haven't been raised in cages.* ❖ ελεύθερης βοσκής

5.138 subsistence farming (n) /səbˈsɪstəns ˈfɑːmɪŋ/
growing food for eating yourself rather than to sell it • *Many people turn to subsistence farming to feed their families during hard times.* ❖ γεωργία διαβίωσης, μη εμπορευματική γεωργία

Writing: a proposal pages 66-67

5.139 venue (n) /ˈvenjuː/
a place where an event takes place • *The venue for the match is the Olympic Stadium.* ❖ τόπος, τοποθεσία

5.140 festive (adj) /ˈfestɪv/
suitable for celebrating sth • *I love preparing food for festive occasions like birthdays.* ➢ festival (n) ❖ γιορτινός

5.141 auditorium (n) /ˌɔːdɪˈtɔːriəm/
the part of a theatre or concert hall where the audience sits • *The auditorium is full and there are no empty seats.* ❖ αμφιθέατρο, αίθουσα (π.χ. θεάτρου)

5.142 take in (phr v) /teɪk ɪn/
include sth • *We took in a trip to the Acropolis Museum when we were in Athens.* ❖ περιλαμβάνω, απολαμβάνω

Phrasal verbs

clean sth out	pig out
cut down on	pile on
cut out	polish off
dine out	pull through
eat up	put up with
go off	take after sb
live on	take in
look down on sb	tuck in
pack away	warm up
pick at	whip up

Video 5: The Smelliest Fruit page 68

5.143 odour (n) /ˈəʊdə/
smell • *A terrible odour was coming from the dustbin.* ❖ μυρωδιά

5.144 bedspread (n) /ˈbedˌspred/
a cover on top of bed sheets and blanket/duvet • *She made the bed and then covered it with a bedspread.* ❖ κουβερλί

5.145 rotten (adj) /ˈrɒtən/
decayed and so cannot be eaten • *The rotten fish smelt absolutely disgusting.* ➢ rot (v, n) ❖ σάπιος

5.146 smuggle (v) /ˈsmʌgl/
take sth secretly to a place where it is not allowed to be • *The little boy smuggled a kitten into the house without his mum knowing.* ❖ μεταφέρω κρυφά/λαθραία

5.147 custard (n) /ˈkʌstəd/
a sweet sauce made from milk, sugar, eggs and flour • *We had apple pie and custard for dessert.* ❖ κρέμα (ζαχαροπλαστικής), κρεμ ανγκλέζ

5.148 charcoal (n) /ˈtʃɑːkəʊl/
a black substance formed from burning wood • *He draws portraits in charcoal.* ❖ κάρβουνο

5.149 absorb (v) /əbˈsɔːb/
take in; soak up • *The rainwater was slowly absorbed by the ground.* ➢ absorption (n) ❖ απορροφώ

5.150 ioniser (n) /ˈaɪənaɪzə/
a machine that cleans the air in a room • *She uses an ioniser to clear the air of dust because she has allergies.* ➢ ionise (v) ❖ ιονιστής

5.151 contaminating (adj) /kɒnˈtæmɪneɪtɪŋ/
making dirty • *A contaminating smell of burning plastic came from the fire at the factory.* ➢ contaminate (v), contamination (n) ❖ μολυσματική, ρυπαρή

5.152 ban (v) /bæn/
not allow • *Smoking is banned here so please extinguish your cigarette.* ➢ ban (n) ❖ απαγορεύω

Vocabulary Exercises

A Match.

1. Surely you realise that Janet isn't interested in you.
2. No, you can't use my car and then ask me to pay for petrol.
3. I love this new gadget.
4. Don't worry about breaking that old vase.
5. I can't believe he treated the boss like a new employee.
6. You spilt coffee all over my laptop, you idiot.
7. The kids are jumping up and down on the trampoline.
8. Nobody wants to be the one to announce the redundancies.

a. There's no use crying over spilt milk.
b. Wake up and smell the coffee!
c. You are toast!
d. I suppose it is a hot potato.
e. He really has got egg on his face now.
f. They are always full of beans.
g. It's the best thing since sliced bread.
h. You can't have your cake and eat it too!

B Complete the sentences with these adjectives.

bland   culinary   edible   famished   fizzy   mouldy   peckish   scrumptious   sharp   sizzling   stale   staple

1. I was a little _____ so I ate an apple.
2. Grapefruits are too _____ for me. I prefer sweeter fruit.
3. Having missed lunch he was _____ by supper time and gobbled down his meal.
4. Rice is a(n) _____ food in Asia.
5. The chef added a pinch of salt to the sauce as it was too _____ .
6. I won't have lemonade as I don't like _____ drinks.
7. You really should try the new restaurant. The food there is absolutely _____ .
8. We were impressed with his _____ skills and recommended he become a chef.
9. This bread is so _____ I can't bite through the hard crust.
10. The cake was _____ and covered in green dots.
11. If you aren't sure that a mushroom is _____, don't pick it.
12. We had _____ sausages and bacon for breakfast.

C Read the definitions and complete the words.

1. a substance added to food for flavour   c _ _ _ _ _ _ _ _
2. cook quickly in boiling water   b _ _ _ _ _
3. food not eaten at the end of a meal   l _ _ _ _ _ _ _ _
4. a smell   o _ _ _ _
5. a special formal meal   b _ _ _ _ _ _
6. a towel you dry plates with   d _ _ _ _ _ _ _ _
7. a dried red grape   r _ _ _ _ _
8. prepare a hot beverage   b _ _ _
9. drink to stop being thirsty   q _ _ _ _ _
10. eat or chew noisily   m _ _ _ _

D Complete the phrasal verbs in these sentences. Use one or two words.

1. Shall we dine _____ at our favourite restaurant tonight?
2. She's cutting _____ sugar in order to lose weight.
3. Grandpa is very ill, but we all hope he pulls _____ soon.
4. I can't put _____ my awful neighbours any longer.
5. Why are you picking _____ your food? Don't you like it?
6. The boys can really pack _____ a large meal in no time at all.
7. This milk smells a bit sour. Has it gone _____?
8. Make sure you eat _____ all your vegetables.
9. We really pigged _____ at the buffet and had huge helpings.
10. If you feel cold, I can warm _____ some soup for you.

5 Grammar

5.1 Transitive και Intransitive Phrasal Verbs

Τα transitive phrasal verbs (μεταβατικά) ακολουθούνται από αντικείμενο, ενώ τα intransitive phrasal verbs (αμετάβατα) δεν έχουν αντικείμενο.
→ *I prefer my tea **laced with** honey.* (transitive, αντικείμενο = honey)
→ *Malnutrition can be fatal but the doctor says he'll **pull through**.* (intransitive, δεν έχει αντικείμενο)

5.2 Separable και Inseparable Phrasal Verbs

Αν το αντικείμενο ενός phrasal verb μπορεί να μπει ανάμεσα στο ρήμα και το μόριο/την πρόθεση, τότε το phrasal verb είναι separable, δηλαδή χωρίζεται. Αν το αντικείμενο πρέπει οπωσδήποτε να μπει μετά από το μόριο/την πρόθεση, το phrasal verb είναι inseparable, δηλαδή δε χωρίζεται.
→ *You haven't eaten all day so don't **pick at** your food.* (inseparable)
→ *If you're hungry, I can warm up the leftovers. / If you're hungry, I can **warm** the leftovers **up**.* (separable)

Αν το αντικείμενο ενός separable phrasal verb είναι ουσιαστικό, τότε συνήθως μπαίνει μετά το μόριο/την πρόθεση. Αν το αντικείμενο είναι αντωνυμία, συνήθως μπαίνει ανάμεσα στο ρήμα και το μόριο/την πρόθεση.
→ *After cooking, she always **cleans up** the kitchen.* (αντικείμενο = the kitchen)
→ *After cooking, she always **cleans it up**.* (αντικείμενο = η αντωνυμία 'it')
→ *After cooking, she always **cleans up it**.* ✗

Γενικά, τα phrasal verbs που έχουν δύο μόρια (particles) δε χωρίζονται, είναι inseparable. Μπορούν όμως να ακολουθούνται από αντωνυμία.
→ *The dietician advised him to **cut down on** fizzy drinks.*
→ *The dietician advised him to **cut down on them**.*

5.3 Same-way Question Tags

Όταν μια πρόταση είναι καταφατική, η question tag συνήθως είναι αρνητική, και όταν η πρόταση είναι αρνητική, η question tag συνήθως είναι καταφατική. Μερικές φορές, όμως, μια καταφατική πρόταση έχει καταφατική question tag και μια αρνητική πρόταση έχει αρνητική question tag (same-way question tags). Χρησιμοποιούμε τα same-way question tags για να εκφράσουμε ενδιαφέρον, έκπληξη, θυμό, χαρά κλπ., και όχι για να κάνουμε πραγματική ερώτηση.
→ *So, **you're** opting for water instead of a fizzy drink, **are you**?*
→ ***You think** you can have your cake and eat it too, **do you**?*

5.4 Question Tags for polite requests

Μπορούμε να χρησιμοποιήσουμε question tags για να εκφράσουμε ευγενικά ένα αίτημα.
→ *You **couldn't** beat these eggs for me, **could** you?*

5.5 Reinforcement Tags

Τα reinforcement tags μπαίνουν στο τέλος της πρότασης και ενισχύουν (reinforce) αυτό που είπε ο ομιλητής. Σχηματίζονται ως εξής: υποκείμενο + auxiliary/modal verb, σε αντίθεση με ένα κανονικό question tag (auxiliary/modal verb + υποκείμενο).
→ *Teens should avoid all those unhealthy snacks, **they should**.*
→ *Organic produce is tastier and healthier for us, **it is**.*

Grammar Exercises

A Choose the correct answers.

1 The meal was so good we ___ in no time.
 a polished off it
 b polished it off

2 John cooked the recipe, but I ___ as an idea.
 a came up it with
 b came up with it

3 I think she ___ but she disagrees.
 a takes after her mother
 b takes her mother after

4 Supper is ready, so ___ all of you.
 a tuck in
 b tuck it in

5 We wanted to hold a party, but ___ at the last minute.
 a our plans fell through
 b fell through our plans

6 I wasn't hungry, so I only ___.
 a picked my food at
 b picked at my food

7 He was late, so he ___ and ran out the door.
 a gulped down
 b gulped his breakfast down

8 The milk was off and I ___.
 a threw up
 b threw up it

B Match.

1 So you've cooked us a meal,
2 He won't wash the dishes you know.
3 So I'm the worst cook in the world,
4 Let's try out that new Japanese place,
5 After getting sick she'll never eat there again,
6 So Katy got a new oven,
7 I couldn't have some sugar,
8 I don't suppose I could see the menu again,

a am I? You can just make your own supper then!
b have you? That's great.
c could I? I've run out.
d did she? That must have been expensive.
e shall we? The food there looks appetising.
f Oh won't he? We'll see about that!
g could I? I'd like a dessert.
h will she? What a terrible experience!

C Circle the correct reinforcement tag.

1 That's a scrumptious meal, that is / that isn't.
2 Greg works too hard, does he / he does.
3 This lemon pie is too tart, it is / this is.
4 We would love a meal out, we would / we should.
5 They had a lovely spread, they had / they did.
6 You should take care of yourself, you should / you shall.
7 I'd better get some lunch, I had / I better.
8 You drink too many soft drinks, you drink / you do.

5 Grammar

Exam Task

For questions 1-12, read the text below and decide which answer (A, B, C or D) best fits each gap.

Weight loss camps for children

With the problem of child (1) ___ becoming a serious health matter in western countries, weight loss camps for youngsters are gaining popularity. Once their child has (2) ___ the pounds, parents resort to outside help. The goal of many camps is not only to help children to (3) ___ weight. They realise that obese children are often (4) ___ on and have issues of self-esteem. The aim is to raise their confidence and self-image as well as teach responsible choices about food. Research has been (5) ___ into the success of camps that deal with children's (6) ___ as well as food intake. It appears that successful camps are those that appeal to children's intelligence in order to help them control food (7) ___ . A thoughtful child is made aware of food choices and continues to choose responsibly after he or she goes home.

Another major factor for success is the support of family at home. If children return home to a family that (8) ___ large (9) ___ of food, they are unlikely to keep off the weight they lost at camp. Encouragement and support are key. Kind vigilance is also important as hungry children may try to (10) ___ food into their rooms. In addition, (11) ___ to fast food and snacks should be limited as they can (12) ___ havoc with children's willpower. All in all, weight loss camps are as much about parents as children.

1	A obesity	B	consumption	C	cuisine	D	appetite
2	A whipped up	B	piled on	C	taken on	D	lived on
3	A shed	B	ban	C	skim	D	absorb
4	A put up	B	cleaned out	C	taken after	D	looked down
5	A conducted	B	navigated	C	carried	D	renovated
6	A nutrition	B	cognition	C	counterparts	D	nutrients
7	A helpings	B	platters	C	cravings	D	feasts
8	A gobbles	B	nibbles	C	sips	D	chops
9	A banquets	B	napkins	C	portions	D	odours
10	A brew	B	swap	C	smuggle	D	blend
11	A nutrient	B	habituation	C	incident	D	exposure
12	A do	B	play	C	make	D	pay

6 Living Planet

page 69

6.1 **luminous** (adj) /ˈluːmɪnəs/
shining • *My alarm clock has luminous hands so I can see the time in the dark.* ❖ φωτεινός

Word Focus   page 70

6.2 **magma** (n) /ˈmægmə/
hot liquid rock below the Earth's surface • *The magma below the ground was red hot.* ❖ μάγμα

6.3 **microbe** (n) /ˈmaɪkrəʊb/
a tiny living thing you can see with a microscope • *The scientist examined the microbes under the microscope.* ❖ μικροοργανισμός

6.4 **photosynthesis** (n) /fəʊtəʊˈsɪnθəsɪs/
process in plants where carbon dioxide and water are turned into food using the sun's energy • *We learned about photosynthesis in biology lessons in secondary school.* ➢ photosynthesise (v) ❖ φωτοσύνθεση

6.5 **by-product** (n) /ˈbaɪˌprɒdʌkt/
a substance produced during the process of making or destroying sth else • *Asphalt is a by-product of oil refining.* ❖ υποπροϊόν

6.6 **molten** (adj) /ˈməʊltən/
(metal or rock that is) in a liquid state due to high temperature • *Molten rock was pouring out of the volcano.* ➢ melt (v) ❖ λιωμένος, τετηγμένος

6.7 **oxidation** (n) /ɒksɪˈdeɪʃn/
process of a substance combining with oxygen • *If you leave that metal tool out in the rain, oxidation will take place.* ❖ οξείδωση

Reading   pages 70-71

6.8 **spark** (v) /spaːk/
cause to start • *The argument between the two fans sparked a bigger fight between many supporters.* ➢ spark (n) ❖ προκαλώ

6.9 **formation** (n) /fɔːˈmeɪʃn/
shaping • *The formation of this lake took place millions of years ago.* ➢ form (v) ❖ σχηματισμός

6.10 **harness** (v) /ˈhaːnɪs/
control and use the power of sth • *This solar panel harnesses energy from the sun to heat up water.* ➢ harness (n) ❖ χρησιμοποιώ, δαμάζω

6.11 **consist of** (v) /kənsɪst ɒv/
be made of • *This report consists of an introduction, a presentation and recommendations.* ❖ αποτελούμαι από

6.12 **composition** (n) /kɒmpəˈzɪʃn/
the way sth is made • *The geologist studied the composition of the rock to see how it was formed.* ➢ compose (v) ❖ σύνθεση

6.13 **trigger** (v) /ˈtrɪgə/
cause to start • *The lightning strike triggered a blackout.* ➢ trigger (n) ❖ προκαλώ

6.14 **iron** (n) /aɪən/
a dark red/brown mineral • *Iron is used to make steel.* ❖ σίδηρος

6.15 **ferrous** (adj) /ˈferəs/
containing iron • *Steel is a ferrous metal.* ❖ σιδηρούχος, υποσιδηρούχος

6.16 **ferric** (adj) /ˈferɪk/
containing iron • *When you leave iron out in the rain, it forms ferric oxide, or rust.* ❖ σιδηρικός

6.17 **version** (n) /ˈvɜːʃn/
type of sth • *I saw the black and white version of this film.* ❖ εκδοχή

6.18 **coincidental** (adj) /kəʊɪnsɪˈdentəl/
happening by chance • *Meeting you here was coincidental. I hadn't planned to go out today.* ➢ coincidence (n), coincide (v) ❖ συμπτωματικός

6.19 **subject (to)** (v) /sʌbˈdʒekt (tʊ)/
cause to experience • *The class was subjected to extra homework as a punishment for cheating.* ❖ υποβάλλω σε (δοκιμασία, εγχείρηση, κλπ), εκθέτω σε

6.20 **turmoil** (n) /ˈtɜːmɔɪl/
great trouble and confusion • *There was great turmoil after the tsunami struck the coastal areas.* ❖ αναταραχή

6.21 **greenhouse gas** (n) /ˈgriːnˌhaʊs gæs/
a gas which causes the greenhouse effect • *Greenhouse gases are increasing in the Earth's atmosphere.* ❖ αέριο του θερμοκηπίου

6.22 **chain of events** (expr) /tʃeɪn ɒv ɪˈvents/
things happening one after another • *The history students studied the chain of events that led to the First World War.* ❖ αλυσίδα γεγονότων

6.23 **endure** (v) /ɪnˈdjʊə/
continue to exist through sth difficult • *He endured two days at sea in the storm before he took to his cabin with seasickness.* ➢ endurance (n), endurable (adj) ❖ αντέχω

6.24 **shift** (n) /ʃɪft/
a change • *Greenhouse gases have caused*

a shift in average temperatures. ➢ shift (v) ❖ αλλαγή

6.25 emerge (v) /ɪˈmɜːdʒ/
come out • *The rabbit emerged from its hole in the field and hopped away.* ➢ emergence (n) ❖ βγαίνω, εμφανίζομαι, αναδύομαι

6.26 thrive (v) /θraɪv/
grow; do well • *The crops thrived this year with the good weather.* ➢ thriving (adj) ❖ ακμάζω, ευημερώ

6.27 ozone layer (n) /ˈəʊzəʊn ˈleɪə/
a layer of gases in the atmosphere that prevents harmful radiation from the sun from reaching the Earth • *The ozone layer blocks the sun's dangerous rays from reaching Earth.* ❖ στρώμα του όζοντος

6.28 shield (n) /ʃiːld/
protection • *Use this umbrella as a shield against the sun.* ➢ shield (v) ❖ ασπίδα, προστασία

6.29 solar radiation (n) /ˈsəʊlə reɪdɪˈeɪʃn/
heat and energy from the sun • *Solar radiation would destroy life on Earth without the protection of the ozone layer.* ❖ ηλιακή ακτινοβολία

6.30 emit (v) /ɪˈmɪt/
send out • *That factory chimney emits a lot of smoke that pollutes the area.* ➢ emission (n) ❖ εκπέμπω

6.31 spew (v) /spuː/
throw out in large amounts • *Molten rock was spewed into the sky from the volcano.* ❖ ξερνώ

6.32 element (n) /ˈelɪmənt/
a substance that consists of atoms of only one type • *Oxygen is an element in air that is essential for our survival.* ❖ στοιχείο

Vocabulary pages 72-73

6.33 clear (adj) /klɪə/
sunny, with no clouds • *It was a clear day so it was perfect for the beach.* ❖ αίθριος

6.34 gusty (adj) /ˈgʌsti/
windy • *The gusty weather kept blowing my hat away.* ➢ gust (n) ❖ ανεμώδης

6.35 overcast (adj) /ˌəʊvəˈkɑːst/
cloudy • *It is overcast so it might rain later.* ❖ συννεφιασμένος

6.36 pouring (adj) /ˈpɔːrɪŋ/
raining hard • *It was pouring and we got absolutely soaked.* ➢ pour (v) ❖ βρέχει πολύ

6.37 roasting (adj) /ˈrəʊstɪŋ/
very hot • *It was a roasting day in Athens. The temperature reached 40 degrees.* ➢ roast (v) ❖ πολύ ζεστός

6.38 sticky (adj) /ˈstɪki/
(weather that is) hot and wet • *I get sweaty in this sticky weather.* ❖ ζεστός και υγρός

6.39 drizzly (adj) /ˈdrɪzli/
raining a little • *It's a drizzly day again, so wear a raincoat.* ➢ drizzle (v, n) ❖ ψιχαλίζει

6.40 showery (adj) /ˈʃaʊəri/
raining on and off • *It was showery in the afternoon, but we went into shops to keep dry.* ➢ shower (n) ❖ βροχερός

6.41 blistering (adj) /ˈblɪstərɪŋ/
very hot • *We need to turn on the air-conditioning in this blistering weather.* ❖ πολύ ζεστός

6.42 sweltering (adj) /ˈsweltərɪŋ/
very hot • *It was sweltering in the desert and the tourists found it hard to cope with the heat.* ➢ swelter (v) ❖ ασφυκτικά ζεστός

6.43 oppressive (adj) /əˈpresɪv/
(weather that is) hot and wet • *The atmosphere is oppressive; I think it's going to rain later.* ➢ oppress (v) ❖ πνιγηρός, αποπνικτικός

6.44 bright (adj) /braɪt/
sunny • *A bright day like this is perfect for holiday photographs.* ➢ brightness (n) ❖ ηλιόλουστος

6.45 fair (adj) /feə/
(weather that is) good • *The weather is usually fair in Greece in May.* ❖ αίθριος

6.46 fine (adj) /faɪn/
sunny and dry • *We went for a walk in the country because it was a fine day.* ❖ αίθριος

6.47 dull (adj) /dʌl/
grey; not sunny at all • *Our holiday was ruined by dull weather. It wasn't sunny once.* ➢ dullness (n) ❖ γκρίζος, μουντός, σκοτεινός

6.48 gloomy (adj) /ˈgluːmi/
(weather that is) grey and miserable • *This gloomy weather is depressing.* ➢ gloom (n) ❖ γκρίζος, σκοτεινός

6.49 humid (adj) /ˈhjuːmɪd/
damp • *The evening was humid but it didn't rain.* ➢ humidity (n) ❖ υγρός

6.50 muggy (adj) /ˈmʌgi/
unpleasantly warm and wet • *The washing won't dry in this muggy weather.* ➢ mugginess (n) ❖ ζεστός και υγρός

6.51 sultry (adj) /ˈsʌltri/
warm and damp • *We left the windows open on the sultry summer night.* ❖ ζεστός και υγρός

6.52 blowy (adj) /ˈbləʊi/
windy • *The blowy weather dried the clothes quickly.* ➢ blow (v) ❖ ανεμώδης

6.53 blustery (adj) /ˈblʌstəri/
very windy • *The weather is often blustery near the coast in winter.* ❖ με αέρα που λυσσομανά

6.54 breezy (adj) /ˈbriːzi/
a little windy • *It's breezy, so we can fly our kite today.* ➢ breeze (n) ❖ με αεράκι

6.55 dump (v) /dʌmp/
throw away • *Somebody had dumped their household rubbish by the side of the road.* ➢ dumping (n) ❖ πετώ

6.56 **dirt** (n) /dɜːt/
substances such as dust or mud that make things dirty • *Don't sit down in the dirt.* ➢ dirty (adj) ❖ βρομιά

6.57 **soil** (n) /sɔɪl/
the substance on the surface of the earth where plants, trees, etc. grow • *The soil here is ideal for cultivating olive trees.* ❖ χώμα

6.58 **drill** (v) /drɪl/
dig deep holes in the ground or under the sea for oil • *They are drilling for oil in the North Sea.* ➢ drill (n) ❖ τρυπώ (με τρυπάνι), κάνω γεώτρηση

6.59 **mine** (v) /maɪn/
dig tunnels underground to find coal, diamonds, etc. • *They used to mine for coal in many parts of Europe.* ➢ mine (n) ❖ εξορύσσω, σκάβω

6.60 **sulphur dioxide** (n) /ˈsʌlfə daɪˈɒksaɪd/
a poisonous gas that causes air pollution • *Carbon dioxide, sulphur dioxide and other poisonous gases pollute the atmosphere.* ❖ διοξείδιο του θείου

6.61 **polluter** (n) /pəˈluːtə/
sb or a company that pollutes • *This factory is the worst polluter in the area.* ➢ pollute (v), pollutant (n), pollution (n), polluted (adj) ❖ ρυπαίνων

6.62 **pollutant** (n) /pəˈluːtənt/
a substance that pollutes • *The chemicals that come from your car exhaust are pollutants that contaminate the air we breathe.* ➢ pollute (v) ❖ ρυπογόνος ουσία

6.63 **be up in arms** (expr) /bi ʌp ɪn ɑːmz/
be very angry and protest about it • *People were up in arms about the increase in taxes.* ❖ ξεσηκώνομαι, επαναστατώ

6.64 **landfill** (n) /ˈlændfɪl/
a hole in the ground where rubbish is buried • *There is a landfill near here and it often smells terrible because of the rubbish.* ❖ χώρος υγειονομικής ταφής

6.65 **wasteland** (n) /ˈweɪstˌlænd/
an unattractive area with little life • *The place was a wasteland after the tornado destroyed it.* ❖ ερημότοπος, ξερότοπος

6.66 **outskirts** (pl n) /ˈaʊtskɜːts/
the parts of a town that are furthest from the centre • *He lives on the outskirts of town so he has to take a bus to the centre.* ❖ περίχωρα

6.67 **oil spill** (n) /ɔɪl spɪl/
an accident where oil pollutes the sea and/or land • *The oil spill from the tanker killed many fish and birds.* ❖ πετρελαιοκηλίδα

6.68 **slip** (n) /slɪp/
sliding on sth wet • *That was a nasty slip on the wet floor. Did you hurt yourself?* ➢ slip (v) ❖ γλίστρημα

6.69 **landfall** (n) /ˈlændfɔːl/
the land you arrive at after a sea voyage • *The ship made landfall on an island in the middle of the ocean.* ❖ προσέγγιση σε ξηρά

6.70 **landslide** (n) /ˈlændslaɪd/
rocks and earth falling down the side of a mountain • *The heavy rain caused a landslide that blocked the road with rocks.* ❖ κατολίσθηση

6.71 **hunter-gatherer** (n) /ˈhʌntə-ˈɡæðərə/
sb who lives by hunting animals and gathering fruit and nuts • *Hunter-gatherers moved from place to place in search of food.* ❖ κυνηγός-τροφοσυλλέκτης

6.72 **live off the land** (expr) /lɪv ɒf ðə lænd/
eat what grows naturally • *The subsistence farmer lives off the land and has no need for supermarkets.* ❖ ζω από τη γη

6.73 **berry** (n) /ˈberi/
a small round fruit • *The two berries in this jam are strawberry and blackberry.* ❖ μούρο

6.74 **suffice** (v) /səˈfaɪs/
be enough • *If this money does not suffice, you can apply to the bank for a loan.* ➢ sufficient (adj) ❖ αρκώ, επαρκώ

6.75 **nomad** (n) /ˈnəʊmæd/
sb who travels from place to place instead of living in one place all the time • *The nomads travelled in the desert on camels.* ➢ nomadic (adj) ❖ νομάς

6.76 **migrate** (v) /maɪˈɡreɪt/
go to live in another area or country • *The birds migrated to warmer places in the south to spend the winter.* ➢ migration (n) ❖ μεταναστεύω

6.77 **territory** (n) /ˈterətri/
land that is owned or controllled by sb/sth • *Male animals defend their territory against other males.* ➢ territorial (adj) ❖ περιοχή

6.78 **seek** (v) /siːk/
look for • *If it rains, we should seek a dry place to spend the night.* ❖ αναζητώ

6.79 **refuge** (n) /ˈrefjuːdʒ/
shelter or protection • *The travellers sought refuge from the storm at a small hotel.* ❖ καταφύγιο

6.80 **shelter** (n) /ˈʃeltə/
a structure made or built to protect you from the weather • *The explorers made a shelter of branches to keep dry.* ➢ shelter (v) ❖ καταφύγιο

6.81 **fashion** (v) /ˈfæʃn/
make sth • *Early humans used tools they had fashioned out of rocks and bones.* ❖ φτιάχνω, διαμορφώνω

6.82 **beat down** (phr v) /biːt daʊn/
shine strongly • *The sun was beating*

down so we had to find some shade.
❖ (ο ήλιος) βαράει

6.83 blow up (phr v) /bləʊ ʌp/
begin suddenly with force • *A storm blew up at sea and endangered the fishermen.*
❖ φουσκώνω, ξεσπώ

6.84 bucket down (phr v) /ˈbʌkɪt daʊn/
rain heavily • *It's bucketing down. You're going to get very wet if you go out.* ❖ βρέχει πολύ δυνατά

6.85 clear up (phr v) /klɪə ʌp/
stop raining and become fine • *If the weather clears up later, let's go out for a walk.*
❖ καθαρίζω

6.86 blow over (phr v) /bləʊ ˈəʊvə/
go away without causing damage • *The storm blew over and the sun came out.* ❖ περνώ

6.87 dry up (phr v) /draɪ ʌp/
If a lake, pond, river, etc. dries up, the water in it disappears. • *When it didn't rain for two months the stream dried up.* ❖ ξεραίνω

6.88 disperse (v) /dɪˈspɜːs/
move apart • *The clouds dispersed and the sun appeared.* ➣ dispersal (n)
❖ (δια)σκορπίζομαι

6.89 prolonged (adj) /prəˈlɒŋd/
continuing for a long time • *There was a prolonged heat wave and everyone suffered.*
➣ prolong (v) ❖ παρατεταμένος, διαρκείας

6.90 drought (n) /draʊt/
a period of time when there is no rain
• *The long drought meant that animals died and crops failed.* ❖ ανομβρία, ξηρασία

6.91 weary (adj) /ˈwɪəri/
tired • *I felt terribly weary after walking around the shops all day.* ➣ weariness (n)
❖ κουρασμένος

6.92 safe and sound (expr) /seɪf ænd saʊnd/
unharmed after being in danger • *Despite the storm, the sailors got back to port safe and sound.* ❖ σώος και αβλαβής

6.93 soaked (adj) /səʊkt/
completely wet • *I forgot my umbrella and got soaked in the rain.* ➣ soak (v)
❖ μουσκεμένος

6.94 unaware (adj) /ʌnəˈweə/
not knowing • *The teacher was unaware of the cheating when she marked the tests.*
❖ ανήξερος, που έχει άγνοια

6.95 indifferent (adj) /ɪnˈdɪfərənt/
uninterested • *She was indifferent to the fate of the planet and didn't even recycle.*
➣ indifference (n) ❖ αδιάφορος

6.96 viable (adj) /ˈvaɪəbl/
capable of working successfully; feasible
• *Buying a huge petrol-guzzling car was not economically viable for us.* ❖ βιώσιμος

6.97 alternative (n) /ɔːlˈtɜːnətɪv/
a different choice • *A good alternative to going to the cinema is renting a DVD from a video club.* ➣ alternative (adj)
❖ εναλλακτική λύση

6.98 fossil fuel (n) /fɒsl fjʊəl/
fuel like coal or oil • *Coal was the fossil fuel used in the Industrial Revolution.*
❖ ορυκτό καύσιμο

6.99 interfere (v) /ɪntəˈfɪə/
get involved in sth that is not your affair
• *Don't interfere; it's none of your business.*
➣ interference (n) ❖ παρεμβαίνω

6.100 insistence (n) /ɪnˈsɪstəns/
saying that sth must be done • *Insistence on good behaviour has led to a good environment at this school.* ➣ insist (v) ❖ επιμονή

6.101 drove of cattle (expr) /drəʊv ɒv ˈkætl/
a group of cattle • *The rancher led a drove of cattle across the plains.* ❖ κοπάδι βοοειδών

6.102 tower of giraffes (expr) /ˈtaʊə ɒv dʒɪˈrɑːfs/
a group of giraffes • *A tower of giraffes were eating the leaves of the trees.* ❖ αγέλη καμηλοπαρδάλεων

6.103 bed of snakes (expr) /bed ɒv sneɪks/
a group of snakes • *There was a bed of snakes under a rock in the desert.*
❖ κοπάδι φιδιών

6.104 army of ants (expr) /ˈɑːmi ɒv ænts/
a group of ants • *We watched an army of ants going in and out of their nest.* ❖ στρατός μυρμηγκιών, αποικία μυρμηγκιών

6.105 parliament of owls (expr) /ˈpɑːləmənt ɒv aʊlz/
a group of owls • *A parliament of owls made soft noises in the night.* ❖ ομάδα κουκουβαγιών

6.106 pride of lions (expr) /praɪd ɒv ˈlaɪənz/
a group of lions • *We saw a pride of lions when we were on safari in Kenya.*
❖ αγέλη λιονταριών

6.107 continental United States (n) /kɒntɪˈnentəl juˈnaɪtɪd steɪts/
all the states of the Unites States except Hawaii and Alaska • *There are 48 states in the continental United States.*
❖ ηπειρωτικές Ηνωμένες Πολιτείες

6.108 hostile (adj) /ˈhɒstaɪl/
difficult to live in • *It isn't easy to live in the hostile environment of the desert.*
➣ hostility (n) ❖ εχθρικός για τη ζωή

6.109 forbidding (adj) /fəˈbɪdɪŋ/
frightening • *The explorers were determined to cross the forbidding desert.* ➣ forbid (v)
❖ απειλητικός, τρομακτικός

6.110 scorched (adj) /skɔːtʃt/
burnt by the sun • *The scorched grass was brown and dry.* ➣ scorch (v) ❖ καμένος

6.111 **barren** (adj) /ˈbærən/
dry and bare, with few plants • *The barren plot of land had no trees and few plants.* ❖ άγονος

6.112 **startlingly** (adv) /ˈstɑːtlɪŋli/
surprisingly • *We had a startlingly beautiful view of the sea from our cheap hotel.*
➢ startle (v), startling (adj) ❖ καταπληκτικά, εντυπωσιακά

6.113 **searing** (adj) /ˈsɪərɪŋ/
extremely hot • *I couldn't bear the searing heat so I went indoors.* ➢ sear (v) ❖ έντονα καυτός

6.114 **soar** (v) /sɔː/
rise very high • *The temperature soared to over 40 degrees in the afternoon.* ❖ ανεβαίνω στα ύψη

6.115 **nap** (n) /næp/
a short sleep • *She had a nap in the afternoon after arriving home from work.* ➢ nap (v)
❖ υπνάκος

6.116 **elevation** (n) /eləˈveɪʃn/
height • *We climbed to the highest elevation to admire the city from above.* ➢ elevate (v)
❖ ανύψωση

Grammar pages 74-75

6.117 **charity** (n) /ˈtʃærəti/
an organisation that raises money to help people or animals in need • *Oxfam is a well-known British charity that helps people in need.* ➢ charitable (adj)
❖ φιλανθρωπικό ίδρυμα

6.118 **principal** (n) /ˈprɪnsɪpl/
a head teacher • *The principal announced that we could leave school early that day.* ❖ διευθυντής/διευθύντρια σχολείου

6.119 **feel sth in one's bones** (expr)
/fiːl sʌmθɪŋ ɪn wʌnz bəʊnz/
be certain about sth even though you cannot explain why you are certain • *I know she's lying. I feel it in my bones.* ❖ έχω προαίσθημα για κάτι, νιώθω κάτι 'στο πετσί μου'

6.120 **lonesome** (adj) /ˈləʊnsəm/
unhappy because you are alone • *The lonesome child played by himself in a corner.*
❖ (που νιώθει) μόνος, θλιμμένος λόγω μοναξιάς

6.121 **sadden** (v) /ˈsædən/
make sad • *The news that your grandmother passed away saddened us all.* ➢ sad (adj), sadness (n) ❖ στεναχωρώ

6.122 **subspecies** (n) /ˈsʌbspiːʃɪz/
a group of plants or animals within a species that have particular characteristics • *The European subspecies of wolf has longer ears than the North American subspecies.*
❖ υποείδος

6.123 **demise** (n) /dɪˈmaɪz/
death • *The zoo is sad to announce the demise of its giant panda.* ❖ θάνατος

Listening page 76

6.124 **laid-back** (adj) /leɪd-bæk/
relaxed; not strict • *The teacher is laid-back so he won't mind if your homework is a day late.*
❖ χαλαρός, άνετος

6.125 **reclining** (adj) /rɪˈklaɪnɪŋ/
tilting backwards • *I tipped back the reclining seat on the plane and tried to sleep.*
➢ recline (v) ❖ ανακλινόμενος

6.126 **unrushed** (adj) /ˈʌnˌrʌʃt/
relaxed • *I prefer an unrushed holiday by the sea.* ❖ χαλαρός, ξεκούραστος

6.127 **resemble** (v) /rɪˈzembl/
look or behave like sb • *He resembles his dad physically but they have different personalities.*
➢ resemblance (n) ❖ μοιάζω

6.128 **hide out** (phr v) /haɪd aʊt/
make sure you are not found • *The robbers hid out all weekend in the forest before they were caught.* ➢ hide-out (n) ❖ κρύβομαι

6.129 **bizarre** (adj) /bɪˈzɑː/
very strange • *His behaviour was bizarre; I can't explain it.* ❖ παράξενος, αλλόκοτος

6.130 **weird** (adj) /wɪəd/
strange • *This weird animal was a flying dinosaur.* ❖ παράξενος

6.131 **juvenile** (adj) /ˈdʒuːvənaɪl/
still growing; under the age of 18 • *Police often give talks at schools to try to fight juvenile crime.* ➢ juvenile (n) ❖ ανήλικος

6.132 **pay homage to** (expr) /peɪ ˈhɒmɪdʒ tuː/
show respect towards • *On November 11th, people pay homage to those who died in World War I.* ❖ αποδίδω φόρο τιμής σε

6.133 **commemorate** (v) /kəˈmeməreɪt/
do sth to show that you remember an important past event • *Parades on March 25th commemorate the Greek Revolution of 1821.* ➢ commemoration (n)
❖ τιμώ τη μνήμη

6.134 **be in two minds** (expr) /biː ɪn tuː maɪndz/
be undecided • *I am in two minds about whether to move abroad to find work as I would miss my friends and family.*
❖ είμαι αναποφάσιστος

6.135 **inconclusive** (adj) /ɪnkənˈkluːsɪv/
not having a clear result • *The results were inconclusive so the scientists did more experiments.*
❖ αναποτελεσματικός, μη οριστικός

6.136 **be pushed for time** (expr) /biː pʊʃt fə taɪm/
have a very limited period of time to do sth

- We'll try to finish the work today, but we're pushed for time. ❖ με πιέζει ο χρόνος, έχω πολύ λίγο χρόνο για κάτι

6.137 **work against the clock** (expr) /wɜːk əˈɡenst ðə klɒk/
work quickly because you do not have much time • *The builders are working against the clock to finish the house before the winter.* ❖ δουλεύω γρήγορα, με αντίπαλο τον χρόνο

Phrasal verbs

beat down	bucket down	dry up
blow over	clear up	hide out
blow up		

Speaking page 77

6.138 **urban** (adj) /ˈɜːbən/
in/of a town or city • *This urban area needs more greenery for the residents to enjoy.* ❖ αστικός

6.139 **biodiversity** (n) /baɪəʊdaɪˈvɜːsɪti/
the variety of animals and plants in an area • *The biodiversity of the sea is being threatened by pollution.* ❖ βιοποικιλότητα

6.140 **food chain** (expr) /fuːd tʃeɪn/
all living things in a group in which one creature eats another, and then is eaten by another • *The introduction of new species of fish in the lake is affecting the food chain.* ❖ τροφική αλυσίδα

6.141 **survival of the fittest** (expr) /səˈvaɪvl əv ðə ˈfɪtəst/
the principle that only the creatures that are best adapted to their environment will survive and reproduce • *During the last ice age, it was a struggle to live. It was a case of the survival of the fittest.* ❖ ο νόμος του ισχυρού, επιβίωση των ικανοτέρων

Writing: a contribution pages 78-79

6.142 **lagoon** (n) /ləˈɡuːn/
an area of sea water that is separated from the sea by a reef, a sandbank or rocks • *We went swimming in the warm blue water of the lagoon.* ❖ λιμνοθάλασσα

6.143 **hospitality** (n) /ˌhɒspɪˈtæləti/
friendly behaviour to one's guests • *The Greeks are famous for their hospitality to strangers.* ➢ hospitable (adj) ❖ φιλοξενία

6.144 **picturesque** (adj) /ˌpɪktʃəˈresk/
(of a place) pretty in an old-fashioned way • *The picturesque village was high in the mountains.* ❖ γραφικός

6.145 **nestle** (v) /ˈnesəl/
be situated in a half-hidden or sheltered position • *The old town nestles at the foot of the hill.* ❖ φωλιάζω, κουρνιάζω

6.146 **stunning** (adj) /ˈstʌnɪŋ/
very beautiful or impressive • *The view from the top of the mountain was stunning.* ➢ stun (v) ❖ εκπληκτικός, εκθαμβωτικός

6.147 **stove** (n) /stəʊv/
sth that burns coal, wood, etc. and is used to heat a room or for cooking • *The old lady lit the stove to make tea.* ❖ σόμπα, εστία μαγειρέματος κουζίνα

6.148 **draw** (v) /drɔː/
take from • *In the past, we drew water from the river.* ❖ αντλώ, τραβώ

6.149 **well** (n) /wel/
a hole in the ground from where water can be drawn • *The water in the well in the garden is drinkable.* ❖ πηγάδι

6.150 **fragrant** (adj) /ˈfreɪɡrənt/
smelling nice • *I love walking in the garden and smelling the fragrant flowers.* ➢ fragrance (n) ❖ αρωματικός

6.151 **underestimate** (v) /ʌndəˈestɪmeɪt/
not realise how important sth is • *Do not underestimate the ability of your opponent.* ❖ υποτιμώ

6.152 **natural resource** (n) /ˈnætʃrəl rɪˈsɔːs/
sth such as a forest, coal, etc. which exists in a place and can be used by people • *Oil is a natural resource that will run out in the near future.* ❖ φυσικός πόρος

6.153 **tranquillity** (n) /træŋˈkwɪləti/
peace • *They love the tranquillity of the countryside.* ➢ tranquil (adj) ❖ ηρεμία, γαλήνη

6.154 **contemplation** (n) /kɒntemˈpleɪʃn/
deep reflective thought • *He sat in quiet contemplation of the summer evening.* ➢ contemplate (v) ❖ περισυλλογή, στοχασμός, ενατένιση

Video 6: Holland Water page 80

6.155 **global warming** (n) /ˈɡləʊbl ˈwɔːmɪŋ/
an increase in world temperatures caused by increased amounts of carbon dioxide in the atmosphere • *Global warming is threatening our survival.* ❖ υπερθέρμανση του πλανήτη

6.156 **low-lying** (adj) /ləʊ-ˈlaɪɪŋ/
not far above sea level or below sea level • *Low-lying islands are in danger of flooding because of rising sea levels.* ❖ που βρίσκεται σε χαμηλό υψόμετρο

6.157 **be at odds** (expr) /bi ət ɒdz/
disagree with sb about sth • *Sarah and her father are at odds and can't agree on anything.* ❖ διαφωνώ, έρχομαι σε αντίθεση/ αντιπαράθεση

6.158 **flood** (v) /flʌd/
become covered in water • *The river overflowed and flooded the high street.* ➢ flood (n) ❖ πλημμυρίζω

6.159 **sink** (v) /sɪŋk/
go under water • *The stone sank to the bottom of the lake when I threw it in.* ❖ βυθίζομαι

6.160 **pump** (v) /pʌmp/
force water out of a place with a special machine • *After the flood, we had to pump water out of our basement* ➢ pump (n) ❖ αντλώ

6.161 **marshland** (n) /ˈmɑːʃlænd/
a wet muddy area of land • *Thousands of waterbirds live in the marshlands.* ❖ βαλτότοπος

6.162 **recreation** (n) /rekrɪˈeɪʃn/
an activity you do for pleasure • *For recreation I play tennis and go for long walks.* ➢ recreational (adj) ❖ αναψυχή

6.163 **radical** (adj) /ˈrædɪkəl/
differing from tradition; innovative or progressive • *Banning cars from the city centre and introducing bike lanes was a radical move.* ➢ radical (n), radically (adv) ❖ ριζοσπαστικός

6.164 **regardless of** (expr) /rɪˈɡɑːdləs ɒv/
without being affected or influenced by sth • *Regardless of what you may say, I am going to sell the car.* ❖ άσχετα από

6.165 **elaborate** (adj) /ɪˈlæbərət/
complex • *The elaborate system of roads was hard to navigate.* ➢ elaborate (v) ❖ περίπλοκος

6.166 **dyke** (n) /daɪk/
a wall which stops water flooding an area • *Many dykes were built in the Netherlands to protect the land from floods.* ❖ ανάχωμα

6.167 **windmill** (n) /ˈwɪndmɪl/
a building with wooden blades that turn in the wind • *This windmill used to provide the whole community with flour.* ❖ ανεμόμυλος

6.168 **reclaim** (v) /riːˈkleɪm/
make an area suitable for farming or building • *The land here used to be under the sea, but it was reclaimed.* ❖ αποξηραίνω, εκχερσώνω

6.169 **sand dune** (n) /sænd djuːn/
a hill of sand formed by the wind in a desert or near the sea • *The children chased each other up and down the sand dunes.* ❖ αμμόλοφος

6.170 **tide** (n) /taɪd/
the regular rise and fall of the level of the sea caused by the pull of the moon and sun • *We'll go for a walk along the beach when the tide goes out.* ➢ tidal (adj) ❖ παλίρροια

6.171 **floating** (adj) /ˈfləʊtɪŋ/
lying on the surface of water • *The floating markets of Thailand are very colourful with all the fresh fruit and vegetables in the canoes.* ➢ float (v) ❖ που επιπλέει

6.172 **recreation** (n) /ˌriːkriˈeɪʃn/
an activity you do for pleasure • *What do you like doing for recreation?* ❖ αναψυχή, ψυχαγωγία

Earth and its atmosphere

dyke	natural resource
fossil fuel	ozone layer
global warming	sand dune
greenhouse gas	solar radiation
lagoon	tide
landslide	wasteland
magma	

Verbs whose nouns do not change form

balance	nap	shift
drill	pump	slip
harness	shelter	spark
mine	shield	trigger

Vocabulary Exercises

A Match.

1 A strange chain of
2 We should try living off
3 This axe head was fashioned out
4 The hikers arrived back safe and
5 An army of
6 There was a pride of
7 The people came to pay
8 I'm in two

a sound after the storm.
b the land to save money.
c lions in the distance.
d homage to the king.
e of a piece of rock.
f minds about it; I can't decide.
g ants moved across the lawn.
h events led to the incident.

B Complete the table.

Verb	Noun
form	1
2	emergence
compose	3
insist	4
5	endurance
6	migration
7	emission
8	dominance
9	sadness
10	shift
11	pollutant
12	interference

C Complete the phrasal verbs in the sentences.

1 The criminals were _____ out in a small cabin in the woods.
2 The sun _____ down on the sandy beach.
3 If it _____ down like this tomorrow, we will have to cancel the cricket match.
4 The pond has _____ up in this hot weather and my fish are dead.
5 A storm _____ up while we were on the ferry and I got very seasick.
6 I hope the weather _____ up soon so we can sit in the garden.
7 Luckily the storm _____ over quickly and it didn't ruin our day.

D Choose the correct answers.

1 An umbrella is no use on such a ___ day.
   a showery   b blustery   c drizzly
2 I need my sunglasses in this ___ sunshine.
   a bright   b muggy   c humid
3 We got ___ in the downpour.
   a soaked   b scorched   c searing
4 The crops grew well in the rich ___ of the region.
   a dirt   b marshland   c soil
5 The hooligans' rude comments ___ a fight in the stands.
   a harnessed   b sparked   c mined
6 When people heard about the incident, they were up in ___ .
   a arms   b guns   c rocks
7 The ___ of the baby elephant is very sad and the zoo keepers will miss him.
   a slip   b turmoil   c demise
8 Is solar power a ___ alternative to fossil fuels?
   a precious   b viable   c sultry
9 He saw a ___ of snakes in the desert.
   a parliament   b drove   c bed
10 There was a ___ drought, so there was very little water in the lakes and rivers.
   a soaked   b prolonged   c unrushed

6 Grammar

6.1 Modal Verbs

Modal	Use
can	για να μιλήσουμε για γενική ικανότητα στο παρόν και στο μέλλον για να ζητήσουμε κάτι για να δώσουμε την άδεια μας σε κάποιον να κάνει κάτι → She **can** water the plants and she's only six! → **Can** you put the rubbish in the bin? → Sure, you **can** go out if it's not rainy.
can't	για να δείξουμε πως είμαστε σίγουροι ότι κάτι δεν ισχύει → It **can't** be organic olive oil. It doesn't taste right.
could	για να μιλήσουμε για γενική ικανότητα στο παρελθόν (αόριστος του can) για να μιλήσουμε για μια πιθανότητα στο μέλλον για να ζητήσουμε κάτι ευγενικά για να προτείνουμε κάτι → My grandmother **could** predict the weather in the village. → Another ice age **could** happen in the future. → **Could** you explain photosynthesis to me? → You **could** seek refuge in a cave if a storm breaks out.
may	για να μιλήσουμε για μια πιθανότητα στο μέλλον για να ζητήσουμε κάτι ευγενικά για να δώσουμε την άδεια μας με ευγενικό τρόπο σε κάποιον να κάνει κάτι → She **may** volunteer at the animal shelter. → **May** I ask you something? → Yes, you **may** organise a recycling campaign at school.
might	για να μιλήσουμε για μια πιθανότητα στο μέλλον σαν τον αόριστο του may → I **might** sell my car and get a bike. → Andy said he **might** watch the documentary.
must	για να πούμε ότι κάτι είναι απαραίτητο για να μιλήσουμε για κάτι που είναι υποχρεωτικό για να εκφράσουμε βεβαιότητα ότι κάτι ισχύει για να προτείνουμε κάτι → We **must** try to help animals in need. → You **must** finish your project by tomorrow. → The heat in Death Valley National Park **must** be really oppressive. → You **must** get some fresh air; you look tired.
mustn't	για να μιλήσουμε για κάτι που δεν επιτρέπεται → We **mustn't** litter the area.
should	για να δώσουμε συμβουλή για να ζητήσουμε συμβουλή → You **should** plant herbs in your garden. → **Should** I try to run when I see a pack of dogs?
would	για πράξεις που κάναμε συχνά στο παρελθόν αλλά δεν κάνουμε πια για να ζητήσουμε κάτι ευγενικά → I **would** throw waste paper in the rubbish, but now I recycle it. → **Would** you take a look at the modem, please?
needn't	για να πούμε ότι κάτι δεν είναι απαραίτητο → We **needn't** buy the book; we can borrow it from George.
be able to	για να μιλήσουμε για γενική ικανότητα για να μιλήσουμε για μια συγκεκριμένη ικανότητα στο παρελθόν → She **is able to** produce her own honey. → The yachtsmen **were able to** reach the shore before the storm broke.

6 Grammar

have to	για να πούμε ότι κάτι είναι απαραίτητο για να μιλήσουμε για υποχρέωση → They **have to** book a place for the seminar. → We **have to** protect endangered species.
mustn't & don't have to	Χρησιμοποιούμε *mustn't* για να πούμε ότι κάτι δεν επιτρέπεται, ενώ χρησιμοποιούμε *don't have to* για να πούμε ότι δεν υπάρχει υποχρέωση ή αναγκαιότητα. → Factories **mustn't** dump their chemical waste in rivers. → You **don't have to** water the plants every day.

Σημειώσεις:
Μπορούμε να χρησιμοποιήσουμε και το *ought to* για να δώσουμε μια συμβουλή, αλλά συνήθως δε χρησιμοποιείται στον ερωτηματικό τύπο.
→ Oil spills **ought to be** prevented.

Μπορούμε να χρησιμοποιήσουμε το *need* και σαν κανονικό ρήμα. Έχει καταφατικό, ερωτηματικό και αρνητικό τύπο, και χρησιμοποιείται συνήθως στον Present Simple και στον Past Simple. Ακολουθείται από full infinitive.
→ They **need to close down** the landfill. It's unhealthy.

6.2 Perfect Modal Verbs

Perfect Modal	Meaning
must have + past participle	Είμαστε βέβαιοι ότι κάτι έγινε στο παρελθόν. → The earthquake **must have triggered** the landslide.
can't have + past participle	Είμαστε βέβαιοι ότι κάτι αποκλείεται να έγινε στο παρελθόν. → The book **can't have vanished** into thin air. It was here a minute ago.
may/might/could have + past participle	Είναι πιθανό κάτι να έγινε στο παρελθόν, αλλά δεν είμαστε σίγουροι. → He **may have gone** to Australia, but we're not sure.
could/might have + past participle	Υπήρχε πιθανότητα να γίνει κάτι στο παρελθόν αλλά δεν έγινε. → I **could have gone** to a tourist resort but I didn't like the idea.
should/ought to have + past participle	Ήταν σωστό να γίνει κάτι, αλλά δεν το κάναμε. Περιμέναμε να γίνει κάτι, αλλά δεν έγινε. → The plants are dead. You **should have watered** them. → They **should have dealt with** the oil spill by now.
would have + past participle	Σκοπεύαμε να κάνουμε κάτι, αλλά δεν το κάναμε. → We **would have called** the local council but it was Sunday.
need't have + past participle	Δεν ήταν απαραίτητο να κάνουμε κάτι αλλά το κάναμε. → You **needn't have brough**t all those candles. The room has electricity.

Grammar Exercises

A Complete the sentences with the words below.

| bound | have | may | might | mustn't | ought | should | won't |

1. You _____ to give in your assignment tomorrow or the teacher will fail you.
2. Mum has agreed and said we _____ go on the school trip to France.
3. You _____ park here as this is a no-parking zone.
4. I believe parents _____ encourage their children to recycle.
5. You are _____ to see John at that restaurant. He goes there every night.
6. Mum thinks I _____ to do a first aid course. What's your advice?
7. I can do this part of the recipe but I _____ need some help with the topping.
8. These children are so noisy. They just _____ calm down.

B Match.

1. That's impossible.
2. What do you suggest I do?
3. It's a real habit with her now.
4. I'm absolutely certain.
5. I hope they are able to do something.
6. She has a request.
7. It's prohibited I'm afraid.
8. It really isn't necessary.

a. That must be Kate at the door.
b. Surely this answer can't be right.
c. You don't have to make me supper.
d. Clients mustn't smoke on the premises.
e. I think you should apologise.
f. Don't worry. With your donation they can save the zoo.
g. She will eat two bananas for breakfast every day.
h. She wants to know if you could help out at the charity event.

C Finish these sentences with your own ideas and the perfect modals in brackets.

1. But I was sure this is George's house. (must have)
   _____
2. That isn't Mary at the door because she is in New York. (can't have)
   _____
3. Jimmy is late home from work. (might have)
   _____
4. You didn't need to cook tonight. (could have)
   _____
5. I'm going to be late for my appointment. (should have)
   _____
6. It wasn't necessary for you to put me up in your flat. (would have)
   _____
7. That was a delicious meal. (needn't have)
   _____
8. Darren has forgotten his phone again. (ought to have)
   _____

6 Grammar

Exam Task

For questions 1-15, read the text below and think of the word which best fits the gap. Use only one word in each gap.

Coping with global warming

Global warming is threatening life on Earth. It's a fact. We **(1)** ____ act now or our own species will soon be endangered. According to experts, we have no choice but to find alternatives **(2)** ____ fossil fuels, because they will soon run **(3)** ____ . This is the message on eco-news bulletins but a large number of people seem quite unaware **(4)** ____ the urgency of the situation. We continue to buy and run petrol-guzzling vehicles and seem indifferent **(5)** ____ the harm exhaust fumes are doing to the atmosphere. We **(6)** ____ to buy hybrid cars but few can follow such advice when these vehicles aren't affordable. If the situation gets worse, we feel that governments are bound **(7)** ____ help us. But will they?

Regardless **(8)** ____ whether governments will or can help their citizens, as individuals we **(9)** ____ be encouraged to do more, couldn't we? Here eco-news reporters don't help. They **(10)** ____ concentrate on the gloom and doom of our situation! It's a bad habit of theirs. Twenty years ago we were constantly warned of the hole in the ozone **(11)** ____ . Today it rarely makes the headlines. **(12)** ____ can't have gone away, can it? Well no, but a little research online reveals that the hole is diminishing. This news could **(13)** ____ made the headlines and woken us up to what can be done. Reporters **(14)** ____ not have to tell us only the woes of our situation. They should encourage us to act positively in order to emerge safe **(15)** ____ sound from this situation.

7 Eureka!

page 83

7.1 **nomination** (n) /nɒmɪˈneɪʃn/
the act of officially suggesting sb for a prize, position, etc. • *My nomination for best sportsman is Usain Bolt.* ➢ nominate (v)
❖ υποψηφιότητα

Word Focus — page 84

7.2 **nickel** (n) /ˈnɪkəl/
a hard silver-white metal • *Nickel is used to make the metal steel.* ❖ νικέλιο

7.3 **hardback** (n) /ˈhɑːdbæk/
a book with a hard cover • *The hardback version of this book costs more but the harder cover will make it last longer.* ❖ βιβλίο με σκληρό εξώφυλλο
✎ Opp: paperback

7.4 **kiln** (n) /kɪln/
a large oven for baking bricks and clay • *The clay pots were heated in the kiln to harden them.* ❖ καμίνι, κλίβανος

7.5 **lunatic** (n) /ˈluːnətɪk/
a mad person • *The man who shot those innocent people must be a lunatic.*
❖ ανισόρροπος, παράφρων

7.6 **reinforce** (v) /riːɪnˈfɔːs/
make a structure or material stronger • *Nowadays we reinforce the materials we build with to make them stronger.*
➢ reinforced (adj) ❖ ενισχύω

7.7 **MDF** (n) /em diː ef/
boards made of wood fibres pressed together • *I bought an MDF table from IKEA.*
❖ ινοσανίδα μεσαίας πυκνότητας
✎ MDF = medium density fibreboard

7.8 **agility** (n) /æˈdʒɪlɪti/
the ability to move in a quick and easy manner • *The agility of the gymnast impressed us all.*
➢ agile (adj) ❖ ευκινησία

Reading — pages 84-85

7.9 **phonograph** (n) /ˈfəʊnəɡrɑːf/
a record player • *The phonograph allowed people to listen to recorded music.*
❖ φωνογράφος

7.10 **irrigation screw** (n) /ɪrɪˈɡeɪʃn skruː/
a device for lifting water, also known as Archimedes' screw • *The irrigation screw made watering crops much easier for farmers.*
❖ κοχλίας του Αρχιμήδη (κοχλίας άρδευσης)

7.11 **windscreen wiper** (n) /ˈwɪndskriːn ˈwaɪpə/
a device that cleans rainwater off the front window of a vehicle • *Use the windscreen wipers so you can see where you are driving in the rain.* ❖ υαλοκαθαριστήρας

7.12 **transform** (v) /trænsˈfɔːm/
change completely • *PCs transformed the world of work and entertainment.*
➢ transformation (n) ❖ μετατρέπω

7.13 **prophecy** (n) /ˈprɒfəsi/
a prediction, often religious • *The prophecy that the world would end in 2012 did not come true.* ❖ προφητεία

7.14 **machinery** (n) /məˈʃiːnəri/
machines • *Tractors are essential farming machinery.* ❖ μηχανήματα

7.15 **manual labour** (n) /ˈmænjuəl ˈleɪbə/
work done by people with their own hands • *Manual labour is still used on fruit farms because people are needed to harvest the delicate berries.* ❖ χειρωνακτική εργασία

7.16 **seamstress** (n) /ˈsiːmstrəs/
a woman who makes and sews clothes • *The seamstress shortened the client's trousers.* ❖ μοδίστρα

7.17 **seam** (n) /siːm/
a line where two pieces of material are sewn together • *The seam on the arm of this sweater has come undone.* ❖ ραφή

7.18 **sewing machine** (n) /ˈsəʊwɪŋ məˈʃiːn/
a device you can sew clothes with • *I made myself a new jacket on the sewing machine.*
❖ ραπτομηχανή

7.19 **mundane** (adj) /mʌnˈdeɪn/
ordinary and uninteresting • *I don't enjoy mundane chores like vacuuming and dusting.*
❖ πληκτικός

7.20 **automated** (adj) /ˈɔːtəmeɪtɪd/
using computers and machines to do a job • *Production in this factory is automated and workers supervise the machinery.* ➢ automation (n) ❖ αυτόματος, αυτοματοποιημένος

7.21 **cost effective** (adj) /kɒst ɪˈfektɪv/
giving the best benefit/profit compared to the money that is spent on sth • *Some employees were fired because the boss wanted to make the business more cost effective.*
❖ αποδοτικός, οικονομικός

7.22 **flexible** (adj) /ˈfleksɪbl/
which bends easily • *This plastic ruler is flexible, so it won't break if you bend it.*
➢ flexibility (n) ❖ εύκαμπτος
✎ Opp: inflexible, stiff

7.23 **give way** (expr) /gɪv weɪ/
be replaced by sth • *Vinyl records gave way to CDs, which have given way to MP3 files.* ❖ αντικαθίσταμαι, δίνω τη θέση μου

7.24 **curl up** (phr v) /kɜːl ʌp/
sit comfortably with your legs close to your body so you are like a ball • *She curled up on the sofa with her favourite book.* ❖ κουλουριάζομαι, αράζω

7.25 **construction** (n) /kənˈstrʌkʃn/
the process of building • *The construction of the building took twelve months.* ➤ construct (v) ❖ κατασκευή

7.26 **steel bar** (n) /stiːl bɑː/
a long straight piece of metal made of steel, often used in buildings • *Steel bars were used to support the weight of the loft extension.* ❖ ατσάλινη μπάρα

7.27 **mansion** (n) /ˈmænʃn/
a very large house • *The celebrity lived in a mansion in Beverly Hills.* ❖ έπαυλη

7.28 **frame** (n) /freɪm/
a structure that surrounds sth like a picture or window and holds it in place • *The frame of the window was made of aluminium.* ❖ πλαίσιο, σκελετός κατασκευής

7.29 **poverty** (n) /ˈpɒvəti/
the state of being very poor • *There was a lot of poverty in the country because so many people had no work.* ➤ poor (adj) ❖ φτώχεια
✎ Opp: wealth

7.30 **proclaim** (v) /prəʊˈkleɪm/
announce • *The prime minister proclaimed on the news that he believed in higher taxes for the rich.* ❖ εξαγγέλλω, ανακηρύσσω

7.31 **do away with** (phr v) /duː əˈweɪ wiːð/
get rid of • *Do you think people will do away with cars to ride bikes instead?* ❖ καταργώ, πετάω

7.32 **spot on** (expr) /spɒt ɒn/
perfectly correct • *Your prediction about good weather today was spot on so let's go for a walk.* ❖ ακριβής, στο στόχο

7.33 **artificial** (adj) /ɑːtɪˈfɪʃl/
not natural but man-made • *Artificial intelligence is used with voice recognition programs on computers.* ❖ τεχνητός

7.34 **bumblebee** (n) /ˈbʌmblˌbiː/
a large hairy bee • *The bumblebee buzzed around the spring flowers.* ❖ ανθηδών, μπούμπουρας

7.35 **aviation** (n) /ˌeɪviˈeɪʃn/
the business of flight • *Aviation has made it much easier to travel around the world.* ➤ aviator (n) ❖ αεροπορία

7.36 **substitute** (n) /ˈsʌbstɪtjuːt/
a replacement • *She uses a sugar substitute to sweeten her coffee as it is not fattening.* ➤ substitute (v) ❖ υποκατάστατο

7.37 **sector** (n) /ˈsektə/
an area of activity • *My dad works in the public sector. He's a civil servant.* ❖ τομέας

7.38 **workforce** (n) /ˈwɜːkfɔːs/
the people who work for a particular organisation • *The company is going to fire ten per cent of its workforce.* ❖ εργατικό/ανθρώπινο δυναμικό

7.39 **acquire** (v) /əˈkwaɪə/
gain; obtain • *The family have acquired great wealth and many possessions over the generations.* ➤ acquisition (n) ❖ αποκτώ

7.40 **aviator** (n) /ˈeɪvieɪtə/
sb who flies a plane • *Amelia Earhart was a great aviator who tried to fly around the world.* ➤ aviation (n) ❖ αεροπόρος, πιλότος

7.41 **prosthetic** (n) /prɒsˈθetɪk/
an artificial part of the body • *He was able to walk again after his accident thanks to prosthetics.* ➤ prosthetic (adj) ❖ προσθετικό μέλος

7.42 **limb** (n) /lɪm/
an arm or leg • *She broke all four limbs when she fell off the balcony.* ❖ άκρο

Building
construction   mansion
frame   steel bar

Phrasal verbs
curl up   do away with

Vocabulary   pages 86-87

7.43 **remodel** (v) /riːˈmɒdəl/
change the structure of sth • *The farm buildings were remodelled to accommodate pigs as well as cows.* ❖ αναδιαμορφώνω

7.44 **revolutionise** (v) /revəˈluːʃənaɪz/
completely change • *Flight revolutionised the way we travel.* ➤ revolution (n), revolutionary (adj) ❖ φέρνω επανάσταση

7.45 **stimulate** (v) /ˈstɪmjʊleɪt/
make sth develop; encourage • *The fascinating documentary stimulated my interest in geography.* ➤ stimulation (n) ❖ διεγείρω

7.46 **apparatus** (n) /æpəˈreɪtəs/
equipment for experiments • *We prepared the apparatus for our chemistry experiment.* ❖ εργαστηριακή συσκευή, εξάρτημα (για επιστημονικά πειράματα)

7.47 **utensil** (n) /juːˈtensəl/
a piece of equipment for cooking and eating, a knife or a spoon, etc. • *I need some new cooking utensils, especially spatulas.* ❖ μαγειρικό σκεύος

7.48 computerised (adj) /kəmˈpjuːtəraɪzd/
using a computer to control the way sth is done • *This computerised system requires internet access.* ➢ computer (n), computerise (v) ❖ ηλεκτρονικός

7.49 mechanical (adj) /mɪˈkænɪkl/
using an engine or machine to do work • *This mechanical egg timer runs on batteries.* ➢ mechanism (n) ❖ μηχανικός

7.50 assumption (n) /æˈsʌmpʃn/
sth you think is true even though you have no proof • *Your assumption that I am a pensioner is wrong as I am only 55.* ➢ assume (v) ❖ υπόθεση

7.51 discard (v) /dɪsˈkɑːd/
throw away • *She looked through her old magazines to decide which to keep and which to discard.* ❖ πετώ

7.52 filter (v) /ˈfɪltə/
remove unwanted substances from water, air, etc. by passing it through a piece of equipment • *This ioniser filters the air so it is dust-free.* ➢ filter (n) ❖ φιλτράρω

7.53 purify (v) /ˈpjʊərɪfaɪ/
remove harmful substances from sth • *The water sold in these bottles is purified so you can drink it.* ➢ purification (n) ❖ καθαρίζω

7.54 sterilise (v) /ˈsterɪlaɪz/
clean sth completely by killing any bacteria in it • *You should sterilise the bottles before making milk formula for the baby to drink.* ➢ sterilisation (n) ❖ αποστειρώνω

7.55 cube (n) /kjuːb/
an object with six equal square sides • *The dice we used to play Monopoly were red cubes.* ➢ cubic (adj) ❖ κύβος

7.56 cylinder (n) /ˈsɪlɪɪndə/
an object with straight sides and circular ends • *Roll up the poster and keep it in this cylinder.* ➢ cylindrical (adj) ❖ κύλινδρος

7.57 rectangle (n) /ˈrektæŋgl/
a shape with four sides, two of which are longer than the other two, and four 90° angles at the corners • *I prefer this wallet; it's a rectangle, so the notes don't get bent in it.* ➢ rectangular (adj) ❖ ορθογώνιο

7.58 sphere (n) /sfɪə/
a round shape like a ball • *Did you know that Earth is not a perfect sphere?* ➢ spherical (adj) ❖ σφαίρα

7.59 displace (v) /dɪsˈpleɪs/
take the place of sb/sth • *The ice I dropped in the glass displaced the water and made it spill over the rim.* ➢ displacement (v) ❖ εκτοπίζω

7.60 copper (n) /ˈkɒpə/
a reddish-brown metal • *The saucepan is made of copper.* ❖ χαλκός

7.61 conductor (n) /kənˈdʌktə/
sth that allows electricity to pass through it • *Copper is an excellent conductor of electricity and is used to make electrical wires.* ➢ conduct (v) ❖ αγωγός

7.62 monitor (n) /ˈmɒnɪtə/
sth that checks the progress of sth • *The patient was attached to a heart monitor to make sure he remained stable.* ➢ monitor (v) ❖ συσκευή (καρδιακής) παρακολούθησης

7.63 component (n) /kəmˈpəʊnənt/
one of the parts of which sth is made • *We need to replace one of the components of the machine.* ❖ συνιστών μέρος, κομμάτι

7.64 periodic table (n) /pɪərɪˈɒdɪk ˈteɪbl/
a list of elements arranged according to their atomic structure • *We learned the gases on the periodic table in chemistry.* ❖ περιοδικός πίνακας των χημικών στοιχείων

7.65 corrode (v) /kəˈrəʊd/
If metal corrodes, it is destroyed by the action of water or chemicals. • *Acids corrode metal.* ➢ corrosion (n), corrosive (adj) ❖ διαβρώνω

7.66 erode (v) /ɪˈrəʊd/
If the soil or rock is eroded by the weather, its surface is destroyed gradually. • *The river is widening because the water flow erodes the river banks.* ➢ erosion (n) ❖ διαβρώνω

7.67 unstable (adj) /ʌnˈsteɪbl/
changeable • *The unstable chemical was handled very carefully by the scientist.* ➢ instability (n) ❖ ασταθής

7.68 explosive (n) /ɪksˈpləʊsɪv/
a substance that can cause an explosion • *Explosives which could be used to make bombs were found in the terrorist's hideout.* ➢ explode (v), explosion (n) ❖ εκρηκτικό

7.69 expand (v) /ɪksˈpænd/
become bigger • *Metals expand when they are heated.* ➢ expansion (n) ❖ διαστέλλω, διαστέλλομαι, επεκτείνω, διευρύνω
✎ Opp: contract

7.70 extend (v) /ɪkˈstend/
become longer • *The bank extended the time he had to pay back the loan.* ➢ extent (n), extension (n), extensive (adj) ❖ εκτείνω

7.71 dense (adj) /dens/
A dense substance has a lot of mass in relation to its size. • *Ice floats because it is less dense than water.* ➢ density (v) ❖ πυκνός

7.72 erupt (v) /ɪˈrʌpt/
When a volcano erupts, it explodes and sends smoke, rocks, lava and ash into the sky. • *Mount Etna erupted again last month.* ➢ eruption (n) ❖ εκρήγνυμαι

7.73 liquefied (adj) /ˈlɪkwɪfaɪd/
turned into liquid • *The lorry was transporting liquefied gas to be used for heating.* ➤ liquefy (v), liquid (n), liquefaction (n) ❖ υγροποιημένος

7.74 gemstone (n) /ˈdʒemstəʊn/
a precious stone; a jewel • *Her favourite gemstones are diamonds.* ❖ πολύτιμος λίθος

7.75 purity (n) /ˈpjʊərɪti/
containing nothing wrong or harmful • *The purity of this diamond increases its value.* ➤ pure (adj) ❖ καθαρότητα

7.76 antiquity (n) /ænˈtɪkwɪti/
the distant past • *The Parthenon is one of antiquity's most famous monuments.* ❖ αρχαιότητα

7.77 derive (v) /dɪˈraɪv/
get from • *The Mercedes derives its name from a relative of the designer.* ➤ derivative (n) ❖ παίρνω, προέρχομαι

7.78 flawless (adj) /ˈflɔːləs/
perfect • *This flawless gemstone is absolutely beautiful.* ➤ flaw (n) ❖ άψογος, αψεγάδιαστος

7.79 control panel (n) /kənˈtrəʊl ˈpænəl/
sth that allows computer users to view and manipulate hardware, add and remove software, etc. • *You can customise your computer settings by going to the control panel.* ❖ πίνακας ελέγχου

7.80 assembly line (n) /æˈsembli laɪn/
a system for making things in a factory: the things move past a line of workers who each make one part • *Working on an assembly line is monotonous.* ❖ γραμμή συναρμολόγησης

7.81 fraction (n) /ˈfrækʃn/
very small amount • *It took a fraction of a second for the cat to pounce on the mouse.* ❖ κλάσμα

7.82 innovation (n) /ɪnəˈveɪʃn/
a new idea or thing being used for the first time • *Smartphones are the latest innovation on the market.* ➤ innovative (adj) ❖ καινοτομία

7.83 plant (n) /plɑːnt/
a factory • *This plant produces cars and other vehicles.* ❖ εργοστάσιο

7.84 efficient (adj) /ɪˈfɪʃnt/
working well, without wasting time, energy or money • *Emma is a very efficient secretary; you can rely on her to do the work well.* ➤ efficiency (n) ❖ αποδοτικός, αποτελεσματικός
✎ Opp: inefficient

7.85 assemble (v) /əˈsembl/
put together the parts of sth • *I found it difficult to assemble the wardrobe.* ➤ assembly (n) ❖ συναρμολογώ

7.86 reinvent the wheel (expr) /ˌriːɪnˌvent ðə wiːl/
waste time trying to develop sth that has already been done • *We don't need to reinvent the wheel; we already have a perfectly good system in place.* ❖ ανακαλύπτω τον τροχό

7.87 forefront (n) /ˈfɔːfrʌnt/
first place • *Japan is at the forefront of robotic research with new ideas.* ❖ πρώτη γραμμή

7.88 cutting edge (n) /ˈkʌtɪŋ edʒ/
the most advanced stage in the development of sth • *Our factory is at the cutting edge as regards the technology we use to make computers.* ❖ εξελιγμένος, προηγμένος, τελευταία λέξη (π.χ. της τεχνολογίας)

7.89 get your wires crossed (expr) /get jɔː ˈwaɪəz krɒst/
become confused about what sb is saying because you think they are talking about sth else • *We got our wires crossed and went to different places to meet.* ❖ μπερδεύομαι

7.90 light years ahead (expr) /laɪt jɪəz əˈhed/
a long way ahead of others • *His brilliant ideas are light years ahead of other researchers.* ❖ πολύ μπροστά, έτη φωτός μπροστά

7.91 glitch (n) /glɪtʃ/
a small problem • *You can solve this glitch by restarting your computer.* ❖ μικροβλάβη

7.92 push the panic button (expr) /pʊʃ ðə ˈpænɪk ˈbʌtən/
become frightened or worried • *Don't push the panic button whenever you have trouble with your laptop.* ❖ πανικοβάλλομαι

7.93 instruction manual (n) /ɪnˈstrʌkʃn ˈmænjuəl/
a book that tells you how to do or use sth • *You need to read the instruction manual to see how the machine works.* ❖ εγχειρίδιο οδηγιών

7.94 not rocket science (expr) /nɒt ˈrɒkɪt ˈsaɪəns/
not difficult to understand • *This chapter on levers in your physics textbook is not rocket science, so you'll understand it easily.* ❖ δεν είναι και πυρηνική φυσική

7.95 lung (n) /lʌŋ/
one of the two organs in your chest that you use to breathe • *If you smoke, you run the risk of getting lung cancer.* ❖ πνεύμονας

7.96 particle (n) /ˈpɑːtɪkl/
a very small piece • *The atmosphere was full of particles of dust from the Sahara desert.* ❖ σωματίδιο

7.97 coin (v) /kɔɪn/
invent a word or phrase • *People first coined the word 'wireless' for radios.* ❖ επινοώ (λέξη ή φράση)

7.98 solely (adv) /ˈsəʊli/
only • *He is solely responsible for the accident. No one else is to blame.* ➤ sole (adj) ❖ μόνο, αποκλειστικά

Mechanisation
assembly line	machinery
automated	mechanical
computerised	plant

Physics and Chemistry

verbs	adjectives	nouns
corrode	dense	apparatus
displace	liquefied	conductor
expand	unstable	periodic table

Grammar — pages 88-89

7.99 split an atom (expr) /splɪt æn 'ætəm/
divide the smallest part of a chemical element
• *A nuclear reaction is the result of splitting an atom.* ❖ διασπώ το άτομο

7.100 disprove (v) /dɪs'pruːv/
show sth is not true • *The scientist disproved the old theory with new findings.*
❖ διαψεύδω

7.101 grant (n) /grɑːnt/
money you get from sb for a particular purpose
• *He got a grant to pay for his university studies.* ❖ υποτροφία, επιχορήγηση

7.102 bronze (n) /brɒnz/
a yellowish-brown metal • *The statue was made of bronze.* ❖ μπρούντζος

7.103 tin (n) /tɪn/
a silvery-white metal • *This food can is made of tin.* ❖ κασσίτερος

7.104 artefact (n) /'ɑːtɪfækt/
an object like a tool that was made in the past and is historically interesting • *We examined the Roman artefacts in the museum exhibition.*
❖ τεχνούργημα, αρχαιολογικό εύρημα

7.105 hue (n) /hjuː/
a colour • *The morning sky was a pale blue hue.* ❖ απόχρωση

7.106 satellite (n) /'sætəlaɪt/
a machine that goes around the Earth and is used for electronic communications • *Satellites are essential for worldwide telecommunications.* ❖ δορυφόρος

7.107 reflective (adj) /rɪ'flektɪv/
able to send light back • *The reflective surface of a mirror was flawed by a crack.*
➢ reflect (v) ❖ ανακλαστικός

7.108 surface (n) /'sɜːfɪs/
the top part of sth • *There was rubbish floating on the surface of the sea.* ❖ επιφάνεια

7.109 engineer (n) /ˌendʒɪ'nɪə/
sb whose job is to design and build roads, bridges, engines, etc. • *She wants to study to be an engineer when she leaves school.*
➢ engineering (n), engine (n) ❖ μηχανικός

7.110 craft (n) /krɑːft/
a boat or a plane • *The old fisherman designed and built his craft himself.*
❖ σκάφος

7.111 nuclear reactor (n) /'njuːklɪə rɪ'æktə/
a machine used to produce nuclear energy
• *This power plant uses a nuclear reactor to produce electricity.* ❖ πυρηνικός αντιδραστήρας

7.112 geyser (n) /'giːzə/
a natural spring that sends hot water or steam into the air • *Don't go near the geyser. You might get burnt.* ❖ θερμοπίδακας

7.113 nail (n) /neɪl/
the thin hard layer that covers the tip of a finger or toe • *Maria bites her nails when she is nervous.* ❖ νύχι

7.114 appliance (n) /ə'plaɪəns/
a machine like a cooker, fridge or iron that is designed to do a particular job in the home
• *This shop sells a wide range of electrical appliances.* ❖ συσκευή

7.115 spiral out of control (expr) /'spaɪrəl aʊt əv kən'trəʊl/
quickly get out of control • *The situation spiralled out of control and there was chaos.*
❖ βγαίνω εκτός ελέγχου (γρήγορα)

7.116 malfunction (v) /mæl'fʌŋkʃn/
work incorrectly • *The DVD player is malfunctioning again, so we can't watch a movie.*
➢ malfunction (n) ❖ έχω βλάβη, δυσλειτουργώ

Metals

bronze	steel
copper	tin
nickel	

Listening — page 90

7.117 solar panel (n) /'səʊlə 'pænl/
piece of equipment which uses the sun's heat to make energy • *We have a solar panel on the roof which heats our water.* ❖ ηλιακός συλλέκτης

7.118 sustainable (adj) /sʌs'teɪnəbl/
able to continue for a long time and not deplete natural resources • *Wind power is a sustainable form of energy as opposed to fossil fuels, which are running out.*
➢ sustain (v) ❖ αειφόρος, βιώσιμος
✎ Opp: unsustainable

7.119 tile (n) /taɪl/
a flat piece of clay on a wall, floor or roof
• *She dried the tiles on the bathroom wall after having a shower.* ❖ κεραμίδι, πλακάκι

Inventions

irrigation screw	satellite
MDF	sewing machine
nuclear reactor	solar panel
phonograph	windscreen wiper

Speaking
page 91

7.120 **restrict** (v) /rɪˈstrɪkt/
limit • *Parking here is restricted to residents only.* ➤ restriction (n) ❖ περιορίζω

7.121 **ultrasound** (n) /ˈʌltrəsaʊnd/
a medical process that uses a sound that is too high for humans to hear in order to produce an image of the inside of your body • *The doctor needs an ultrasound to find out what is wrong with him.* ❖ υπέρηχος

7.122 **scan** (n) /skæn/
a medical test in which a special machine produces an image of the inside of your body: • *The doctor looked at a scan of the man's lungs.* ➤ scan (v) ❖ τομογραφία, σάρωση

Writing: a nomination
pages 92-93

7.123 **worthy** (adj) /ˈwɜːði/
deserving • *He donated money to a worthy charity.* ➤ worth (n) ❖ άξιος, αξιόλογος
✎ Opp: unworthy

7.124 **evaluation** (n) /ɪvæljuˈeɪʃn/
making a judgement • *Students received a fair evaluation of their progress at the end of the first term.* ➤ evaluate (v) ❖ αξιολόγηση, εκτίμηση

7.125 **justification** (n) /dʒʌstɪfɪˈkeɪʃn/
a good reason for doing sth • *The justification for higher prices is the increased cost of production.* ➤ justify (v) ❖ αιτιολόγηση

7.126 **curiosity** (n) /kjʊərɪˈɒsɪti/
desire to know • *His curiosity about the formation of the Earth led him to become a geologist.* ➤ curious (adj) ❖ περιέργεια

7.127 **lay the foundations** (expr) /leɪ ðə faʊnˈdeɪʃnz/
provide the conditions that will make it possible for sth to be successful • *The Wright brothers laid the foundations for the development of aviation.* ❖ θέτω τις βάσεις, τα θεμέλια

7.128 **enquiring mind** (expr) /ɪnˈkwaɪərɪŋ maɪnd/
sb with an enquiring mind is interested in finding out more about everything • *An enquiring mind is essential for somebody who wants to go into research.* ❖ ερευνητικό πνεύμα

7.129 **pave the way** (expr) /peɪv ðə weɪ/
create the conditions for sth to continue • *Walt Disney paved the way for future animation movies.* ❖ ανοίγω το δρόμο

7.130 **reputation** (n) /repjʊˈteɪʃn/
the opinion people have of sb • *Francis Ford Coppola has a reputation as a great director.* ➤ reputable (adj) ❖ φήμη

Video 7: Lighting the Dark
page 94

7.131 **chart** (v) /tʃæt/
make a map • *Early explorers charted the sea and land as they travelled and created the first maps.* ➤ chart (n) ❖ χαρτογραφώ

7.132 **shine light on sth** (expr) /ʃaɪn laɪt ɒn ˈsʌmθɪŋ/
reveal sth new • *Exploration on Mars will shine light on the formation of other planets.* ❖ ρίχνω φως σε κάτι

7.133 **glimpse** (n) /glɪmps/
a momentary look at sb/sth • *I caught a glimpse of a fish before it swam away.* ➤ glimpse (v) ❖ γρήγορη ματιά

7.134 **occurrence** (n) /əˈkʌrəns/
sth that happens • *Earthquakes are a regular occurrence in this area.* ➤ occur (v) ❖ περιστατικό, συμβάν

7.135 **victim** (n) /ˈvɪktɪm/
sb who is hurt or killed • *The victim of the shooting is being treated in hospital.* ❖ θύμα

7.136 **impose** (v) /ɪmˈpəʊz/
have a bad effect on sb/sth • *Climbing in freezing conditions imposed challenges on the men.* ❖ επιβάλλω

7.137 **anglerfish** (n) /ˈæŋglə,fɪʃ/
a fish that attracts its prey with a fleshy structure hanging from a thin filament on its head • *The divers watched the anglerfish catch its prey and then eat it.* ❖ βατραχόψαρο

7.138 **eel** (n) /iːl/
a long fish like a snake • *The eel hid in an underwater cave.* ❖ χέλι

7.139 **drowning** (n) /ˈdraʊənɪŋ/
dying from being under water for too long • *The victim of the drowning was not a strong swimmer.* ➤ drown (v) ❖ πνιγμός

7.140 **facet** (n) /ˈfæsɪt/
an aspect • *A walk in the poorer areas of town revealed facets of life she had never seen before.* ❖ όψη

7.141 **discrete** (adj) /dɪsˈkriːt/
separate from other things • *The photos of discrete areas of the seabed fascinated researchers.* ❖ ξεχωριστός, χωριστός

Vocabulary Exercises

A Complete sentences with one word in each gap.

1 On a cold winter evening I like to _____ up on the sofa with a book.
2 Well done. Your answer is _____ on.
3 If he knew that this app already exists, he would stop trying to reinvent the _____.
4 We got our _____ crossed and I turned up at the wrong time.
5 To fight pollution we should do _____ with cars in city centres.
6 It's not _____ science so you'll understand my theory easily.
7 She is perfect for the research post as she has a(n) _____ mind.
8 George Stephenson laid the _____ for steam powered transport.
9 Apple and Microsoft paved the _____ for personal computers in every home.
10 Scientists hope their study of the sea will shine a(n) _____ on new species.

B Choose the correct answers.

1 She makes her own clothes on her sewing ___.
   a machinery   b machine   c plant

2 The experiment can be conducted using very simple ___.
   a utensil   b apparatus   c frame

3 This factory produces many cars on its ___.
   a assembly line   b work station   c control panel

4 We need to find ___ sources of energy to replace fossil fuels.
   a discrete   b dense   c sustainable

5 You always ___ the panic button instead of staying calm.
   a get   b split   c push

6 The wealthy couple live in a ___ set in a beautiful garden in the countryside.
   a mansion   b skyscraper   c component

7 Phosphorus is ___ and, unless it is kept in water in the lab, it reacts violently with oxygen in the atmosphere.
   a flexible   b unstable   c flawless

8 The sea has ___ the cliffs over thousands of years.
   a eroded   b corroded   c discarded

9 I wonder who first ___ the term Internet?
   a filtered   b charted   c coined

10 The religious ___ was thought by many believers to signal the end of the world.
   a prophecy   b forecast   c prediction

C Choose the correct answers.

1 An **explosive** can be used to make
   a an apparatus.
   b a bomb.

2 You can use a **solar panel**
   a to generate energy.
   b to split an atom.

3 A **geyser** can be dangerous because
   a you can get burnt.
   b it is poisonous.

4 **Manual labour** is not used
   a to pick strawberries.
   b in automated factories.

5 A **conductor** allows electricity
   a to flow through it.
   b to be reflected away from it.

6 If there is a **glitch** in your program,
   a you have a problem.
   b it will run better.

7 Water that is **displaced** in a glass could
   a overflow.
   b freeze.

8 Some jobs are mundane, so the people who do them
   a are stimulated.
   b get bored.

7 Grammar

7.1 Zero Conditional

If clause	Main clause
Present Simple	Present Simple

Χρησιμοποιούμε το **zero conditional** για να μιλήσουμε για το αποτέλεσμα μιας πράξης ή μιας κατάστασης που ισχύει πάντα. Στη θέση του *if* μπορούμε να χρησιμοποιήσουμε το *when*.
→ *If copper **corrodes**, it **becomes** green.*
→ *When copper **corrodes**, it **becomes** green.*

7.2 First Conditional

If clause	Main clause
Present tense	*will, can, could, may, might* + απαρέμφατο χωρίς *to* (bare infinitive)

Χρησιμοποιούμε το **first conditional** για να μιλήσουμε για το αποτέλεσμα μιας πράξης ή μιας κατάστασης που είναι πιθανό να συμβεί τώρα ή στο μέλλον.
→ *If I **find** a Kindle on sale, I **will buy** it for my son.*
→ *If you **look** at the sky at night, you **can see** Venus.*

Μπορούμε επίσης να χρησιμοποιήσουμε προστακτική (imperative) στην κύρια πρόταση.
→ *If you can't set up the PC, **read** the manual again.*

7.3 Second Conditional

If clause	Main clause
Past tense	*would, could, might* + απαρέμφατο χωρίς *to* (bare infinitive)

Χρησιμοποιούμε το second conditional για να μιλήσουμε για κάτι:
που μάλλον δε θα συμβεί τώρα ή στο μέλλον.
→ *If supernovas **weren't** so rare, we **would see** them more often.*
που δε θα συμβεί ή που είναι καθαρά υποθετική στο παρόν ή στο μέλλον.
→ *If we **had** the money, we **would install** solar panels at home.*

Μπορούμε να χρησιμοποιήσουμε το second conditional για να δώσουμε συμβουλή.
→ *If I **were** you, I **would buy** the laser printer.*

Σημείωση: Συνήθως χρησιμοποιούμε *were* για όλα τα πρόσωπα σε προτάσεις του second conditional.
→ *If the chemistry teacher **were** here, she would answer our questions.*

7.4 Third Conditional

If clause	Main clause
Past Perfect	*would, could, might* + *have* + past participle

Χρησιμοποιούμε το third conditional για να μιλήσουμε για γεγονότα ή καταστάσεις που θα μπορούσαν να είχαν συμβεί στο παρελθόν, αλλά δε συνέβησαν. Αυτά είναι πάντα υποθετικά γιατί δεν μπορούμε να αλλάξουμε το παρελθόν.
→ *If Ford **hadn't introduced** the assembly line, cars **wouldn't have become** affordable for most people.*
→ *You **could have transferred** the data easily if you **had brought** a memory stick.*

7.5 Mixed Conditionals

If clause	Main clause
Past Perfect	would + απαρέμφατο χωρίς to (bare infinitive)

Έχουμε mixed conditional όταν τα δύο μέρη της υποθετικής πρότασης αναφέρονται σε διαφορετικό χρόνο. Χρησιμοποιούμε mixed conditional για να εκφράσουμε το αποτέλεσμα που έχει στο παρόν ένα υποθετικό γεγονός ή κατάσταση του παρελθόντος.
→ If he **had made** a major scientific breakthrough, he **would be awarded** a Nobel Prize now.

7.6 Conditionals χωρίς *if*

Μπορούμε να χρησιμοποιήσουμε *provided/providing that, on condition that* και *as long as* στη θέση του *if* σε προτάσεις του first conditional.
→ **Provided** you study the periodic table of the elements, you will do well on the test.
→ **As long as** we recycle properly, electronic waste will not pile up.

Μπορούμε να χρησιμοποιήσουμε *unless* σε προτάσεις του first και του second conditional. Σημαίνει *if not*.
→ We won't be able to see the comet **unless** the sky is clear tomorrow.

Μπορούμε να χρησιμοποιήσουμε το *otherwise* αντί για την *if* clause. Σημαίνει *if not*.
→ Mix the chemicals carefully. **Otherwise**, you'll ruin the experiment.

Μπορούμε να χρησιμοποιήσουμε το *supposing* σε όλες τις υποθετικές προτάσεις. Η κύρια πρόταση συνήθως είναι ερωτηματική. Σημαίνει 'αν υποθέσουμε' ή 'τι θα γινόταν αν'.
→ **Supposing** the lecture is boring, what will you do?
→ **Supposing** they created a landfill on the outskirts of town, would people protest?

Μπορούμε να αντικαταστήσουμε το *if* με απαρέμφατο.
→ **Interrupt** me once more, and I'll have to ask you to leave the class.

Αντί για *if*, μπορούμε να χρησιμοποιήσουμε το *should*.
→ **Should you need** the keys to the lab, please contact Dr Craig.

7.7 Wish & If only

Μπορούμε να χρησιμοποιήσουμε unreal past (μη πραγματικός αόριστος) με *wish* και *if only* για να αναφερθούμε σε επιθυμίες στο παρελθόν, στο παρόν και το μέλλον.

Χρησιμοποιούμε *wish/if only* + past tense για να μιλήσουμε για το παρόν ή το μέλλον.
→ I **wish** we **had** an electric car.
→ **If only** I **could find** a full-time position.
→ I **wish** we **were going** to the science museum next Friday.

Χρησιμοποιούμε *wish/if only* + χρόνο past perfect για να μιλήσουμε για το παρελθόν.
→ I **wish** I **had tried** harder in science class when I was a student.

Χρησιμοποιούμε *wish/if only* + *would* + bare infinitive (απαρέμφατο χωρίς *to*) για να μιλήσουμε για τις ενοχλητικές συνήθειες των άλλων, ή για να πούμε ότι θα θέλαμε κάτι να είναι διαφορετικό στο μέλλον. Το χρησιμοποιούμε για πράξεις και όχι για καταστάσεις.
→ I **wish** you **wouldn't enter** the lab without permission.

7.8 Inversion

Μπορούμε να χρησιμοποιήσουμε ορισμένες λέξεις και φράσεις στην αρχή της πρότασης για να δώσουμε έμφαση σε αυτές. Όταν το κάνουμε αυτό, η σειρά των λέξεων αλλάζει. Αυτό ονομάζεται inversion (αντιστροφή).
→ **Never** have I seen such a beautiful diamond.
→ **Not only** was Da Vinci a great painter, **but** he was **also** an inventor.
→ **Under no circumstances** must you reveal the findings of the experiment.

7 Grammar

→ **At no time** did he stop looking for ways to make daily life easier.
→ **Little** did he realise the impact his discovery would have.
→ **Rarely / Seldom** can you see a flawless diamond.
→ **Not once** did he doubt that his theory would be accepted.
→ I read the instructions again. **Only then** was I able to assemble the telescope.
→ **Only after / Not until** the 1990s did personal computers become widely used.
→ **So** mundane was the work on the assembly line **that** many workers decided to quit.
→ **No sooner / Hardly** had he graduated than he found work as a lab assistant.
→ **Nowhere** can you see such huge geysers as in this National Park.

Grammar Exercises

A Complete the sentences with the words below.

> and   but   if   long   otherwise   provided   supposing   unless

1 I wouldn't be a student here today _____ I hadn't received a grant.
2 You won't be late _____ you leave punctually.
3 The nuclear reactor is safe _____ a human error occurs.
4 Luckily Kate helped him study, _____ he wouldn't have passed his physics exam.
5 As _____ as you replace the battery, you won't have any more problems with this device.
6 _____ for your encouragement, I wouldn't have become so enthusiastic about chemistry.
7 _____ your teacher gave you an F, what would you do?
8 Read out the physics notes to me _____ I will recite them back to you.

B Complete the conditional sentence with your own ideas and the conditional given.

1 If I don't get good grades this year, _____. (first)
2 I wouldn't have learned so much English _____. (third)
3 If penicillin did not exist, _____. (second)
4 If water freezes _____. (zero)
5 The world wouldn't be at risk from global warming _____. (mixed)

C Complete the sentences with the correct form of the verbs in brackets.

1 I wish I _____ (know) the answer to this question.
2 If only he _____ (pass) his chemistry exam last month.
3 I wish you _____ (not treat) me like a child all the time.
4 If only I _____ (can/get) into university next year.
5 If only he _____ (not have to) go away to college.
6 I wish I _____ (can/take) the test again next week.
7 If only I _____ (not choose) physics this year. It's so hard!
8 I wish my parents _____ (stop) nagging me about homework every day.

D Circle the correct words.

1 Not / No only were you late, but you also failed to apologise.
2 Under no / any circumstances should you drink this water.
3 Rarely had I / I had been so absorbed by a documentary.
4 Nowhere else can see you / can you see these migratory birds in such numbers.
5 Little / Seldom did they know that the teacher had set a test for the next class.
6 Only when / then did he shout 'Eureka!'.
7 Not until yesterday I did / did I hear about the bomb scare.
8 Had he / He had known you were busy, he wouldn't have bothered you.

Exam Task

For questions 1-10, read the text below. Use the word at the end of some of the lines to form a word that fits the gap in the same line.

Self-driving cars

The self-driving car is a recent (1) _____ that has not yet reached the market,	INNOVATIVE
but should do so in the not too distant future. It is an (2) _____ vehicle that	AUTOMATION
does not require a driver. Instead, a (3) _____ system navigates around	COMPUTER
obstacles and along roads.	
The (4) _____ for the driverless car is that it will provide a number of benefits.	JUSTIFY
(5) _____ explain that it will be safer because its quicker reactions will reduce	INVENT
traffic accidents. It will also give mobility to those who could not otherwise drive,	
such as blind people, for example, which makes this a (6) _____ invention.	WORTH
The assumption that it will be too expensive may well be (7) _____ by the fact	PROVE
that it will do away with the need for car insurance and road signs. Lower fuel consumption is	
an additional bonus as well as fewer (8) _____ problems because it will run at	MECHANISM
optimum levels.	
However, in a recent survey in the US few drivers were positive about buying a self-driving car	
mainly due to the additional purchase cost of around $3000. The (9) _____ is that	PREDICT
self-driving cars will take a while yet to be accepted by the general public. In the meantime, some	
companies have been using prototypes, the most notable of which is Google. A fleet of autonomous	
vehicles have already been tested with almost no accidents to date, so clearly the (10) _____	EVALUATE
is a positive one.	

8 Money Mad

Word Focus — page 96

8.1 breadline (n) /ˈbredlaɪn/
lowest level of income on which it is possible to live • *They are living on the breadline and can only just afford to feed themselves.*
❖ όριο της φτώχειας

8.2 credit crunch (n) /ˈkredɪt krʌntʃ/
a bad economic situation in which it becomes difficult to borrow money • *The bank has refused to lend him more money since the credit crunch.*
❖ πιστωτική κρίση

8.3 backup (n) /ˈbækʌp/
extra help or support • *We can only do the job if we get some backup.* ➣ back up (phr v)
❖ εφεδρικός

8.4 in tandem with (expr) /ɪn ˈtændəm wɪð/
at the same time as • *You can run this program in tandem with others.*
❖ παράλληλα με

8.5 inflation (n) /ɪnˈfleɪʃn/
the continuing increase in prices • *Because of inflation, bread and milk have risen in price.*
❖ πληθωρισμός

8.6 downgrading (n) /daʊnˈgreɪdɪŋ/
making sth less good, important or valuable than it was • *The downgrading of the country's credit rating has caused massive problems for the government.*
➣ downgrade (v) ❖ υποβάθμιση

8.7 devaluation (n) /diːvæljuːˈeɪʃn/
reduction in the value of a currency compared to another currency • *The devaluation of the currency allowed the country to export goods at cheaper prices.*
➣ devalue (v) ❖ υποτίμηση

Reading — pages 96-97

8.8 bartering (n) /ˈbɑːtərɪŋ/
exchanging goods for other goods rather than money • *Before currency, bartering was the way people traded goods.*
➣ barter (v) ❖ ανταλλακτική οικονομία (χωρίς χρήματα)

8.9 bond (n) /bɒnd/
a document promising that a government will pay back money it has borrowed, usually with interest • *The government bonds fell in value because of the economic crisis.* ❖ ομόλογο

8.10 exchange rate (n) /ɪksˈtʃeɪndʒ reɪt/
the value of one currency compared to the value of another currency • *The exchange rate for one euro is around 120 Japanese yen.* ❖ συναλλαγματική ισοτιμία

8.11 food voucher (n) /fuːd ˈvaʊtʃə/
a coupon used to get food instead of money • *The government provides low-income families with food vouchers.* ❖ κουπόνι για τρόφιμα

8.12 haggling (n) /ˈhæglɪŋ/
arguing over the price of sth before you pay • *Haggling is a way of buying things at lower prices in the market.* ➣ haggle (v) ❖ παζάρεμα

8.13 legal tender (n) /ˈliːgəl ˈtendə/
official money • *The legal tender in Greece is the euro.* ❖ νόμιμο χρήμα

8.14 despair (n) /dɪsˈpeə/
loss of hope • *Fred felt despair when he saw that he had no money in the bank.*
➣ despair (v), desperate (adj) ❖ απελπισία

8.15 recession (n) /rɪˈseʃn/
a period when the economy of a country is doing badly • *The recession led to shops closing and people losing jobs.* ❖ ύφεση

8.16 shockwaves (pln) /ˈʃɒkweɪvz/
the powerful shock people feel when sth bad happens • *The economic problems in the USA sent shockwaves across all the economies of the world.* ❖ κύμα κλονισμού, σεισμικό κύμα

8.17 catapult (v) /ˈkætəpʊlt/
throw suddenly into a situation • *When he lost his income, he was catapulted into serious financial difficulties.* ➣ catapult (n) ❖ εκτινάσσω

8.18 plunge (v) /plʌndʒ/
fall a long way suddenly • *Half the population under 30 was plunged into unemployment because of the recession.* ➣ plunge (n) ❖ βυθίζω

8.19 debt (n) /det/
money you owe sb • *He has a credit card debt of over five thousand euros.* ❖ χρέος

8.20 mount (v) /maʊnt/
increase • *Her debts mounted because she had no money to pay them back.*
❖ ανεβαίνω, αυξάνομαι

8.21 take the bull by the horns (expr) /teɪk ðə bʊl baɪ ðə hɔːnz/
deal with a difficult problem bravely • *He decided to take the bull by the horns by looking for work abroad.*
❖ πιάνω τον ταύρο από τα κέρατα

8.22 currency (n) /ˈkʌrənsi/
money used in a country • *The currency used in Greece is the euro.* ❖ νόμισμα

8.23 **bring to mind** (expr) /brɪŋ tʊ maɪnd/
remind you of sth • *The current recession brings to mind the economic problems of the 1930s.* ❖ θυμίζω, φέρνω στο νου

8.24 **trader** (n) /ˈtreɪdə/
sb who buys and sells things as a job • *The market traders drove a hard bargain.*
➢ trade (n, v) ❖ έμπορος

8.25 **stall-holder** (n) /stɔːl ˈhəʊldə/
sb who sells produce at a market • *My cousin is a stall-holder at this market and sells oranges.* ❖ ιδιοκτήτης (υπαίθριου) πάγκου

8.26 **hard-up** (adj) /hɑːd-ʌp/
having little money • *Jeff is hard-up since losing his job, so he might need to borrow some money.* ❖ άπορος, απένταρος

8.27 **purchase** (n) /ˈpɜːtʃəs/
sth you buy • *My purchases included a new jacket and a pair of socks.* ➢ purchase (v)
❖ αγορά

8.28 **cover one's costs** (expr) /ˈkʌvə wʌnz kɒsts/
pay for the cost of running sth • *When taxes increased, restaurants had to put up their prices to cover their costs.*
❖ καλύπτω τις δαπάνες μου

8.29 **account** (n) /əˈkaʊnt/
an arrangement with a bank whereby the bank keeps your money safe • *She has a PayPal account which she uses when she shops online.* ❖ λογαριασμός

8.30 **credit** (v) /ˈkredɪt/
add money to a bank account • *Your bank account will be automatically credited with your salary every month.* ➢ credit (n)
❖ πιστώνω

8.31 **debit** (v) /ˈdebɪt/
take money out of a bank account • *You can use this card to make purchases and your account will be debited immediately.*
➢ debit (n) ❖ χρεώνω

8.32 **apt** (adj) /æpt/
appropriate • *His comment was very apt and it described the situation perfectly.*
❖ κατάλληλος, εύστοχος

8.33 **transaction** (n) /trænsˈækʃn/
a piece of business • *The details of the transaction are on this receipt.* ❖ συναλλαγή

8.34 **unofficial** (adj) /ʌnəˈfɪʃl/
not approved by an authority • *Bartering is an unofficial way of doing business.* ❖ ανεπίσημος
✎ Opp: official

8.35 **set up** (phr v) /set ʌp/
create; start • *The church set up a number of canteens where the poor can get a free meal.*
❖ ιδρύω, στήνω

8.36 **courgette** (n) /kɔːˈʒet/
a long thin green vegetable • *Let's have fried courgettes and tzatziki to start with.* ❖ κολοκυθάκι

8.37 **interest rate** (n) /ˈɪntrəst reɪt/
the percentage charged by a bank when you borrow money or the percentage you are paid by a bank when you keep your money in an account • *The bank is offering an interest rate of 2.2% if you have a savings account.*
❖ επιτόκιο

8.38 **be made redundant** (expr)
/bi meɪd rɪˈdʌndənt/
lose your job because there is no more work for you • *She was made redundant and has been unemployed for a year.*
❖ απολύομαι

8.39 **let alone** (expr) /let əˈləʊn/
used after saying sth to emphasise that because the first thing is not true, the next thing cannot be true either • *The child can't read let alone write an essay!* ❖ πόσο μάλλον

Problems with the economy

credit crunch	downgrading
debt	inflation
devaluation	recession

Vocabulary pages 98-99

8.40 **circulation** (n) /sɜːkjʊˈleɪʃn/
the exchange of money from one person to another in society • *The euro has been in circulation since 2002.* ➢ circulate (v)
❖ κυκλοφορία

8.41 **counterfeit** (v) /ˈkaʊntəfɪt/
make money that is not genuine • *The criminals who counterfeited euros were caught and arrested.* ➢ counterfeit (n, adj)
❖ πλαστογραφώ

8.42 **denomination** (n) /dɪnɒmɪˈneɪʃn/
value of a coin or paper money • *The denomination of this coin is two euros.*
❖ ονομαστική αξία

8.43 **forgery** (n) /ˈfɔːdʒəri/
an illegal copy of money, a work of art, a document, etc. • *You can tell this money is a forgery because it hasn't got a watermark.*
➢ forge (v) ❖ πλαστογραφία

8.44 **comprise** (v) /kəmˈpraɪz/
consist of • *Her library comprises over a thousand books.* ❖ αποτελούμαι από

8.45 **polymer** (n) /ˈpɒlɪmə/
a substance that consists of large molecules made from combinations of simpler molecules • *The object is made of an artificial polymer.* ❖ πολυμερές

8.46 **enhance** (v) /ɪnˈhɑːns/
improve • *The politician tried to enhance his image by dressing in smarter clothes.*
➢ enhancement (n) ❖ βελτιώνω

8.47 **plummet** (v) /ˈplʌmɪt/
fall by a large amount • *Since the new principal started at the school, the number of pupils playing truant has plummeted.*
❖ πέφτω κατακόρυφα, μειώνομαι αισθητά

8.48 **crash** (v) /kræʃ/
fail suddenly • *When the American stock market crashed in 1929, it was followed by a deep recession.* ➢ crash (n) ❖ χρεοκοπώ, καταρρέω οικονομικά

8.49 **smash** (v) /smæʃ/
break into pieces • *The glass smashed when I dropped it.* ➢ smash (n)
❖ σπάω, κάνω κομμάτια

8.50 **share** (n) /ʃeə/
part of a company you can buy as an investment • *He bought shares in Facebook and hopes to make a profit when they gain value.* ❖ μετοχή

8.51 **fund** (n) /fʌnd/
money collected for a cause • *We donated money to a fund which helps single mothers.*
➢ fund (v) ❖ ταμείο

8.52 **sum** (n) /sʌm/
an amount of money • *This car costs a large sum of money, so I will pay for it in instalments.* ❖ ποσό

8.53 **owe** (v) /əʊ/
have to pay sth back • *Bob still owes me thirty pounds which he borrowed from me last week.* ❖ χρωστώ

8.54 **mortgage** (n) /ˈmɔːɡɪdʒ/
a legal agreement with a bank whereby you borrow money to buy a house and pay back the money over a long period • *They took out a thirty-year mortgage to buy a house.* ➢ mortgage (v)
❖ ενυπόθηκο δάνειο

8.55 **invest** (v) /ɪnˈvest/
buy sth that you hope will give you a profit • *He invested in gold a few years ago and made a huge profit when the price of gold went up.* ➢ investment (n) ❖ επενδύω

8.56 **speculate** (v) /ˈspekjuleɪt/
buy shares, property, etc. hoping to make a large profit when you sell them • *She speculated in property, but lost a lot of money when the market crashed.*
➢ speculation (n) ❖ κερδοσκοπώ

8.57 **bank teller** (n) /bæŋk ˈtelə/
sb who serves clients at a bank, cashier • *I told the bank teller that I wanted to deposit 150 euros into my account.* ❖ ταμίας

8.58 **verify** (v) /ˈverɪfaɪ/
find out if sth is correct or true • *We will have to verify your details before you can open an account at our bank.*
➢ verification (n) ❖ επαληθεύω, εξακριβώνω

8.59 **advantageous** (adj) /ˌædvənˈteɪdʒəs/
favourable • *It will be advantageous to our company if we can find cheaper office space.*
➢ advantage (n) ❖ επωφελής

8.60 **bustling** (adj) /ˈbʌslɪŋ/
lively • *The stall-holders worked hard in the bustling market.* ➢ bustle (v)
❖ πολυσύχναστος

8.61 **leading** (adj) /ˈliːdɪŋ/
the best; the most important • *Samsung is a leading mobile phone manufacturer.*
➢ lead (v) ❖ κύριος, κορυφαίος

8.62 **mutual** (adj) /ˈmjuːtʃuəl/
common • *I buy quality produce grown locally for the mutual benefit of the farmers and myself.* ❖ αμοιβαίος

8.63 **prosperous** (adj) /ˈprɒspərəs/
rich; affluent • *The prosperous businessman donated a large sum of money to charity.*
➢ prosper (v) ❖ εύπορος, που ευημερεί

8.64 **foremost** (adj) /ˈfɔːməʊst/
the best; the most important • *'Fage' is one of Greece's foremost dairy product manufacturers.*
❖ κύριος

8.65 **flourish** (v) /ˈflʌrɪʃ/
do well • *Her business flourished and she soon started exporting goods abroad.*
➢ flourishing (adj) ❖ ακμάζω, προκόβω

8.66 **boom** (v) /buːm/
increase a lot • *Fish farming boomed as demand increased.* ➢ boom (n) ❖ σημειώνω ραγδαία άνοδο, αναπτύσσομαι ραγδαία

8.67 **affluent** (adj) /ˈæfluənt/
rich • *The affluent residents in this area all own very expensive cars.* ➢ affluence (n)
❖ πλούσιος, ευκατάστατος

8.68 **guild** (n) /ɡɪld/
an organisation of people who do the same job • *This certificate shows that he is a member of the bakers' guild.* ❖ συντεχνία

8.69 **chip in** (phr v) /tʃɪp ɪn/
When each person in a group chips in, they give a little money so that they can buy sth together. • *We all chipped in to buy pizza.*
❖ συνεισφέρω

8.70 **fork out** (phr v) /fɔːk aʊt/
spend a lot of money on sth, usually reluctantly • *Despite being a student, he forked out 1000 euros on a new computer.*
❖ πληρώνω πολλά

8.71 **put down (a deposit)** (phr v)
/pʊt daʊn (ə dɪˈpɒzɪt)/
pay part of the cost of sth • *The car cost £5,000, and we had to put down a deposit of £1,500.* ❖ καταβάλλω, πληρώνω (προκαταβολή)

8.72 **set sb back** (phr v) /set ˈsʌmbədi bæk/
cost sb a large amount of money • *The holiday set us back two months' salary.*
❖ στοιχίζω

8.73 **splash out** (phr v) /splæʃ aʊt/
spend a lot of money on sth • *We splashed out for our anniversary and went to an expensive restaurant.* ❖ ξοδεύω πολλά

8.74 **farewell** (n) /feəˈwel/
the act of saying goodbye • *We held a farewell party at the office for John when he retired.*
❖ αποχαιρετισμός

8.75 **black market** (n) /blæk ˈmɑːkɪt/
illegal buying and selling • *She bought a bag on the black market from a street seller.*
❖ μαύρη αγορά

8.76 **flea market** (n) /fliː ˈmɑːkɪt/
a market that sells cheap goods • *Let's go shopping at the flea market in Monastiraki.*
❖ υπαίθρια αγορά

8.77 **stock market** (n) /stɒk ˈmɑːkɪt/
the business of buying and selling stocks and shares • *The value of shares fell on the stock market because of the recession.*
❖ χρηματιστήριο

8.78 **fluid** (adj) /ˈfluːɪd/
changeable • *The political situation is fluid and elections could be held at any moment.*
➢ fluidity (n) ❖ ρευστός

8.79 **old money** (expr) /oʊld ˈmʌni/
wealth that has been inherited rather than earned • *He had old money and looked down on the nouveau riche.* ❖ παλιό χρήμα, παλιά ελίτ

8.80 **pocket money** (n) /ˈpɒkɪt ˈmʌni/
money that parents give their children every week or month • *Betty gets 20 euros pocket money a month from her parents.*
❖ χαρτζιλίκι

8.81 **bank balance** (n) /bæŋk ˈbæləns/
the amount of money you have in your bank account • *He checked his bank balance at the ATM to see how much was in his account.*
❖ υπόλοιπο τραπεζικού λογαριασμού

8.82 **bank statement** (n) /bæŋk ˈsteɪtmənt/
a document that tells you your bank transactions and balance • *The details of this month's transactions will be on your next bank statement.*
❖ κατάσταση λογαριασμού

8.83 **make a fortune** (expr) /meɪk ə ˈfɔːtʃuːn/
make a lot of money • *The band made a fortune with their album and are now very rich.* ❖ βγάζω πολλά χρήματα

8.84 **make a loss** (expr) /meɪk ə lɒs/
If a business makes a loss, it spends more than it earns. • *The company has made a loss for the last five years, so I am afraid we have to close down.* ❖ παθαίνω ζημιά, ζημιώνομαι

8.85 **make a profit** (expr) /meɪk ə ˈprɒfɪt/
money you earn from a business or from selling sth for more than it cost • *The café made a profit of only 500 euros last month.* ❖ έχω κέρδος

8.86 **sales figures** (n) /seɪlz ˈfɪgəz/
statistics showing how much a company sells • *Sales figures show a profit for the first quarter but a loss in the second.*
❖ στοιχεία πωλήσεων

8.87 **sales tax** (n) /seɪlz tæks/
money paid to the government on products sold • *Sales tax rose to 23% on some products.* ❖ φόρος πωλήσεων, φόρος κατανάλωσης

8.88 **credit limit** (n) /ˈkredɪt ˈlɪmɪt/
the maximum amount of money you can borrow on a credit card • *The credit limit on this card is five thousand euros.*
❖ πιστωτικό όριο

8.89 **credit rating** (n) /ˈkredɪt ˈreɪtɪŋ/
how likely you are to pay back money you borrow • *She has an excellent credit rating because she has never fallen behind with any payments.* ❖ πιστοληπτική αξιολόγηση

8.90 **be in the money** (expr) /biː ɪn ðə ˈmʌni/
have a lot of money • *He is in the money because he got a bonus at work.* ❖ έχω χρήματα

8.91 **for my money** (expr) /fə maɪ ˈmʌni/
in my opinion • *For my money, this recession is going to last many more years.*
❖ κατά τη γνώμη μου

8.92 **get one's money's worth** (expr)
/get wʌnz ˈmʌniz wɜːθ/
get good value for your money • *She got her money's worth when she bought a TV and got a DVD player with it for half price.*
❖ παίρνω κάτι που αξίζει τα λεφτά του

8.93 **throw money at** (expr) /θrəʊ ˈmʌni æt/
try to solve a problem by spending money on it • *Throwing money at the house by decorating it won't fix the problem of damp.*
❖ ρίχνω χρήματα σε, πετάω χρήματα σε

8.94 **throw money around** (expr)
/θrəʊ ˈmʌni əˈraʊnd/
spend money carelessly • *He's always throwing money around and buying expensive gifts for everyone.* ❖ σπαταλώ χρήματα

8.95 **extravagantly** (adv) /ɪksˈtrævəgəntli/
more than necessary or more than you can afford • *They spent money extravagantly for their wedding, with champagne and caviar on the menu.* ➢ extravagance (n), extravagant (adj) ❖ πολυδάπανα

8.96 **tighten one's belt** (expr) /ˈtaɪtən wʌnz belt/
spend less money because you have less than you used to • *We'll have to tighten our belts and spend less until I find a job.*
❖ σφίγγω το ζωνάρι

8.97 **line one's pockets** (expr) /laɪn wʌnz ˈpɒkɪts/
make money dishonestly • *The mayor lined his pockets with money from the building fund* ❖ κλέβω

8.98 **have deep pockets** (expr) /hæv diːp ˈpɒkɪts/
have a lot of money • *David must have deep pockets if he can afford a cruise around the world.* ❖ είμαι πλούσιος

8.99 **do sth on a shoestring** (expr) /duː ˈsʌmθɪŋ ɒn ə ˈʃuːstrɪŋ/
do sth using very little money • *She can dress on a shoestring by making all her own clothes.* ❖ κάνω κάτι με ελάχιστο κόστος

8.100 **shanty town** (n) /ˈʃænti taʊn/
an area with lots of roughly built huts made from wood, plastic, cardboard, etc. where poor people live • *The children living in the shanty town had no shoes.* ❖ παραγκούπολη

8.101 **crippling** (adj) /ˈkrɪplɪŋ/
very harmful • *Many innocent people died in the crippling conditions during the war.* ➢ cripple (v) ❖ φρικτός

8.102 **harshly** (adv) /ˈhɑːʃli/
severely • *She was criticised harshly for her bad behaviour.* ➢ harsh (adj), harshness (n) ❖ σκληρά, αυστηρά

8.103 **laundry** (n) /ˈlɔːndri/
clothes that need to be washed • *We do the laundry every Saturday morning.* ➢ launder (v) ❖ άπλυτα (ρούχα)

Phrasal verbs

chip in	set sb back
fall behind	set up
fork out	splash out
put down	turn sb down

Grammar   pages 100-101

8.104 **scales** (pl n) /skeɪlz/
a weighing machine • *He weighed himself on the scales.* ❖ ζυγαριά

8.105 **derive** (v) /dɪˈraɪv/
come from sth else • *Many English words derive from Latin and Greek.* ➢ derivative (adj, n), derivation (n) ❖ προέρχομαι

8.106 **respectively** (adv) /rɪˈspektɪvli/
in the order previously mentioned • *George and Hannah bought a Fiat and a Renault respectively.* ➢ respective (adj) ❖ αντίστοιχα

8.107 **mug** (v) /mʌɡ/
rob sb in the street • *When the woman was mugged in the shopping centre, her bag and car keys were stolen.* ➢ mugger (n), mugging (n) ❖ επιτίθεμαι και ληστεύω

8.108 **nugget** (n) /ˈnʌɡɪt/
a small piece of a valuable metal found in the ground • *The nugget of gold that was found in the mine is worth a fortune.* ❖ ψήγμα χρυσού

Listening   page 102

8.109 **savings account** (n) /ˈseɪvɪŋz əˈkaʊnt/
a bank account in which you keep money that you want to save and which pays you interest • *I have almost £10,000 in my savings account now!* ❖ λογαριασμός ταμιευτηρίου

8.110 **turn sb down** (phr v) /tɜːn ˈsʌmbədi daʊn/
reject sb • *I applied for the job, but they turned me down.* ❖ απορρίπτω

8.111 **VAT** (abbr) /ˌviː eɪ ˈtiː/
a tax added to the price of goods and services • *What is the VAT on books these days?* ❖ ΦΠΑ (Φόρος Προστιθέμενης Αξίας)
✎ VAT = value added tax

8.112 **short (of sth)** (adj) /ʃɔːt (əv ˈsʌmθɪŋ)/
not having enough (of sth) • *I'm afraid I can't lend you any money as I'm short of cash myself.* ❖ (αυτός) που έχει ξεμείνει (από κάτι)

8.113 **in the region of** (expr) /ɪn ðə ˈriːdʒən əv/
approximately • *I'm not sure how many people were at the meeting, but there must have been in the region of 1,000.* ❖ περίπου

8.114 **accountant** (n) /əˈkaʊntənt/
sb whose job is to keep or check financial accounts, calculate taxes, etc. • *The firm employs an accountant to control its finances.* ➢ accounts (pl n), account (n) ❖ λογιστής

8.115 **fall behind** (phr v) /fɔːl bɪˈhaɪnd/
fail to pay sb money that you owe them on time • *She lost her job and fell behind with the rent.* ❖ μένω πίσω (σε πληρωμές)

8.116 **deposit** (v) /dɪˈpɒzɪt/
put money in a bank • *I deposited the money in your account yesterday.* ➢ deposit (n) ❖ καταθέτω

8.117 **cash flow** (n) /kæʃ fləʊ/
the movement of money into and out of a business • *They couldn't pay the mortgage because they had cash flow problems.* ❖ ρευστότητα

Speaking   page 103

8.118 **money is no object** (expr) /ˈmʌni ɪz nəʊ ˈɒbdʒɪkt/
money is not considered a problem because you have lots of it • *Money is no object, so you can spend as much as you like on the wedding.* ❖ υπάρχει άφθονο χρήμα

8.119 down-and-out (adj) /daʊn-ænd-aʊt/
without money, a job or a place to live • *The man was down-and-out and slept on a bench in the park every night.*
❖ άστεγος, πάμφτωχος

8.120 spending spree (expr) /ˈspendɪŋ spriː/
a period of time when you spend a lot of money • *I bought three new pairs of shoes on my spending spree in the sales.*
❖ γλέντι αγορών

8.121 budgeting (n) /ˈbʌdʒɪtɪŋ/
careful planning of what you spend
• *Budgeting is essential if you want to save money for a holiday.* ➣ budget (v, n)
❖ κατάστρωση προϋπολογισμού

8.122 make ends meet (expr) /meɪk endz miːt/
have only just enough money to buy what you need • *We can only make ends meet if we don't spend any money on luxuries.*
❖ τα βγάζω πέρα

8.123 have money to burn (expr) /hæv ˈmʌni tʊ bɜːn/
have more money than you need • *Those rich celebrities have money to burn and throw very extravagant parties.*
❖ έχω λεφτά για πέταμα

8.124 make a killing (expr) /meɪk ə ˈkɪlɪŋ/
make a large profit • *We made a killing on the business deal, so the boss is really pleased.*
❖ βγάζω εύκολο κέρδος

8.125 lavish (adj) /ˈlævɪʃ/
spending/costing a lot of money • *They held a lavish party costing a fortune for their guests*
➣ lavishly (adv)
❖ πολυτελής, πλουσιοπάροχος

8.126 down-to-earth (adj) /daʊn-tə-ˈɜːθ/
practical • *Stan is down-to-earth so his advice will be useful.* ❖ πρακτικός, προσγειωμένος

8.127 abject poverty (expr) /ˈæbdʒekt ˈpɒvəti/
condition of being terribly poor • *The families in the shanty towns were living in abject poverty.* ❖ απόλυτη φτώχεια

8.128 filthy rich (expr) /ˈfɪlθi rɪtʃ/
extremely wealthy • *The filthy rich rock star owns a mansion in Hollywood and three yachts.* ❖ πάμπλουτος

8.129 dirt cheap (expr) /dɜːt tʃiːp/
costing very little money • *This dirt cheap watch only cost five euros.* ❖ πάμφθηνος

Writing: an article (1) pages 104-105

8.130 sweep (v) /swiːp/
spread quickly • *The news that the boss was retiring swept the office.* ❖ εξαπλώνω, απλώνομαι

8.131 smooth sailing (expr) /smuːð ˈseɪlɪŋ/
very easy to do • *The test was smooth sailing for Harry as he had revised well.* ❖ ομαλή πορεία, χωρίς προβλήματα, παιχνιδάκι

8.132 retail industry (n) /ˈriːteɪl ˈɪndəstri/
selling goods to the public • *He works in the retail industry as a clothing store manager.*
❖ βιομηχανία λιανικής πώλησης

8.133 house-bound (adj) /ˈhaʊs-baʊnd/
unable to leave the house • *Katy is house-bound until her bad back gets better.*
❖ κλεισμένος στο σπίτι

8.134 fake (n) /feɪk/
a copy of an object that is intended to deceive people • *The painting is not by Rembrandt; it's a fake.* ➣ fake (adj) ❖ απάτη

8.135 revenue (n) /ˈrevənjuː/
money that a business receives during a certain period • *The company suffered a loss of revenue when their product was recalled.*
❖ έσοδα

8.136 at the expense of (expr) /ət ði ɪkˈspens əv/
If you do sth at the expense sb/sth, you do sth that could harm them. • *The factory owner profited at the expense of his workers.*
❖ εις βάρος

Banking and investing

account	credit rating
bank balance	debit
bank statement	exchange rate
bank teller	owe
bond	revenue
crash	share
credit	stock market
credit limit	transaction

Video 8: Art of the Deal page 106

8.137 vendor (n) /ˈvendə/
sb who sells things • *The market vendor was selling strawberries.* ❖ πωλητής

8.138 alley (n) /ˈæli/
a narrow road between buildings • *We walked down a narrow alley to the next road.*
❖ στενό δρομάκι, σοκάκι

8.139 date (n) /deɪt/
a sweet, sticky brown fruit that grows on a kind of palm tree • *We ate dates for dessert in Egypt.* ❖ χουρμάς

8.140 craftsman (n) /ˈkrɑːftsmən/
sb who makes things skilfully with their hands • *These chairs were made by a local craftsman.* ➣ craftsmanship (n) ❖ τεχνίτης

8.141 **kaftan** (n) /ˈkæftæn/
a long piece of clothing worn in the Middle East countries • *Abdul's white kaftan is made of cotton and linen.* ❖ καφτάνι
✎ Also: caftan

8.142 **auction** (n) /ˈɔːkʃn/
a public sale where the person who offers the highest price buys the item • *I bid for a PlayStation on an online auction and was lucky enough to get it.* ➢ auction (v)
❖ δημοπρασία

Vocabulary Exercises

A Circle the odd one out.

1	customer	vendor	trader
2	mount	crash	plummet
3	fake	forgery	fund
4	flourish	boom	sweep
5	verify	invest	speculate
6	hard-up	affluent	prosperous
7	redundant	favourable	advantageous
8	earn	credit	owe

B Circle the correct words.

1 The pound has been in circulation / inflation for longer than any other currency.
2 I think he spends too inevitably / extravagantly and should tighten his belt.
3 They are living on the breadline / in abject poverty and can just afford food and rent.
4 The wedding was a lavish / crippling affair.
5 The dollar is unofficial / legal tender in America.
6 More and more families need food purchases / vouchers in order to survive.
7 The mutual / bustling port was full of tourists boarding ferries.
8 How much money did you invest in the stock / flea market?

C Match.

1 credit   a holder
2 exchange   b figures
3 stall   c teller
4 bank   d crunch
5 black   e flow
6 sales   f spree
7 shanty   g industry
8 spending   h rate
9 retail   i town
10 cash   j market

D Complete the sentences with one word in each gap.

1 I'm reading this economics book _____ tandem with another one about the recession.
2 She splashed _____ on a new dress for the party.
3 This film about college brings _____ mind my student days.
4 I'm _____ the money because I just got paid!
5 We have very low salaries so we try to do everything _____ a shoestring.
6 The tickets for the concert set him _____ nearly a hundred euros.
7 He looks fit but, _____ my money, his opponent looks stronger.
8 Throwing money _____ your problem won't make it go away.

8 Grammar

8.1 Relative Clauses

Οι relative clauses (αναφορικές προτάσεις) δίνουν περισσότερες πληροφορίες για το υποκείμενο ή το αντικείμενο μιας πρότασης. Εισάγονται με τις παρακάτω λέξεις:

- *who* για πρόσωπα
- *which* για πράγματα ή ζώα
- *whose* για να δείξουμε κτήση ή ιδιοκτησία
- *when* για χρόνο
- *where* για τοποθεσίες

8.2 Defining Relative Clauses

Μια προσδιοριστική αναφορική πρόταση (defining relative clause) μας δίνει πληροφορίες που είναι απαραίτητες ώστε να καταλάβουμε για ποιο πρόσωπο ή ποιο πράγμα μιλάμε. Δε χρησιμοποιούμε κόμμα για να τη χωρίσουμε από την υπόλοιπη πρόταση. Μπορούμε να χρησιμοποιήσουμε *that* αντί για *who* και *which*.
→ That's the journalist **who/that wrote the article on inflation**.

Όταν το *who*, *which* ή το *that* είναι αντικείμενο της προσδιοριστικής αναφορικής πρότασης, μπορούμε να το παραλείψουμε.
→ *He's the man (**who**) they have accused of money laundering.*
→ ***That**'s the second-hand store (**which**) Linda visits every week.*

8.3 Non-defining Relative Clauses

Μια μη-προσδιοριστική πρόταση (non-defining relative clause) μας δίνει παραπάνω πληροφορίες που όμως δεν είναι απαραίτητες για να καταλάβουμε το νόημα της κύριας πρότασης. Χρησιμοποιούμε κόμμα πριν και μετά τη non-defining relative clause για να τη χωρίσουμε από την υπόλοιπη πρόταση. Με τις non-defining relative clauses δε χρησιμοποιούμε *that*, και δεν παραλείπουμε την αναφορική αντωνυμία.
→ *My sister, **who was made redundant**, is trying hard to make ends meet.*
→ *The mall, **which has a huge car park**, is located on the outskirts of town.*

8.4 Prepositions in Relative Clauses

Η αναφορική αντωνυμία μπορεί να αναφέρεται στο αντικείμενο της πρόθεσης. Όταν το ύφος είναι ανεπίσημο, η πρόθεση μπαίνει μετά από το ρήμα. Όταν έχουμε επίσημο ύφος, η πρόθεση μπορεί να μπει πριν από την αναφορική αντωνυμία. Μετά από πρόθεση δεν μπορούμε να χρησιμοποιήσουμε την αναφορική αντωνυμία *that*.
→ *The online store **which** Adam orders **from** is open around the clock.*
→ *The online store **from which** Adam orders is open around the clock.*
→ *The charity, **which** I donate money **to**, helps the homeless.*
→ *The charity, **to which** I donate money, helps the homeless.*

8.5 Participle clauses

Υπάρχουν δύο είδη participles (μετοχές). Η present participle – ενεργητική μετοχή (verb + *-ing*), και η past participle – παθητική μετοχή (verb + *-ed* ή άλλος ανώμαλος τύπος ρήματος).

Χρησιμοποιούμε participles σε participle clauses (μετοχικές προτάσεις) ώστε να κάνουμε μια πρόταση συντομότερη. Μπορούν να αντικαταστήσουν το υποκείμενο και το ρήμα σε μια πρόταση, όταν το υποκείμενο της κύριας και της δευτερεύουσας πρότασης είναι το ίδιο. Χρησιμοποιούμε present participle όταν το ρήμα είναι ενεργητικό (active), και past participle όταν το ρήμα είναι παθητικό (passive).
→ *Before **filling** out my tax forms, I asked an accountant for advice.*
→ ***Given** a Jaguar for his graduation, Ken felt like a millionaire.*

Μπορούμε να χρησιμοποιήσουμε μετοχή για να αντικαταστήσουμε την αναφορική αντωνυμία και το ρήμα.
→ *The employees (**who were not paid**) were very disappointed.*
→ *The employees **not paid** were very disappointed.*
→ *People **who live** below the poverty line often rely on food vouchers.*
→ *People **living** below the poverty line often rely on food vouchers.*

8 Grammar

Μπορούμε επίσης να χρησιμοποιήσουμε perfect participle (μετοχή αορίστου), δηλαδή *having* + past participle για να ενώσουμε δύο προτάσεις που έχουν το ίδιο υποκείμενο.
Αυτό το κάνουμε:
όταν μια πράξη έχει ολοκληρωθεί πριν από μια άλλη πράξη.
→ **He withdrew** money from the bank and then paid his bills.
→ **Having withdrawn** money from the bank, he paid his bills.
όταν μια πράξη συνεχιζόταν για ένα χρονικό διάστημα πριν αρχίσει μια άλλη πράξη.
→ **He had been investing** part of his salary for years so he was financially secure.
→ **Having invested** part of his salary for years, he was financially secure.

Χρησιμοποιούμε την perfect participle στην ενεργητική και στην παθητική φωνή.
ενεργητική φωνή (active voice): *having* + past participle
→ **Having asked** the bank teller to check her account, she waited.

παθητική φωνή (passive voice): *having been* + past participle
→ **Having been asked** to check her account, the bank teller did it quickly.

8.6 Cleft Sentences

Χρησιμοποιούμε cleft sentences για να δώσουμε έμφαση σε αυτά που θέλουμε να πούμε. Οι cleft sentences μοιάζουν με τις relative clauses. Στις cleft sentences χρησιμοποιούμε φράσεις όπως: *the reason why, the thing that, the person/people who, the place where, the day when* και προτάσεις με το *what* και το *is/was*.
→ **The reason (why)** Carol wanted to see me **was** to ask for a small loan.
→ **The people who** truly deserve our support **are** the unemployed.
→ **What really worries me is** that investing in stocks and bonds is quite unpredictable.

Grammar Exercises

A Choose the correct answers. Sometimes more than one answer is possible.

1 John has taken the parking space – / who / that I always use.
2 The shop assistant – / who / that spoke to me was very polite.
3 This is the bank – / where / that I first opened an account.
4 Catherine, who / whom / whose husband is my cousin, is an excellent financial advisor.
5 The reason – / why / which I bought some shares is to earn some money on my savings.
6 The affluent community, – / that / which we are not a part of, are always throwing extravagant parties.
7 Those were the times – / when / why I was happiest.
8 You are the second person who / that / – has asked to borrow money from me today.

B Circle the correct words.

1 Established / Establishing after World War II, the EEC eased trade in Europe.
2 Having stolen / Having been stolen, my credit card was cancelled.
3 Being / Been hard-up, we have to budget carefully all the time.
4 The money raising / raised for the children's hospital fund was an enormous help.
5 Smiling / Smiled kindly, the lady offered the elderly gentleman a seat on the bus.
6 Rudely interrupting / interrupted again, the speaker refused to carry on talking.
7 Having filled / Having been filled in my tax return, I posted it the next morning.
8 Not having introduced / having been introduced, the Englishmen did not strike up a conversation.

C Match.

1 The reason
2 What
3 The thing
4 2002 was the year
5 It was her sister
6 London is a city
7 All that is required
8 It was last Sunday

a depressed us were all our bills.
b the euro was officially launched.
c where many banks have their headquarters.
d why he rang was to ask for money.
e when I finally got some rest.
f is your signature on these forms.
g that worries me the most is my credit rating.
h who couldn't pay her back.

Exam Task

For questions 1-6, complete the second sentence so that it has a similar meaning to the first sentence, using the word given. Do not change the word given. You must use between three and six words, including the word given.

1 The charity was founded in 1997.
   UP
   The charity _____ in 1997.

2 They made a deposit of one thousand euros for the new car.
   PUT
   They _____ for the new car.

3 The company lost money the first year of the recession.
   LOSS
   The company _____ of the recession.

4 He earns money designing landscape gardens.
   LIVING
   He _____ landscape gardens.

5 She must have a lot of money to be able to afford a Porsche.
   POCKETS
   She must _____ to be able to afford a Porsche.

6 The students studied all day and all night in preparation for their exams.
   CLOCK
   The students _____ in preparation for their exams.

9 All That Jazz!

Word Focus — page 110

9.1 culture vulture (n) /ˈkʌltʃə ˈvʌltʃə/
sb who is very interested in culture and the arts • *As a culture vulture, I love going to the theatre every weekend.* ❖ λάτρης της τέχνης, του πολιτισμού

9.2 pilot project (n) /ˈpaɪlət ˈprɒdʒekt/
a project set up to test sth • *The pilot project for youth theatre went so well that it became a regular event.* ❖ πιλοτικό πρόγραμμα

9.3 highbrow (adj) /ˈhaɪbraʊ/
serious and difficult to understand • *This highbrow exhibition is about tragedy in theatre.* ❖ διανοούμενος, διανοουμενίστικος
✎ Opp: lowbrow

9.4 mission (n) /ˈmɪʃn/
an important job • *The comedian's mission is not only to entertain but also to make the audience think.* ❖ αποστολή

9.5 instigate (v) /ˈɪnstɪgeɪt/
bring about • *We hope this play about old age will instigate change in the treatment of the elderly.* ➣ instigation (n) ❖ προκαλώ

9.6 plight (n) /plaɪt/
an extremely difficult situation • *The plight of the homeless should not be ignored.* ❖ χάλι

9.7 detention centre (n) /dɪˈtenʃn ˈsentə/
a prison • *The fourteen-year-old thief was taken to a detention centre.* ❖ κέντρο κράτησης

9.8 abridged (adj) /əˈbrɪdʒd/
shortened • *The abridged version of the novel is 100 pages shorter than the original.* ➣ abridge (v) ❖ συντομευμένος

Reading — pages 110-111

9.9 playwright (n) /ˈpleɪraɪt/
sb who writes theatrical plays • *Shakespeare is the most famous English playwright of all.* ❖ θεατρικός συγγραφέας

9.10 free-for-all (n) /ˈfriː-fə-ɔːl/
a situation where anything can happen because there is total freedom • *The guests treated the buffet as a free-for-all and took as much food as they could.* ❖ όλοι εναντίον όλων

9.11 cost an arm and a leg (expr) /kɒst æn ɑːm ænd ə leg/
be extremely expensive • *The tickets for the show cost an arm and a leg so I really can't afford them.* ❖ είναι πανάκριβο, κοστίζει μια περιουσία

9.12 check out (phr v) /tʃek aʊt/
look at sb/sth because they are interesting • *You should check out the new Bond film at the cinema.* ❖ εξετάζω

9.13 courtesy of sb (expr) /ˈkɜːtəsi ɒv ˈsʌmbədi/
kindly provided by • *The refreshments have been provided courtesy of my brother's catering firm.* ❖ με την ευγενική προσφορά

9.14 mushroom (v) /ˈmʌʃruːm/
grow enormously • *Gangnam Style started in South Korea but soon mushroomed into a worldwide phenomenon.* ❖ αυξάνομαι

9.15 stage (v) /steɪdʒ/
organise and present a play • *The drama club decided to stage a play by Shakespeare.* ➣ stage (n) ❖ ανεβάζω (θεατρικό έργο)

9.16 cater for (phr v) /ˈkeɪtə fɔː/
provide • *This fitness club caters for people of all ages.* ❖ καλύπτω τις ανάγκες

9.17 distinguished (adj) /dɪsˈtɪŋgwɪʃt/
respected; admired • *The distinguished pianist gave a performance that was widely admired.* ➣ distinguish (v) ❖ διαπρεπής, σεβαστός

9.18 be on the go (expr) /bi ɒn ðə gəʊ/
be busy and active • *She's very energetic and she's always on the go.* ❖ είμαι εν κινήσει/στο πόδι

9.19 erase (v) /ɪˈreɪz/
get rid of • *International sporting events should erase racial prejudice if all athletes are treated equally.* ➣ erasure (n) ❖ σβήνω

9.20 endeavour (n) /ɪnˈdevə/
an attempt to do sth new • *Our English teacher's endeavour to set up a drama group failed because of lack of interest.* ➣ endeavour (v) ❖ προσπάθεια

9.21 disability (n) /dɪsəˈbɪlɪti/
a condition that makes it difficult for sb to use a part of their body properly • *The Paralympics are an inspirational sporting event for people with disabilities.* ➣ disabled (adj) ❖ αναπηρία

9.22 core (adj) /kɔː/
central • *The core message of this play is equality for women.* ➣ core (n) ❖ κεντρικός

9.23 on tour (expr) /ɒn tʊə/
performing at different venues • *The band are on tour around North America and will play first in New York.* ❖ σε περιοδεία

9.24 listings (pl n) /ˈlɪstɪŋz/
information in a newspaper or magazine about what films, plays, shows, etc. are on • *Look at the listings to what's on at the cinema this weekend.* ❖ πρόγραμμα (κινηματογράφων, θεάτρων κλπ.)

9.25 deprived (adj) /dɪˈpraɪvd/
not having the things that are necessary for a comfortable life • *We are raising money to buy food for deprived families.* ➢ deprive (v), deprivation (n) ❖ στερημένος

9.26 intellect (n) /ˈɪntəlekt/
sb's mind • *Children need to have their intellect stimulated.* ➢ intellectual (adj, n) ❖ μυαλό, νοημοσύνη

9.27 culminate (v) /ˈkʌlmɪneɪt/
end with • *The show culminated with the whole cast on stage singing a farewell song.* ➢ culmination (n) ❖ κορυφώνομαι, καταλήγω

Vocabulary   pages 112-113

9.28 chart (n) /tʃɑːt/
an official list of how many songs or albums are sold every week • *Adele's new song is number 1 in the charts.* ❖ τσαρτ

9.29 decibel (n) /ˈdesɪbel/
a unit for measuring the loudness of sound • *The sound of a jet engine is around 140 decibels.* ❖ ντεσιμπέλ

9.30 download (n) /ˈdaʊnləʊd/
a computer file that has been moved from a computer network to a small computer • *I have a download of U2's album from iTunes.* ➢ download (v) ❖ κατέβασμα

9.31 record label (n) /ˈrekɔːd ˈleɪbəl/
a company that publishes music • *Capitol Records is a well-known American record label that has worked with bands like the Beatles and Duran Duran.* ❖ δισκογραφική εταιρεία

9.32 pianist (n) /ˈpiːənɪst/
sb who plays the piano • *Stevie Wonder, despite being blind, is a talented blues pianist.* ❖ πιανίστας

9.33 single (n) /ˈsɪŋgl/
a recording of a song sold by itself • *Her favourite Madonna single is* Material Girl. ❖ τραγούδι, σινγκλ

9.34 solo artist (n) /ˈsəʊləʊ ˈɑːtɪst/
sb who sings or plays music alone • *Amy Winehouse was a talented solo artist who sadly died at the age of 27.* ❖ σόλο καλλιτέχνης

9.35 whistle (n) /ˈwɪsl/
a high sound made by blowing air out through your lips • *The sheep dog obeyed its master's whistles and commands.* ➢ whistle (v) ❖ σφύριγμα

9.36 air raid siren (n) /eə reɪd ˈsaɪrən/
a warning sound before an attack from war planes • *The residents of London would take cover underground when they heard the air raid sirens during World War II.* ❖ σειρήνα συναγερμού (αεροπορικής επίθεσης)

9.37 lyrics (pl n) /ˈlɪrɪks/
words of a song • *She knows the lyrics of all Adele's songs.* ❖ στίχοι τραγουδιού

9.38 verse (n) /vɜːs/
part of a song or poem • *There are three verses in this song and a chorus that is repeated.* ❖ στροφή, στιχάκι

9.39 apathy (n) /ˈæpəθi/
lack of enthusiasm • *The students' apathy annoyed the teacher, who could not understand why they were not more enthusiastic.* ➢ apathetic (adj) ❖ απάθεια

9.40 set to music (expr) /set tʊ ˈmjuːzɪk/
write or play music to go with words • *I write lyrics which my friend sets to music.* ❖ μελοποιώ

9.41 beat (n) /biːt/
the main rhythm of a piece of music • *The band was OK but they kept losing the beat.* ❖ ρυθμός

9.42 pulse (n) /pʌls/
an amount of sound that is produced by sth for a short time • *The satellite sent out a pulse which was used to map its position.* ➢ pulse (v) ❖ παλμός, σφυγμός, δόνηση

9.43 read music (expr) /riːd ˈmjuːzɪk/
be able to understand written musical notes • *I learned to read music when I started piano lessons.* ❖ διαβάζω μουσική

9.44 stroke (n) /strəʊk/
a movement of a brush • *The painter used short brush strokes to produce this effect.* ❖ πινελιά

9.45 tint (n) /tɪnt/
a small amount of a colour • *She added a red tint to her hair.* ➢ tint (v), tinted (adj) ❖ απόχρωση

9.46 doodle (n) /ˈduːdl/
a drawing you do when you are thinking about sth else • *I drew doodles on my textbook during the boring lesson.* ➢ doodle (v) ❖ πρόχειρο σκιτσάκι, μουντζούρωμα

9.47 carving (n) /ˈkɑːvɪŋ/
a decorative object made by cutting into wood or stone • *There were carvings of flowers on the wooden bowls.* ➢ carve (v) ❖ σκάλισμα

9.48 clay (n) /kleɪ/
a substance used to make pots • *Shape the clay into a pot and then we can put it in the kiln to harden.* ❖ πηλός

9.49 easel (n) /ˈiːzl/
a frame for resting a painting on while you paint • *The artist put a fresh canvas on an easel and started to paint.* ❖ καβαλέτο

9.50 palette (n) /ˈpælɪt/
a flat surface for mixing paints on • *She mixed blue and red on the palette to make a shade of purple.* ❖ παλέτα

9.51 ink (n) /ɪŋk/
coloured liquid used for writing • *In the past we wrote with feathers dipped in ink.* ❖ μελάνι

9.52	**oil** (n) /ɔɪl/ thick paint that contains oil • *The artists used oils to paint the portrait.* ❖ λαδομπογιά	9.66	**backing singer** (n) /ˈbækɪŋ ˈsɪŋə/ a singer who provides extra vocals for the main singer • *Pink Floyd have great backing singers to accompany them at their concerts.* ❖ τραγουδιστής για φωνητικά
9.53	**plaster** (n) /ˈplɑːstə/ a white powder mixed with water that becomes hard when it dries • *She made a plaster copy of the statue.* ❖ σοβάς	9.67	**lead vocalist** (n) /liːd ˈvəʊkəlɪst/ the main singer in a group • *Mick Jagger is still the lead vocalist for the Rolling Stones.* ❖ κύριος τραγουδιστής
9.54	**water colour** (n) /ˈwɔːtə ˈkʌlə/ a mixture of paint and water • *He used water colours to paint a picture of the sea.* ❖ ακουαρέλα	9.68	**microphone stand** (n) /ˈmaɪkrəfəʊn stænd/ equipment used to hold a microphone • *The tall singer had to raise the microphone stand.* ❖ βάση μικροφώνου
9.55	**reproduction** (n) /riːprəˈdʌkʃn/ a copy of a work of art • *I bought a cheap reproduction of the Mona Lisa by da Vinci.* ➢ reproduce (v) ❖ αντίγραφο	9.69	**performing arts** (n) /pəˈfɔːmɪŋ ɑːts/ acting, dancing and playing music • *She is studying performing arts at drama school.* ❖ τέχνες του θεάματος
9.56	**landscape** (n) /ˈlændskeɪp/ a picture of the countryside • *The landscapes she paints of the English countryside are beautiful.* ❖ τοπίο	9.70	**cover version** (n) /ˈkʌvə ˈvɜːʒn/ a new recording of a song originally sung by sb else • *Jessica Simpson sung a cover version of Nancy Sinatra's 1966 song* These Boots Are Made For Walking *in 2005.* ❖ επανεκτέλεση τραγουδιού
9.57	**fresco** (n) /ˈfreskəʊ/ a painting on wet plaster on a wall • *Michelangelo painted beautiful frescoes on the ceiling of the Sistine Chapel.* ❖ νωπογραφία, τοιχογραφία	9.71	**opening act** (n) /ˈəʊpənɪŋ ækt/ a band that plays before the main band at a concert • *Marina and the Diamonds were the opening act for Coldplay on their Mylo Xyloto tour.* ❖ συγκρότημα που εμφανίζεται πριν το κύριο συγκρότημα σε συναυλία
9.58	**still life** (n) /stɪl laɪf/ a painting of objects like fruit or flowers • *I think the fruit in this still life is very well executed.* ❖ νεκρή φύση		
9.59	**commission** (n) /kəˈmɪʃn/ a request for an artist to create a piece of art for which they will be paid • *The artist received a commission to paint the king's portrait.* ➢ commission (v) ❖ ανάθεση	9.72	**mainstream** (adj) /ˈmeɪnstriːm/ generally accepted by most people • *Mainstream music is generally what you hear on daytime radio.* ❖ που ανήκει στο κύριο ρεύμα, της επικρατούσας τάσης
9.60	**concept** (n) /ˈkɒnsept/ an idea • *The concept of graffiti as art is not accepted by everyone.* ❖ ιδέα, έννοια	9.73	**middling** (adj) /ˈmɪdlɪŋ/ average • *The actor gave a middling performance which did not impress the critics.* ❖ μέτριος, καλούτσικος
9.61	**movement** (n) /ˈmuːvmənt/ a group of people who share the same ideas • *The feminist movement took off in the 1970s.* ❖ κίνημα	9.74	**debut** (n) /ˈdeɪbjuː/ a performer's first public appearance in a play, film, show, etc. • *The actor made his debut in the new play.* ❖ ντεμπούτο, πρώτη εμφάνιση
9.62	**subject** (n) /ˈsʌbdʒɪkt/ a thing or person that you paint a picture of • *Children are a difficult subject to draw as they won't sit still.* ❖ θέμα	9.75	**play by ear** (expr) /pleɪ baɪ ɪə/ play music you have heard without having to read written music • *He plays by ear, so he listens to pieces to learn them.* ❖ παίζω απ' έξω, χωρίς παρτιτούρα
9.63	**pop art** (n) /pɒp ɑːt/ modern art that uses bright colours and takes themes from everyday life • *I love the famous pop art picture of Marilyn Monroe by Andy Warhol.* ❖ ποπ αρτ	9.76	**under contract** (expr) /ˈʌndə ˈkɒntrækt/ required to do sth because you have signed an official agreement • *The band is under contract to produce one more album with this record label.* ❖ με σύμβαση
9.64	**socialite** (n) /ˈsəʊʃəlaɪt/ sb who goes to a lot of fashionable parties • *The socialite was photographed at the party wearing lots of jewellery.* ❖ μέλος της κοσμικής κοινωνίας, σοσιαλιτέ	9.77	**in harmony** (expr) /ɪn ˈhɑːməni/ using musical notes combined together in a pleasant way • *The choir sang beautifully in harmony.* ❖ αρμονικά
9.65	**silkscreen** (n) /ˈsɪlkˌskriːn/ silk printed with paint to make a picture • *The silkscreen painting had to be handled carefully.* ❖ μεταξοτυπία		

9.78 **on display** (expr) /ɒn dɪsˈpleɪ/
on show • *Many new paintings were on display at the art gallery.* ❖ σε έκθεση

9.79 **wing** (n) /wɪŋ/
a part of a building that sticks out at an angle to the main part • *They are building a new wing at the hospital.* ❖ πτέρυγα

9.80 **under new management** (expr) /ˈʌndə njuː ˈmænɪdʒmənt/
being controlled by a new boss or company • *The restaurant is under new management so we have a new menu.* ❖ υπό νέα διεύθυνση

9.81 **by heart** (expr) /baɪ hɑːt/
If you know sth by heart, you remember all of it. • *I had to learn the poem by heart for the recital.* ❖ απέξω

9.82 **change one's tune** (expr) /tʃeɪndʒ wʌnz tjuːn/
start to express a different opinion after sth has happened • *Will the politician change his tune if he wins the election?* ❖ αλλάζω γνώμη

9.83 **face the music** (expr) /feɪs ðə ˈmjuːzɪk/
accept the consequences of bad actions • *I failed the exam and now I must face the music.* ❖ αντιμετωπίζω τις συνέπειες των πράξεών μου

9.84 **sell sth for a song** (expr) /sel ˈsʌmθɪŋ fɔːr ə sɒŋ/
sell sth very cheaply • *The shop is selling everything for a song in its closing down sale.* ❖ πουλώ σε πολύ χαμηλή τιμή

9.85 **music to one's ears** (expr) /ˈmjuːzɪk tʊ wʌnz ɪəz/
If sb's words are music to your ears, they make you very happy. • *It was music to our ears when we heard you hadn't been hurt in the train crash.* ❖ μουσική στα αυτιά, κάτι που ευχαριστεί

9.86 **blow one's own trumpet** (expr) /bləʊ wʌnz əʊn ˈtrʌmpɪt/
boast about your achievements • *You should be more modest and not blow your own trumpet.* ❖ περιαυτολογώ

9.87 **boast** (v) /bəʊst/
talk proudly about yourself in an annoying way • *The actor boasted about all the awards he had won.* ❖ περηφανεύομαι, καυχιέμαι

9.88 **sing like a canary** (expr) /sɪŋ laɪk ə kəˈneəri/
confess everything (to the police) • *The thief sang like a canary when the police questioned him.* ❖ ομολογώ/παραδέχομαι τα πάντα

9.89 **sing sb's praises** (expr) /sɪŋ ˈsʌmbədiz ˈpreɪzɪz/
express admiration for sb • *The cast admired the director and sang his praises.* ❖ εκφράζω θαυμασμό

9.90 **make a song and dance about sth** (expr) /meɪk ə sɒŋ ænd dɑːns əˈbaʊt ˈsʌmθɪŋ/
make a big deal about sth that is not important • *He made a song and dance about the water on the carpet.* ❖ κάνω φασαρία για κάτι, το κάνω θέμα

9.91 **make a big deal out of sth** (expr) /meɪk ə bɪg diːl aʊt əv ˈsʌmθɪŋ/
make sth seem more important than it really is • *It was a minor accident. Don't make a big deal out of it.* ❖ κάνω κάτι (ασήμαντο) ολόκληρο ζήτημα

Art
easel	palette
landscape	still life
oil	water colour

Music
backing singer	on tour
beat	pianist
chart	record label
cover version	single
leading vocalist	solo artist
lyrics	verse

Grammar pages 114-115

9.92 **subjective** (adj) /sʌbˈdʒektɪv/
based on personal feelings • *Everyone's opinion is subjective so it is unfair to say a work of art is rubbish.* ➢ subjectivity (n) ❖ υποκειμενικός
✏ Opp: objective

9.93 **brand** (n) /brænd/
a product made by a particular company • *My favourite brand of jeans is Levi's.* ❖ μάρκα

9.94 **pricey** (adj) /ˈpraɪsi/
expensive • *The dress I bought for the party was quite pricey.* ➢ price (n) ❖ ακριβός

9.95 **scale** (n) /skeɪl/
the extent or size of sth compared with sth else • *They entertain on a grand scale, and have dozens of guests at their parties.* ❖ κλίμακα

9.96 **phenomenally** (adv) /fəˈnɒmənəli/
incredibly • *The phenomenally successful tour attracted large audiences at every venue.* ➢ phenomenon (n), phenomenal (adj) ❖ εκπληκτικά, εξαιρετικά

9.97 **line up** (n) /laɪn ʌp/
a group of performers who are involved in an event • *The line up for the event includes Dalaras and Parios.* ❖ λίστα καλλιτεχνών

9.98 lines (pl n) /laɪnz/
the words an actor must learn for a role • *I had to learn my lines for the main part in this play.* ❖ ατάκες/λόγια σεναρίου

9.99 put sb off (phr v) /pʊt ˈsʌmbədi ɒf/
discourage • *The bad weather put us off going to the beach.* ❖ αποθαρρύνω

9.100 bomb (v) /bɒm/
fail badly • *The film bombed because the acting was bad and the special effects unimpressive.* ❖ αποτυγχάνω παταγωδώς

Listening page 116

9.101 carpenter (n) /ˈkɑːpɪntə/
sb who makes things out of wood • *The carpenter made a wooden table and four chairs.* ❖ ξυλουργός

9.102 chest of drawers (n) /tʃest əv drɔːz/
a piece of furniture with drawers where you can keep your clothes • *He puts his T-shirts and underwear in this chest of drawers.* ❖ σιφονιέρα

9.103 scrutiny (n) /ˈskruːtəni/
careful study • *The company's accounts came under scrutiny by the tax office when fraud was suspected.* ➢ scrutinise (v) ❖ λεπτομερής έλεγχος

9.104 authority (n) /ɔːˈθɒrəti/
sb with special knowledge of a subject • *She is an authority on paintings and says this one is a forgery.* ❖ αυθεντία

9.105 authenticity (n) /ɔːθenˈtɪsəti/
being genuine • *Experts were brought in to check the authenticity of the painting.* ➢ authentic (adj) ❖ αυθεντικότητα

Speaking page 117

9.106 graphic artist (n) /ˈɡræfɪk ˈɑːtɪst/
an artist who designs images for the publishing industry • *The graphic artist designed the cover of the book.* ❖ γραφίστας

9.107 handicrafts (pl n) /ˈhændɪˌkrɑːfts/
sth made skilfully by sb using their hands • *This shop sells local handicrafts to tourists.* ❖ χειροτεχνήματα

9.108 objects of art (expr) /ˈɒbdʒekts ɒv ɑːt/
objects with some value as art, which are used for decoration • *The collector has many objects of art at his home.* ❖ αντικείμενα τέχνης

9.109 street artist (n) /striːt ˈɑːtɪst/
sb who performs in the street to entertain passers-by • *A crowd watched the street artist juggle balls in the main square.* ❖ καλλιτέχνης του δρόμου

9.110 performing artist (n) /pəˈfɔːmɪŋ ˈɑːtɪst/
sb who performs music or a dramatic work for an audience • *Most performing artists do not make much money.* ❖ καλλιτέχνης

9.111 wall mural (n) /wɔːl ˈmjʊərəl/
artwork on a wall • *There is a striking wall mural of a ball of string near the Neos Kosmos tram stop.* ❖ τοιχογραφία

9.112 sculpted wall (n) /ˈskʌlptɪd wɔːl/
a wall which has a pattern carved onto it • *He commissioned an artist to create a sculpted wall in his garden.* ❖ τοίχος με ανάγλυφο

9.113 representative (adj) /reprɪˈzentətɪv/
typical of a particular group of people or things • *This painting is representative of the artist's mature work.* ➢ representative (n), represent (v) ❖ αντιπροσωπευτικός

9.114 stand out (phr v) /stænd aʊt/
be noticeable • *The painting that stands out from the rest is this one of a young child.* ❖ ξεχωρίζω

Phrasal verbs
cater for   put sb off
check out   stand out

Writing: a report pages 118-119

9.115 edgy (adj) /ˈedʒi/
intense; new and exciting • *Jimi Hendrix performed edgy music that inspired a generation of musicians.* ❖ έντονος, συναρπαστικός

9.116 turn back the clock (expr) /tɜːn bæk ðə klɒk/
go back to an earlier time or situation • *You can't turn back the clock. You have to get used to the present situation.* ❖ γυρίζω το χρόνο πίσω

9.117 deafening (adj) /ˈdefənɪŋ/
extremely loud • *The music was deafening because we were right next to the speakers.* ➢ deafen (v), deaf (adj) ❖ εκκωφαντικός

9.118 ease (v) /iːz/
reduce • *The ring road around town should ease traffic in the centre.* ❖ διευκολύνω, ελαττώνω

9.119 the down side (expr) /ðə daʊn saɪd/
the negative aspect of sth • *Not everything turned out well. There's also a down side.* ❖ η κακή/αρνητική πλευρά

9.120 traffic congestion (n) /ˈtræfɪk kənˈdʒestʃn/
full of traffic • *Traffic congestion is terrible during the rush hour and it takes me ages to drive to work.* ❖ κυκλοφοριακή συμφόρηση

Video 9: Eye Trick Town page 120

9.121 trompe l'oeil (n) /ˌtrɒmp ˈlɔɪ/
art that creates the illusion of sth real
• We could not believe the doors and windows on the wall were trompe l'oeil art because they looked so real. ❖ τέχνη της ψευδαίσθησης, της οφθαλμαπάτης

9.122 façade (n) /fəˈsɑːd/
the front wall of a building • The façade of the hotel was covered in bougainvillea flowers.
❖ πρόσοψη

9.123 terrace (n) /ˈterɪs/
a paved or grass area next to a building where people can sit • Let's drink our sparkling water on the terrace outside. ❖ βεράντα

Vocabulary Exercises

A Complete the sentences with the correct form of the words.

1 Sophocles was one of the most famous _____ of Ancient Greece.   PLAY
2 He did a beautiful wood _____ of a rose.   CARVE
3 You can buy a _____ of this painting for £100.   REPRODUCE
4 His third play is _____ good.   PHENOMENON
5 There was an atmosphere of _____ in the classroom.   APATHETIC
6 He is a _____ author whose books are greatly admired.   DISTINGUISH

B Match.

1 Steve is a culture ☐   a centre felt cut off from society.
2 The boys at the detention ☐ b label have you signed with?
3 This drama tour is a pilot ☐ c vulture and never misses a new play.
4 She bought two water ☐   d artist she has more freedom.
5 Which record ☐   e colours from the gallery.
6 She feels that as a solo ☐   f siren put fear into our hearts.
7 The sound of the air raid ☐ g life paintings with care.
8 He chooses fruit for his still ☐ h project we hope will take place every year.

C Complete the sentences with one word in each gap.

1 I checked _____ that new restaurant you recommended and liked it a lot.
2 It's a lovely car, but it must have cost and arm and a(n) _____.
3 I don't need the words because I have learnt the poem by _____.
4 The composer set the poem _____ music.
5 I'll have to _____ the music when I tell mum I lost my phone.
6 I know you are a good singer, but you shouldn't blow your own _____ so much.

D Circle the correct words.

1 He has a good memory and can play music by ear / ears.
2 Do you like the pop / hop art that appeared in the 1960s?
3 Everyone is singing his praise / praises since he won a scholarship to a music school.
4 The concert is brought to you courtesy of / to Omega TV.
5 Why are you making a song and dancing / dance about one broken CD?
6 The art gallery has some interesting works by art students in / on display.
7 The wall terrace / mural was not to my taste.
8 There was so much traffic congestion / institution that I was late for the play.

9 Grammar

9.1 Comparison of Adjectives and Adverbs

Χρησιμοποιούμε comparative (συγκριτικό βαθμό) για να συγκρίνουμε δύο πρόσωπα ή πράγματα. Συνήθως σχηματίζουμε το comparative προσθέτοντας την κατάληξη -er στο επίθετο ή το επίρρημα. Αν το επίθετο ή το επίρρημα έχει περισσότερες από δύο συλλαβές, τότε χρησιμοποιούμε τη λέξη *more*. Συχνά χρησιμοποιούμε τη λέξη *than* μετά από το comparative.
→ Are modern plays **more popular than** classic ones?
→ This time they booked their tickets **earlier than** last time.

Χρησιμοποιούμε superlative (υπερθετικό βαθμό) για να συγκρίνουμε ένα πρόσωπο ή πράγμα με άλλα ομοειδή πρόσωπα ή πράγματα. Συνήθως σχηματίζουμε το superlative προσθέτοντας την κατάληξη -est στο επίθετο ή το επίρρημα. Αν το επίθετο ή το επίρρημα έχει περισσότερες από δύο συλλαβές, τότε χρησιμοποιούμε τη λέξη *most*. Πριν από το superlative χρησιμοποιούμε τη λέξη *the*.
→ That's **the most famous** of Picasso's paintings.
→ Sarah spoke **the most loudly** of all the actors on stage.

Υπάρχουν επίθετα και επιρρήματα που είναι ανώμαλα και σχηματίζουν το comparative και superlative με διαφορετικούς τρόπους.

Adjective/Adverb	Comparative/Συγκριτικός	Superlative/Υπερθετικός
good/well	better	the best
bad/badly	worse	the worst
many/more	more	the most
much	more	the most
little	less	the least
far	farther/further	the farthest/furthest

Σημείωση:
1 Κάποιες λέξεις όπως *hard, late, straight* και *fast* είναι και επίθετα και επιρρήματα.
   → She can't draw a **straight** line!
   → After the office she went **straight** to the theatre.

2 Υπάρχουν λέξεις που τελειώνουν σε -ly, όπως *friendly, lovely, silly* και *ugly*, αλλά δεν είναι επιρρήματα, είναι επίθετα.
   → I don't believe there is such a thing as an **ugly** painting.

3 Οι λέξεις *hardly* (= barely, μόλις, σχεδόν δεν) και *lately* (= recently, πρόσφατα) δεν είναι τα επιρρήματα των λέξεων *hard* και *late*.
   → Because she couldn't find a taxi, she came **late**.
   → I haven't visited any museums **lately**.

9.2 Other ways of comparing

Χρησιμοποιούμε *as* + επίθετο/επίρρημα + *as* για να πούμε ότι δύο πρόσωπα ή πράγματα είναι με κάποιο τρόπο παρόμοια.
→ Was this festival **as successful as** last year's?

Χρησιμοποιούμε *not as/so* + επίθετο/επίρρημα + *as* για να πούμε ότι ένα πρόσωπο ή πράγμα έχει μια ιδιότητα σε μικρότερο βαθμό από ένα άλλο.
→ Some people think street art is**n't so difficult** to do **as** a painting.

Χρησιμοποιούμε *the* + comparative (συγκριτικός), *the* + comparative (συγκριτικός) για να πούμε ότι όσο κάτι αυξάνεται ή μειώνεται, τόσο επηρεάζει κάτι άλλο.
→ **The more famous** the painter, **the more expensive** it is to buy their work.

9.3 Qualifiers

Χρησιμοποιούμε qualifiers (προσδιορισμούς) πριν από ένα επίθετο ή επίρρημα για να πούμε πόσο καλός, όμορφος, ικανός κλπ είναι κάποιος ή κάτι, ή πόσο άσχημα, γρήγορα, καλά κλπ έγινε κάτι. Τα πιο συνηθισμένα qualifiers στην αγγλική γλώσσα είναι *very, quite, rather, somewhat, far more, most, less, least, more or less, too, so, just, enough, indeed, still, almost, fairly, really, pretty, even, a bit, a little, a (whole) lot, a good deal, a great deal, much, kind of, sort of*.
→ I like the Doors **far more** than the Rolling Stones.
→ This performance is **a whole lot** better than the one we saw last week.

9.4 *Too* & *Enough*

Χρησιμοποιούμε *too* + επίθετο/επίρρημα για να πούμε ότι κάτι είναι περισσότερο από αυτό που θέλουμε ή χρειαζόμαστε.
→ Sometimes it's **too difficult** to find a parking space near the club.
→ It's **too crowded** to sit here tonight, we'd better leave.

Χρησιμοποιούμε επίθετο/επίρρημα + *enough* ή *enough* + ουσιαστικό για να πούμε ότι κάτι είναι ή δεν είναι τόσο όσο θέλουμε ή χρειαζόμαστε.
→ I'm sorry, but he's not **talented enough**.
→ I have **enough time** to learn my part by heart.

9.5 *So* & *Such*

Χρησιμοποιούμε *so* (τόσο) και *such* (τόσο) για να τονίσουμε κάτι. Είναι πιο εμφατικά από το *very* (πολύ).
Χρησιμοποιούμε *so* + επίθετο/επίρρημα.
→ This dance club is **so amazing**!
Χρησιμοποιούμε *such* + (επίθετο +) ουσιαστικό.
→ This is **such an amazing dance club**!

Μπορούμε επίσης να χρησιμοποιήσουμε *so* και *such* για να δώσουμε έμφαση στα χαρακτηριστικά που οδηγούν σε ένα συγκεκριμένο αποτέλεσμα ή πράξη.
→ The album was **such** a huge success that it went gold in a week.
→ The hot dogs here are **so** tasty that we always eat more than we should.

Grammar Exercises

A Choose the correct answers.

1 *Cats* is the ___ amazing show I have ever seen.
   a more
   b most

2 Why do you think some songs are ___ catchy than others?
   a less
   b the less

3 The paintings aren't ___ good as you made out.
   a such
   b as

4 This fresco is ___ well restored as the others.
   a so
   b as

5 I hope fame allows me to live as normal ___ as I possibly can.
   a a life
   b life

6 The backing singer sang more ___ than the lead vocalist!
   a loud
   b loudly

7 I think that was ___ concert I have ever been to.
   a the worst
   b worst

8 Was the performance as ___ as last night's?
   a better
   b good

9 Grammar

B Complete the sentences with one word in each gap.
1. Your book is good _____ to be accepted by a publisher.
2. The audience was _____ impressed that they gave the cast a standing ovation.
3. Some Shakespeare plays are _____ long for a three-hour performance so they have to be abridged.
4. The musical was _____ a great success that it went to Broadway.
5. I am so busy _____ I will never finish my review.
6. He has so _____ albums that he doesn't know where to store them anymore.
7. The young actor has faced so _____ criticism that he is thinking of giving up.
8. The film was just short _____ to be shown on a two-hour flight.

C Put the words in order to make sentences.
1. great deal / is / more interesting / a / the artist's other works / than / this El Greco

2. he boasts / not / as / performer / good / a / as / he is

3. not / it is / so / poem / bad / a / you claim / as

4. was / popular enough / the top ten / of the charts / the single / to / get into

5. too / are / just / expensive / to / afford / these tickets

6. he could / not / little / had / so / inspiration / all day / the writer / write a word

7. artist / Michelangelo / a / was / wonderful / such

8. not / a / does / light comedy / praise / receive / such / usually

D Complete the sentences with your own ideas and the words given.
1. The latest film I saw _____ (more)
2. Acting isn't _____ (as . . . as)
3. The Parthenon _____ (such)
4. Participants on shows like *Pop Idol* _____ (than)
5. Street artists _____ (less)
6. The longer you take to read a book, _____ (the)
7. Theatre tickets _____ (bit)
8. The literature we study at school _____ (too)

Exam Task

For questions 1-12, read the text below and decide which answer (A, B, C or D) best fits each gap.

THE BEGINNINGS OF A THEATRE

Chichester Festival Theatre is one of the most (1) ___ venues for the (2) ___ arts in England. Founded a little over 50 years ago, what started as the simple (3) ___ of former mayor of Chichester, Leslie Evershed-Martin, for a summer theatre festival later (4) ___ into an event of national importance.

The (5) ___ not only involved raising money for the construction of the theatre, but also the (6) ___ to find a suitable artistic director. The theatre was built (7) ___ of local people and businesses who donated the necessary funds of £105,000. Evershed-Martin wanted the respected actor Laurence Olivier for artistic director, despite people telling him this would be impossible. Their views did not (8) ___ him off, however, so he wrote to Olivier, who accepted the job.

The theatre opened in 1962, and stood (9) ___ as the first of its kind. Audiences were impressed with the simple but (10) ___ design of a central stage which was in the style of those in Greek and Elizabethan theatres.

Olivier created a theatre company of actors, many of whom had their (11) ___ performances there. The (12) ___ of actors since then has included the likes of Patrick Stewart and Joseph Fiennes.

1 A middling   B distinguished   C deprived   D core
2 A performing   B performers'   C performance D forming
3 A commission   B tint   C plight   D concept
4 A mushroomed   B bombed   C boasted   D eased
5 A works   B pulse   C venture   D award
6 A endeavour   B scrutiny   C exhibition   D institution
7 A backing   B free-for-all   C courtesy   D mission
8 A stand   B give   C set   D put
9 A out   B in   C over   D back
10 A mainstream   B highbrow   C innovative   D abridged
11 A pilot   B deafening   C debut   D subjective
12 A tint   B line up   C chart   D artist

10 Modern Living

Word Focus — page 122

10.1 **galley** (n) /ˈgæli/
a ship's kitchen • *The ship's cook prepared lunch for the crew in the galley.* ❖ μαγειρείο (πλοίου)

10.2 **tagged** (adj) /tægd/
labelled • *Make sure your luggage is tagged with your name and phone number.*
➢ tag (v, n) ❖ με ετικέτα

10.3 **realm** (n) /relm/
an area of activity • *New discoveries in the realm of astronomy are very exciting.* ❖ σφαίρα, τομέας

10.4 **hippodrome** (n) /ˈhɪpədrəʊm/
a place where horse races took place in ancient Greece and Rome • *Spectators would cheer the horses on at the hippodrome.* ❖ ιπποδρόμιο

10.5 **fortification** (n) /ˌfɔːtɪfɪˈkeɪʃn/
a tower or wall built to protect an area from enemy attacks • *The thick castle walls were a strong fortification which the enemy could not breach.* ➢ fortify (v) ❖ οχύρωση

Reading — pages 122-123

10.6 **juggle** (v) /ˈdʒʌgl/
give your attention to many things • *Susan juggles a full-time job and voluntary work at a charity shop.* ❖ καταφέρνω

10.7 **born and bred** (expr) /bɔːn ænd bred/
born and having grown up in a particular place • *You can tell he was born and bred in Texas from his accent.* ❖ είμαι γέννημα-θρέμμα

10.8 **chop and change** (expr) /tʃɒp ænd tʃeɪndʒ/
change your mind many times • *He chopped and changed about which course to do before finally deciding on biochemistry.* ❖ αλλάζω γνώμη πολλές φορές

10.9 **marine** (adj) /məˈriːn/
of the sea • *He studies marine life in the Pacific Ocean.* ❖ θαλάσσιος

10.10 **arrowhead** (n) /ˈærəʊˌhed/
the sharp end of an arrow • *Early humans made arrowheads out of stone which they used to hunt with.* ❖ κεφαλή βέλους

10.11 **submarine** (n) /ˌsʌbməˈriːn/
a ship that can travel underwater • *The submarine dived deep into the sea.* ❖ υποβρύχιο

10.12 **formative years** (n) /ˈfɔːmətɪv jɪəz/
years which influence the way sb develops • *He was taught to love the sea during the formative years of his childhood.*
❖ εύπλαστη ηλικία, διαμορφωτικά χρόνια

10.13 **field work** (n) /fiːld wɜːk/
research done in the real world and not in a laboratory • *The geologist collected soil from the mountain as part of his field work.*
❖ εργασία εκτός έδρας, πρακτική έρευνα

10.14 **gather** (v) /ˈgæðə/
collect • *I gathered together my hiking boots, bag and map for the walk in the hills.*
❖ συγκεντρώνω

10.15 **in good shape** (expr) /ɪn gʊd ʃeɪp/
fit and healthy • *He's in good shape because he works out at the gym three times a week.*
❖ σε καλή φόρμα

10.16 **make for** (phr v) /meɪk fə/
go towards a place • *After a busy day at work, Dad made for home.* ❖ ξεκινάω για, πηγαίνω

10.17 **a bite to eat** (expr) /ə baɪt tʊ iːt/
a snack; a meal • *I had a bite to eat in the canteen at lunch time.* ❖ κάτι να φάω

10.18 **head (for)** (v) /hed (fə)/
go in a particular direction • *It's a sunny day and they're heading for the beach.*
❖ κατευθύνομαι (προς)

10.19 **anchor** (v) /ˈæŋkə/
drop an anchor in the sea to keep a boat in one place • *We anchored the yacht in a pretty cove for the afternoon.* ➢ anchor (n)
❖ αγκυροβολώ

10.20 **brief** (v) /briːf/
give sb information about sth • *The principal briefed the staff about the changes to the timetable.* ➢ brief (n) ❖ πληροφορώ

10.21 **on board** (expr) /ɒn bɔːd/
on a plane, ship or train • *When all the passengers were on board, the ship was able to leave port.* ❖ επιβιβασμένος (σε αεροπλάνο, πλοίο ή τρένο)

10.22 **gear** (n) /gɪə/
equipment • *The camping gear he bought included a tent, a torch and a sleeping bag.*
❖ εξοπλισμός

10.23 **aboard** (adv) /əˈbɔːd/
on or onto a plane, ship, bus or train • *There are three hundred passengers aboard this ship.* ❖ επιβιβασμένος

10.24 **carry out** (phr v) /ˈkæri aʊt/
do a task • *The scientist carried out an experiment in the lab.* ❖ εκτελώ, διενεργώ

10.25 **excavation** (n) /ˌekskəˈveɪʃn/
digging to find ancient objects, bones, etc. • *In 2013, an excavation in Leicester successfully revealed the skeleton of King Richard III of England.* ➢ excavate (v) ❖ ανασκαφή

10.26 **field notes** (pl n) /fiːld nəʊtz/
notes taken by a scientist to record their work in progress • *The marine biologist went through her field notes and prepared her report.* ❖ σημειώσεις ερευνητών

10.27 **safekeeping** (n) /ˈseɪfˈkiːpɪŋ/
being in a safe place where it will not be damaged or lost • *I locked my jewellery in a drawer for safekeeping.* ❖ (δια)φύλαξη, διασφάλιση

10.28 **undergo** (v) /ˌʌndəˈgəʊ/
If sb/sth undergoes a test, an experience, etc., it happens to them. • *The skeleton must undergo DNA tests to see if it really is King Richard III.* ❖ υφίσταμαι

10.29 **rigorous** (adj) /ˈrɪgərəs/
thorough • *The athletes followed a rigorous training routine.* ➢ rigour (n), rigorously (adv) ❖ αυστηρός, σκληρός

10.30 **dedicated** (adj) /ˈdedɪkeɪtɪd/
devoted • *She is dedicated to her job and always works hard.* ➢ dedicate (v), dedication (n) ❖ αφοσιωμένος

10.31 **lend a hand** (expr) /lend ə hænd/
help • *Can you lend me a hand with my heavy suitcase?* ❖ δίνω ένα χεράκι

10.32 **snail** (n) /ˈsneɪl/
a small soft animal with a shell that moves slowly • *A snail crawled along the wet path.* ❖ σαλιγκάρι

10.33 **rinse** (v) /rɪns/
wash with clean water • *He rinsed the washing powder out of his shirt and then hung it up to dry.* ➢ rinse (n) ❖ ξεπλένω

10.34 **eager** (adj) /ˈiːgə/
keen; willing • *Eager to help, I offered to wash the dishes.* ➢ eagerness (n), eagerly (adv) ❖ πρόθυμος

10.35 **day-care** (n) /deɪ-keə/
when young children are looked after during the day because their parents are at work • *When Shirley goes back to work, she'll take her toddler to day-care.* ❖ παιδικός σταθμός

10.36 **commute** (v) /kəˈmjuːt/
travel to work • *He commutes to work because he lives in the suburbs but works in the city centre.* ➢ commuter (n) ❖ μετακινούμαι (από και προς τη δουλειά)

10.37 **crusader** (n) /kruːˈseɪdə/
a European Christian who fought against the Muslims in one of the wars in Palestine in the Middle Ages • *The crusaders were finally driven out of the Holy Land.* ➢ crusade (n, v) ❖ σταυροφόρος

10.38 **fragile** (adj) /ˈfrædʒaɪl/
delicate; easily damaged • *The fragile ecosystem of the coral reef was damaged by pollution.* ➢ fragility (n) ❖ εύθραυστος

10.39 **make up one's mind** (expr) /meɪk ʌp wʌnz maɪnd/
decide • *He made up his mind about what to study at university in his last year at school.* ❖ αποφασίζω

10.40 **occupation** (n) /ˌɒkjuˈpeɪʃn/
a job • *People in professional occupations have to dress very smartly.* ❖ ενασχόληση, επάγγελμα

10.41 **reflect** (v) /rɪˈflekt/
think about sth • *I need some time to reflect on the problem.* ➢ reflection (n) ❖ σκέφτομαι, αναλογίζομαι

10.42 **uneventful** (adj) /ˌʌnɪˈventfəl/
with nothing interesting or unusual happening • *It was an uneventful day and nothing unusual happened.* ❖ ήσυχος

10.43 **sheltered** (adj) /ˈʃeltəd/
protected • *He had a sheltered childhood because his family never socialised with anyone outside the neighbourhood.* ➢ shelter (v, n) ❖ προστατευμένος

10.44 **tie up loose ends** (expr) /taɪ ʌp luːs endz/
complete unfinished tasks • *Before starting her new job, Liz had to tie up some loose ends.* ❖ τακτοποιώ εκκρεμότητες

10.45 **in working order** (expr) /ɪn ˈwɜːkɪŋ ˈɔːdə/
working well • *The lift isn't in working order, so you'll have to use the stairs.* ❖ σε σωστή λειτουργία
✎ Opp: out of order

10.46 **trawler** (n) /ˈtrɔːlə/
a fishing boat that drags nets behind it to catch fish • *The trawler got caught in a storm at sea.* ➢ trawl (v) ❖ τράτα

10.47 **devastation** (n) /ˌdevəˈsteɪʃn/
great damage • *The earthquake caused utter devastation in the area.* ➢ devastate (v) ❖ όλεθρος

Vocabulary pages 124-125

10.48 **hectic** (adj) /ˈhektɪk/
very busy • *The teacher had a hectic Saturday morning cleaning, shopping, cooking and marking.* ❖ πυρετώδης

10.49 **provincial** (adj) /prəˈvɪnʃl/
in/of the country • *The couple moved to a provincial town far from the busy capital.* ➢ province (n) ❖ επαρχιακός

10.50 **sedentary** (adj) /ˈsedəntri/
spending a lot of time sitting down and not moving very much • *Sitting all day on the sofa or in front of a laptop is too sedentary a lifestyle for me.* ❖ καθιστικός

10.51 **solitary** (adj) /ˈsɒlɪtri/
alone • *She leads a solitary existence living on her own on an island.* ❖ μοναχικός

10.52 unsophisticated (adj) /ʌnsəˈfɪstɪkeɪtɪd/
simple • *An unsophisticated lifestyle keeps costs down as you only need basic things.*
➢ sophistication (n) ❖ απλός, απλοϊκός
✎ Opp: sophisticated

10.53 cosmopolitan (adj) /kɒzməˈpɒlɪtən/
with many people from different places and of different cultures • *London is a cosmopolitan city with people of many nationalities living there.* ❖ κοσμοπολίτικος

10.54 reasonable (adj) /ˈriːzənəbl/
fairly priced; not expensive • *Five pounds is a reasonable price for a pizza in London.*
➢ reason (n) ❖ λογικός
✎ Opp: unreasonable

10.55 metropolitan (adj) /metrəˈpɒlɪtən/
of the city • *Living in a metropolitan area, I can enjoy everything a city offers.*
❖ μητροπολιτικός

10.56 sociable (adj) /ˈsəʊʃəbl/
enjoying spending time with other people
• *Being sociable, he got to know many people at the party.* ➢ socialise (v) ❖ κοινωνικός
✎ Opp: unsociable

10.57 devoid (of) (adj) /dɪˈvɔɪd (ɒv)/
lacking; without • *Living in the middle of nowhere, she feels her life is devoid of excitement.* ❖ χωρίς, άνευ

10.58 newcomer (n) /ˈnjuːkʌmə/
sb who has just come to a place to live or work
• *Friendly neighbours welcomed the newcomers to the street with an apple pie.* ❖ νεοφερμένος

10.59 pedestrianise (v) /pəˈdestriənaɪz/
make a street into an area that is used only by people who are walking • *They pedestrianised the high street and it's a pleasure to walk there now.* ➢ pedestrianisation (n), pedestrian (n)
❖ πεζοδρομώ

10.60 graduate (v) /ˈɡrædʒueɪt/
get a university degree • *Bob graduated from Harvard with a law degree.* ➢ graduate (n), graduation (n) ❖ αποφοιτώ

10.61 live out of a suitcase (expr)
/lɪv aʊt əv ə ˈsuːtkeɪs/
stay somewhere temporarily with only a few of your belongings in your suitcase because you are travelling • *I travel as part of my job, but I hate living out of a suitcase.*
❖ είμαι συνέχεια με μια βαλίτσα στο χέρι, ταξιδεύω συνέχεια

10.62 crime rate (n) /kraɪm reɪt/
the amount of crime in an area • *Crime rates increased during the financial crisis.*
❖ εγκληματικότητα

10.63 recovery (n) /rɪˈkʌvəri/
becoming well after an illness or injury
• *We were happy to hear of your quick recovery from the flu.* ➢ recover (v) ❖ ανάρρωση

10.64 hit the road (expr) /hɪt ðə rəʊd/
start out on a journey • *We should hit the road early tomorrow before the rush hour.*
❖ ξεκινώ (ταξίδι)

10.65 income (n) /ˈɪnkʌm/
the money you earn from work • *The family struggle to survive on a low income.*
❖ χαμηλό εισόδημα

10.66 hardship (n) /ˈhɑːdʃɪp/
difficulties • *They are facing hardship in the cold winter because they cannot afford heating.* ❖ ταλαιπωρία, δυσκολίες

10.67 get by (phr v) /ɡet baɪ/
have just enough money to live on
• *The elderly couple try to get by on 500 euros a month.* ❖ τα βγάζω πέρα

10.68 excel (v) /ɪkˈsel/
do very well • *He excels at maths and won an award in the school maths competition.*
➢ excellence (n), excellent (adj)
❖ αριστεύω, είμαι πρώτος

10.69 outdo (v) /ˌaʊtˈduː/
perform better than sb • *He tried to outdo his classmates by getting the highest mark.*
❖ ξεπερνώ

10.70 climb the corporate ladder (expr)
/klaɪm ðə ˈkɔːpərət ˈlædə/
get promotion within a company
• *The young employee climbed the corporate ladder and was promoted to personal assistant to the boss.*
❖ αναρριχώμαι στην εταιρική κλίμακα

10.71 colleague (n) /ˈkɒliːɡ/
sb you work with • *My colleagues organised an office party for Christmas.*
❖ συνάδελφος

10.72 ruin (v) /ˈruːɪn/
destroy • *The injury ruined the athlete's chances of competing at the Olympics.*
➢ ruin (n) ❖ καταστρέφω

10.73 spoil (v) /spɔɪl/
give a child everything it wants • *Charlie is difficult and rude because his mother spoils him.* ➢ spoilt (adj) ❖ κακομαθαίνω

10.74 fledgling (adj) /ˈfledʒlɪŋ/
new and inexperienced • *The fledgling online store gradually started to receive orders.*
❖ αρχάριος, χωρίς πείρα
✎ NB a fledgling is a baby bird

10.75 susceptible (adj) /sʌˈseptɪbl/
easily influenced or harmed • *I'm susceptible to colds so I stay indoors when it's snowing.* ➢ susceptibility (n)
❖ επιρρεπής, ευάλωτος

10.76 siren's call (expr) /ˈsaɪrənz kɔːl/
the temptation to do sth that seems attractive but that will have bad consequences • *You must turn your back on the siren's call of an easy life.*
❖ πειρασμός, το κάλεσμα των Σειρήνων

10.77 culprit (n) /ˈkʌlprɪt/
sb/sth blamed for sth • *I returned to the car park to find that my car had been damaged and the culprit had fled.* ❖ ένοχος

10.78 to a lesser extent (expr) /tʊ ə ˈlesə ɪkˈstent/
to a smaller degree • *They were eager to visit Paris and, to a lesser extent, London.*
❖ σε μικρότερο βαθμό

10.79 couch-bound (adj) /ˈkaʊtʃ-baʊnd/
sitting on a sofa for a long time • *We were couch-bound in front of the TV all day as it was too wet to go out.*
❖ κολλημένος στον καναπέ

10.80 obsess (v) /ɒbˈses/
think about only one thing • *The model obsessed so much about her weight that she became anorexic.* ➢ obsession (n), obsessive (adj) ❖ έχω έμμονη ιδέα, σκέπτομαι ένα μόνο πράγμα

10.81 browse (v) /ˈbraʊz/
search for information on the Internet
• *Browsing online can be fun as you surf from one website to another.*
➢ browser (n) ❖ αναζητώ

10.82 irritable (adj) /ˈɪrɪtəbl/
bad-tempered • *The irritable teacher shouted at the pupils.* ➢ irritability (n) ❖ ευέξαπτος, οξύθυμος

10.83 mood-altering (adj) /muːd-ˈɔːltərɪŋ/
a drug capable of causing changes of mood
• *This is a highly-addictive, mood-altering drug.* ❖ ψυχοτρόπος, που αλλάζει τη διάθεση

10.84 bounce back (phr v) /baʊns bæk/
recover from a bad situation • *The company bounced back in the second quarter and made a profit.* ❖ ανακάμπτω, επανέρχομαι σε προηγούμενη κατάσταση

10.85 do without (phr v) /duː wɪðˈaʊt/
cope well despite not having sth • *We must learn to do without a car since we can't afford to run it.* ❖ τα βγάζω πέρα χωρίς

10.86 pull together (phr v) /pʊl təˈgeðə/
work as a team to achieve sth
• *The employees pulled together to make the company more successful.*
❖ συνεργάζομαι

10.87 wear sb down (phr v) /weə ˈsʌmbədi daʊn/
make sb weaker • *The long commute to work every day really wears me down.*
❖ με κουράζει, με φθείρει

10.88 strain (n) /streɪn/
pressure • *The stress and strain of the new job is too much for him to cope with.* ❖ ζόρι

10.89 burn the candle at both ends (expr)
/bɜːn ðə ˈkændl æt bəʊθ endz/
live a hectic life • *Diana is burning the candle at both ends by going out every night after work.* ❖ ζω με πυρετώδη ρυθμό

10.90 hit rock bottom (expr) /hɪt rɒk ˈbɒtəm/
become as unsuccessful or unhappy as it is possible to be • *He hit rock bottom when he ended up homeless.* ❖ πιάνω πάτο

10.91 keep your head above water (expr)
/kiːp jɔː hed əˈbʌv ˈwɔːtə/
survive financially • *She got a second job to keep her head above water.* ❖ επιβιώνω (οικονομικά)

10.92 run yourself into the ground (expr)
/rʌn jəˈself ˈɪntʊ ðə graʊnd/
become extremely tired because you work too hard • *Geena ran herself into the ground working day and night on her project.* ❖ εξαντλώ τον εαυτό μου

10.93 throw in the towel (expr) /θrəʊ ɪn ðə ˈtaʊəl/
realise you must give up • *The athlete threw in the towel when he came last in the semi-final.*
❖ τα παρατάω, παραιτούμαι

10.94 pace (n) /peɪs/
speed • *You must work at a faster pace to finish the task.* ➢ pace (v) ❖ ρυθμός, ταχύτητα

10.95 admit defeat (expr) /ædˈmɪt dɪˈfiːt/
realise you cannot win or do sth • *The football team admitted defeat when they were down 5-0.* ❖ παραδέχομαι την ήττα

Grammar pages 126-127

10.96 promotion (n) /prəˈməʊʃn/
a move to a more important job in a company or organisation • *His promotion from assistant manager to manager was expected.*
➢ promote (v) ❖ προαγωγή

10.97 shopping district (n) /ˈʃɒpɪŋ ˈdɪstrɪkt/
a part of a city or town where there are lots of shops • *The main shopping district in Athens is around Ermou Street.*
❖ εμπορικό κέντρο

10.98 hard to come by (expr) /haːd tə kʌm baɪ/
difficult to find • *Well-paid jobs are hard to come by these days.* ❖ δύσκολο να βρω

10.99 think outside the box (expr)
/θɪŋk aʊtˈsaɪd ðə bɒks/
think of different or unusual ways of doing sth
• *In order to innovate, you need to think outside the box.* ❖ σκέφτομαι διαφορετικά

10.100 initiative (n) /ɪˈnɪʃətɪv/
the ability to act without being told what to do
• *The student showed initiative when he did some research alone in the library.* ❖ πρωτοβουλία

10.101 assess (v) /əˈses/
make a judgement • *The teacher assessed the students' progress by setting a test.*
➢ assessment (n) ❖ αξιολογώ

10.102 pursue (v) /pəˈsjuː/
follow • *The employer decided to pursue two candidates and called them in for a second interview.* ➢ pursuit (n) ❖ ακολουθώ, αναζητώ

10.103 **brand new** (adj) /brænd njuː/
completely new • *These shoes are brand new, so don't dirty them.* ❖ ολοκαίνουργιος

10.104 **tonsils** (pl n) /ˈtɒnsəlz/
glands at the back of the throat • *The doctor says I've got swollen tonsils.* ➢ tonsilitis (n)
❖ αμυγδαλές

10.105 **satellite dish** (n) /ˈsætəlaɪt dɪʃ/
equipment that receives signals from a satellite and enables people to watch satellite television • *We have just installed a satellite dish on our roof.* ❖ δορυφορικό πιάτο

10.106 **rail** (n) /reɪlz/
metal bar that is part of a fence
• *I chained my bicycle to the rails at the front of the station.* ❖ κάγκελο

Work-related words

Verbs	Nouns	Adjectives
brief	colleague	dedicated
commute	occupation	eager
juggle	promotion	hectic
retire		

Listening
page 128

10.107 **slog it out** (expr) /slɒg ɪt aʊt/
work hard • *He slogged it out all week preparing the sales figures.*
❖ δουλεύω σκληρά

10.108 **land a part** (expr) /lænd ə pɑːt/
get a role • *The actress was very pleased to land a part in a BBC series.* ❖ παίρνω ένα ρόλο

10.109 **climb up the career ladder** (expr) /klaɪm ʌp ðə kəˈrɪə ˈlædə/
get promoted • *You'll be climbing up the career ladder if you get the post of department supervisor.* ❖ παίρνω προαγωγή

10.110 **agricultural** (adj) /ˌægrɪˈkʌltʃərəl/
connected with farming • *Greece is an agricultural country and produces olives, grapes and lot of other crops.* ➢ agriculture (n)
❖ γεωργικός, αγροτικός

10.111 **fulfil** (v) /fʊlˈfɪl/
manage to do sth you hoped for • *I fulfilled the ambition of a lifetime when I visited New York.*
➢ fulfilment (n) ❖ εκπληρώνω

10.112 **disinterest** (n) /dɪsˈɪntrəst/
lack of interest • *Fred showed complete disinterest in music, even though his dad was a musician.* ➢ disinterested (adj)
❖ αδιαφορία

10.113 **prospect** (n) /ˈprɒspekt/
the possibility that sth will happen • *The prospect of another war is frightening.* ➢ prospective (adj)
❖ προοπτική

10.114 **rat race** (expr) /ræt reɪs/
the stressful way of life in a large city, competing to be successful, earn money, etc.
• *The pressure of the rat race exhausted him so he quit his job.* ❖ σκληρός ανταγωνισμός στον επαγγελματικό τομέα, αλληλοφάγωμα

10.115 **live in the fast lane** (expr) /lɪv ɪn ðə fɑːst leɪn/
have a hectic and pressured lifestyle • *She lives in the fast lane and is always travelling abroad for business meetings.*
❖ ζω έντονη ζωή

10.116 **rural** (adj) /ˈrʊərəl/
of or in the countryside • *We stayed in an old farmhouse on our holiday in rural France.*
❖ αγροτικός, της υπαίθρου

Speaking
page 129

10.117 **strict** (adj) /strɪkt/
demanding that rules concerning behaviour are obeyed • *The strict teacher demanded that all assignments be handed in on time.*
❖ αυστηρός

10.118 **mother tongue** (n) /ˈmʌðə tʌŋ/
language you learn from your parents
• *My mother tongue is English but I also speak German because I learnt it at school.*
❖ μητρική γλώσσα

10.119 **interactive whiteboard** (n) /ˌɪntərˈæktɪv ˈwaɪtbɔːd/
a classroom board which is connected to a computer • *The teacher displayed some photos from his computer on the interactive whiteboard.* ❖ διαδραστικός πίνακας

10.120 **retire** (v) /rɪˈtaɪə/
stop working and become a pensioner • *John retired at 65 but feels bored staying at home instead of working.* ➢ retirement (n), retired (adj) ❖ συνταξιοδοτούμαι

10.121 **MA** (abbr) /ˌem ˈeɪ/
a second university degree in an arts subject
• *She has an MA in French from the University of Newcastle.* ❖ μεταπτυχιακό δίπλωμα (μάστερ)
✎ MA = Master of Arts

10.122 **incorporate** (v) /ɪnˈkɔːpəreɪt/
include more than one thing • *This course incorporates lectures and field work.* ➢ incorporation (n) ❖ ενσωματώνω

10.123 **discipline** (n) /ˈdɪsəplɪn/
obeying rules and being punished if you do not • *My school has a reputation for strict discipline.* ➢ discipline (v), disciplined (adj), disciplinary (adj) ❖ πειθαρχία

10.124 **high-powered** (adj) /haɪ-ˈpaʊəd/
important and having a lot of responsibility
• *The president of the USA has a high-powered position.* ❖ υψηλής ισχύος

Writing: an article (2) pages 130-131

10.125 convenience (n) /kənˈviːnɪəns/
sth useful and suitable • *The convenience of being able to phone somebody wherever you are is what a mobile phone provides.* ➢ convenient (adj) ❖ ευκολία
✎ Opp: inconvenience

10.126 impact (n) /ˈɪmpækt/
an effect; a result • *Being fired had a terrible impact on her life.* ❖ αποτέλεσμα, αντίκτυπος

10.127 privilege (n) /ˈprɪvɪlɪdʒ/
a special advantage • *In the past, education was a privilege for the rich only.*
➢ privileged (adj) ❖ προνόμιο

10.128 walk of life (expr) /wɔːk əv laɪf/
sb's job or position in society • *People from all walks of life attended the meeting.* ❖ κοινωνικό στρώμα/επίπεδο

10.129 slash (v) /slæʃ/
cut violently • *As we slash away at the rainforests, do we realise how the loss of the trees will affect our planet?* ❖ πετσοκόβω

10.130 bleak (adj) /bliːk/
without anything to make you feel hopeful • *The future looks bleak for a whole generation of unemployed graduates.* ❖ ζοφερός

Phrasal verbs
carry out	make for
do without	pull together
get by	wear sb down

-ible or –able?
inevitable	sociable
irritable	susceptible
reasonable	

Video 10: Zoo Dentists page 132

10.131 filling (n) /ˈfɪlɪŋ/
metal that a dentist puts into a tooth to cover a hole • *The dentist gave him a filling in a tooth that had decayed.* ➢ fill (v) ❖ σφράγισμα

10.132 molar (n) /ˈməʊlə/
a large tooth at the back of the mouth • *The molar at the back of my mouth was painful, so I went to the dentist.* ❖ τραπεζίτης

10.133 anaesthetise (v) /əˈniːsθətaɪz/
give someone a drug so that they do not feel pain • *The surgery began as soon as the patient was anaesthetised.*
➢ anaesthetic (n) ❖ αναισθητοποιώ

10.134 tusk (n) /tʌsk/
one of the two pointed teeth that come out of the mouth of some animals like an elephant • *The elephant's large tusks were what the hunters were after.* ❖ χαυλιόδοντας

10.135 life expectancy (n) /laɪf ɪksˈpektənsi/
the length of time that a person is likely to live • *The life expectancy of Cretans is higher than average.* ❖ προσδόκιμο ζωής

10.136 sea lion (n) /siː ˈlaɪən/
a large seal (sea animal) • *The sea lion moved awkwardly on land, but swam effortlessly once it was in the water.* ❖ θαλάσσιος λέων

10.137 root canal (n) /ruːt kəˈnæl/
removal of the nerve of a tooth • *Your tooth has decayed badly and I'm afraid you need a root canal.* ❖ απονεύρωση

Vocabulary Exercises

A Complete the sentences with the correct verbs.

1. Who can _____ me a hand with the filing?
2. I still can't _____ up my mind about which evening class to choose.
3. I can't come home just now because I have to _____ up some loose ends at the office.
4. He's very ambitious, so he's sure to _____ the corporate ladder fast.
5. Don't _____ the candle at both ends with late nights out and work the next day.
6. He _____ rock bottom when he lost his job and was evicted from his flat.
7. I know I won't get the contract, so I'll have to _____ in the towel.
8. Why not _____ outside the box for once?

B Circle the correct words.

1. He leads a very hectic / sedentary lifestyle and is always on the go.
2. It is often hard for parents to outdo / juggle home life and work.
3. He graduated / tagged from university with a business degree.
4. The family pulled / ruined together to help each other during the recession.
5. That's not expensive. In fact, the price is quite reasonable / irritable.
6. You will run / wear yourself into the ground if you don't take a break.
7. They moved to a provincial / cosmopolitan town in the country in search of tranquillity.
8. The office supervisor will fulfil / brief newcomers about their duties.

C Complete the table.

Nouns	Adjectives
dedication	1
rigour	2
eagerness	3
fragility	4
province	5
shelter	6
susceptibility	7
agriculture	8

D Complete the sentences with these words.

bite   brand   bred   change   district   expectancy   rat   rate

1. The average life _____ of a person in the UK is 79.
2. She was born and _____ in Germany.
3. Why do you chop and _____ so often?
4. Would you like a(n) _____ to eat in the canteen?
5. The crime _____ tends to be higher in inner city areas.
6. This is an expensive shopping _____.
7. If you don't like the _____ race, find a different profession.
8. I can't afford a(n) _____ new car, so I'm looking for a second-hand one.

10 Grammar

10.1 Passive Voice: Tenses

Χρησιμοποιούμε την passive voice (παθητική φωνή):
όταν η πράξη είναι πιο σημαντική από αυτόν ή αυτό που την κάνει (agent/ποιητικό αίτιο).
→ *I **was warned** about internet addiction.*
όταν δε γνωρίζουμε το ποιητικό αίτιο (agent), ή δεν είναι σημαντικό.
→ *The park **was vandalised** last night.*

Σημείωση: Όταν είναι σημαντικό να αναφέρουμε το ποιητικό αίτιο (agent) στην παθητική πρόταση, χρησιμοποιούμε τη λέξη *by*. Όταν θέλουμε να αναφέρουμε το εργαλείο ή το υλικό με το οποίο έγινε κάτι, χρησιμοποιούμε τη λέξη *with*.
→ *The research **was carried out by** a team of geologists.*
→ *She **was attacked with** a knife.*

Σχηματίζουμε την passive voice με το ρήμα *be* και past participle (παθητική μετοχή). Οι ενεργητικοί τύποι του ρήματος (active verbs) μετατρέπονται σε παθητικούς τύπους ρήματος (passive verbs) ως εξής.

Tense / Χρόνος	Active / Ενεργητική	Passive / Παθητική
Present Simple	offer/offers	am/are/is offered
Present Continuous	am/are/is offering	am/are/is being offered
Past Simple	offered	was/were offered
Past Continuous	was/were offering	was/were being offered
Present Perfect Simple	have/has offered	have/has been offered
Past Perfect Simple	had offered	had been offered
Future Simple	will offer	will be offered

Σημείωση: Δεν υπάρχει παθητικός τύπος για τους χρόνους Future Continuous, Present Perfect Continuous και Past Perfect Continuous.

Μετατρέπουμε μια ενεργητική πρόταση σε παθητική με τον παρακάτω τρόπο:
Το αντικείμενο του ρήματος της ενεργητικής πρότασης γίνεται υποκείμενο του ρήματος της παθητικής πρότασης. Το ρήμα *be* χρησιμοποιείται στον ίδιο χρόνο με το κύριο ρήμα της ενεργητικής πρότασης, μαζί με την παθητική μετοχή (past participle) του κυρίου ρήματος της ενεργητικής πρότασης.
→ *She **was teaching** them about ocean life.*
→ *They **were being taught** about ocean life.*

Σημείωση: Όταν θέλουμε να μετατρέψουμε μια πρόταση με δύο αντικείμενα στην παθητική, τότε το ένα αντικείμενο γίνεται υποκείμενο της παθητικής πρότασης και το άλλο παραμένει αντικείμενο. Επιλέγουμε το υποκείμενο της παθητικής πρότασης ανάλογα με το ποιό θέλουμε να τονίσουμε. Αν το προσωπικό αντικείμενο (personal object) παραμείνει αντικείμενο στην παθητική πρόταση, χρησιμοποιούμε και την κατάλληλη πρόθεση (*to, for* κλπ).
→ *We offered **her** the teaching **position**.*
→ ***She** was offered the teaching **position**.*
→ *The teaching **position** was offered to **her**.*

10.2 Passive Voice: Gerunds, Infinitives & Modal Verbs
(Γερούνδια, Απαρέμφατα, Modal Verbs)

Tense / Χρόνος	Active / Ενεργητική	Passive / Παθητική
Gerund / Γερούνδιο	offering	being offered
Bare Infinitive / Απαρέμφατο χωρίς *to*	offer	be offered
Full Infinitive / *to* + Απαρέμφατο	to offer	to be offered
Modal	may offer	may be offered

→ *She looked forward to **being moved** to a new office.*
→ *These files **had better be locked up** when we leave.*

10 Grammar

→ Charles wished **to be relocated** to a rural area.
→ A teen's unusual behaviour **should be discussed** with the parents.

Σημείωση: Κάποια ρήματα έχουν και αντίστοιχο ουσιαστικό που μπορεί να χρησιμοποιηθεί σαν υποκείμενο της παθητικής πρότασης με ένα διαφορετικό παθητικό ρήμα.
→ **They're training** Sue for the new position this week.
→ Sue **is being trained** for the new position this week.
→ Sue's **training** for the new position **will be completed** by the end of this week.

10.3 Reporting with Passive Verbs

Συχνά χρησιμοποιούμε ρήματα όπως *believe, consider, know, expect, say, suppose* και *think* για να αναφέρουμε κάτι στην παθητική φωνή. Μπορούν να χρησιμοποιηθούν με απρόσωπη ή με προσωπική σύνταξη (impersonal or personal structure)

Η απρόσωπη παθητική σύνταξη (impersonal passive structure) σχηματίζεται με *it* + παθητικό ρήμα (passive verb) + *that* + πρόταση.
→ **It is said that** the crime rate is rising.

Η προσωπική σύνταξη σχηματίζεται με ουσιαστικό + παθητικό ρήμα (passive verb) + απαρέμφατο με *to* (full infinitive).
→ **The elderly are believed to live** lonely lives.

10.4 *Seem & Appear*

Τα ρήματα *seem* και *appear* μπορούν να χρησιμοποιηθούν με παρόμοιους τρόπους για να μιλήσουμε για την εντύπωση που μας κάνει κάποιος ή κάτι. Μετά τα ρήματα *seem* και *appear* πολλές φορές χρησιμοποιούμε full infinitive (*to* + απαρέμφατο) ή perfect infinitive για γεγονότα και καταστάσεις του παρελθόντος.
→ The accident doesn't **appear to be** serious. Nobody is hurt. (παρόν)
→ Dylan **appears to have stopped** blogging so much. (παρελθόν)

Μετά από τα ρήματα *seem* και *appear* μπορούμε να χρησιμοποιήσουμε δευτερεύουσα πρόταση με *that*.
→ **It seems that** she can't stop using social networking sites on the Net.
→ **It appears that** people in rural areas are more welcoming.

Μετά από το ρήμα *seem* μπορούμε να χρησιμοποιήσουμε *as if* ή *like*. Δεν μπορούμε να χρησιμοποιήσουμε *as if* και *like* με *appear*.
→ It **seems as if** they will install interactive whiteboards at school.
→ It **seems like** modern lifestyles have their disadvantages.

Σημείωση: Μετά από τα ρήματα *seem* και *appear* μπορούμε να χρησιμοποιήσουμε επίθετο αλλά όχι επίρρημα.
→ He seems **honest**.
→ The new teacher appears (to be) **strict**.

10.5 Passive Causative

Χρησιμοποιούμε causative:
για να πούμε ότι κάποιος έχει αναθέσει μια δουλειά σε κάποιον άλλο.
→ I **had** all the emails **sent**.
για να πούμε ότι κάτι δυσάρεστο συνέβη σε κάποιον.
→ We **had** our car **stolen** while we were on holiday.

Σχηματίζουμε την causative με το ρήμα *have* + αντικείμενο + past participle (παθητική μετοχή). Μπορεί να χρησιμοποιηθεί σε πολλούς χρόνους. Όταν θέλουμε να αναφέρουμε το ποιητικό αίτιο (agent), χρησιμοποιούμε τη λέξη *by*.
→ They **had** a new satellite dish **installed**.
→ I **used to have** the newspaper **delivered** every day.
→ I'**m having** all my emails **checked by** my assistant.

Σημείωση: Μπορούμε επίσης να χρησιμοποιήσουμε *get* + αντικείμενο + past participle. Αυτή η σύνταξη έχει λιγότερο επίσημο ύφος. Όταν όμως περιγράφουμε δυσάρεστα γεγονότα, πρέπει να χρησιμοποιήσουμε το ρήμα *have*.
→ She **got** her new TV **replaced** as it was not working properly.
→ She **had** her new TV **stolen** while she was at work.

Μπορούμε να σχηματίσουμε και άλλους passive causative τύπους χρησιμοποιώντας *need/prefer/want/would like* + αντικείμενο + past ή present participle (παθητική ή ενεργητική μετοχή).
→ I **need** the notes to be **written** today.
→ We **prefer** the alarm to be **installed** soon.
→ I **want** the artefacts (to be) **tagged**, please.
→ The car **needs servicing** so I'll take it to the mechanic today.

Grammar Exercises

A Finish the second sentence using a passive construction.

1 The boss will give David a report to write.
   David will _____.

2 The teacher will give us more homework.
   More homework _____.

3 She explained the schedule to the newcomers.
   The schedule _____.

4 They have agreed to open a new shopping mall.
   It _____.

5 They expect the job situation to improve.
   The job situation _____.

6 They know that the burglar is a local man.
   It _____.

7 We think there are plans to close the school.
   It _____.

8 Imagine somebody asking you to fire an employee.
   Imagine _____.

B Match.

1 The car appears ☐   a car has broken down.
2 Oh no! It seems that the ☐ b to be getting better.
3 My cold seems ☐   c depressed, Betty.
4 It seems as ☐   d be crying.
5 Are you OK? You seem ☐   e if my cold is getting better.
6 Is he OK? He appears to ☐   f left work already.
7 They appear to have ☐   g to have broken down.
8 It seems like ☐   h they have left work already.

10 Grammar

C Complete the second sentence in each pair so that it has a similar meaning to the first sentence. Use the words in bold.

1. The new furniture is being delivered tomorrow. **having**
   I _____ tomorrow.

2. The dentist has removed two molars. **had**
   You _____ by the dentist.

3. I prefer the local garage to service my car. **serviced**
   I prefer _____ the local garage.

4. Please finish the filing by four o'clock. **finished**
   I would _____ by four o'clock.

5. Somebody stole my phone yesterday. **had**
   I _____ yesterday.

6. I locked my brother out of the house for an hour. **got**
   My brother _____ for an hour.

7. They are building a new extension on our kitchen. **are**
   We _____ on our kitchen.

8. They are building a new car park in town. **is**
   A new car park _____ in town.

Exam Task

For questions 1-15, read the text below and think of the word which best fits the gap. Use only one word in each gap.

Working from home

Recently a memo (1) _____ sent to employees at Yahoo asking them to no longer work from home but commute to the office instead. It had (2) _____ decided that the company would become more competitive if employees had actual contact with each other. It seemed as (3) _____ employees were not excelling when they were out of the office. But is this true?

Over the last decade, working from home appears (4) _____ have become more popular with many professionals. People have (5) _____ remote connections installed on their PCs and laptops so they can access their work station from home and slog (6) _____ out all night and weekend if necessary. Far from taking a break and putting their feet up at home, they now live (7) _____ the fast lane all the time.

Working from home is not only for workaholics, however. A number of men and women with young families prefer to (8) _____ allowed to work from home so they can juggle parenting and careers. It is known (9) _____ employers who do not want to lose valuable members of staff are quite happy to (10) _____ without employees for a short term, as long as they still work.

But how do companies react to employees working permanently from home? An office devoid (11) _____ people seems rather odd, and few companies appear to (12) _____ fully accepted the idea. But if fewer people worked at an office, there (13) _____ be less reason to rent large office space, which would cut costs, and lower operating costs mean more profits. All in all, it seems (14) _____ if working from home is here to stay, whatever policy (15) _____ adopted at Yahoo.

11 Sports Crazy!

Word Focus — pages 136

11.1 stuntman (n) /'stʌntmæn/
sb whose job is to do dangerous things instead of an actor • *The stuntman jumped from the building and landed safely on a mattress.* ❖ κασκαντέρ

11.2 don (v) /dɒn/
put on • *He donned his coat and hat and went out.* ❖ φορώ

11.3 make-up (n) /'meɪk-ʌp/
the qualities that form sb's personality • *Honesty and reliability are part of her make-up.* ❖ προσωπικότητα

11.4 adrenaline (n) /ə'drenəlɪn/
a hormone that is released into your body when you are scared or excited • *Her adrenaline flowed when she parachuted out of the plane.* ❖ αδρεναλίνη

11.5 rush (n) /rʌʃ/
a sudden strong feeling • *Doing a bungee jump gave him an adrenaline rush.* ❖ ένταση, έκρηξη

11.6 specification (n) /spesɪfɪ'keɪʃn/
a detailed instruction about how sth should be made • *The specifications say this bike has five gears.* ➢ specify (v) ❖ προδιαγραφές

11.7 rung (n) /rʌŋ/
a step on a ladder • *I climbed to the top rung of the ladder to clean the top of the cupboard.* ❖ σκαλί

11.8 rim (n) /rɪm/
the outside edge of sth circular • *The rim of the wheel got damaged when I rode over a stone.* ❖ ζάντα

11.9 intact (adj) /ɪn'tækt/
undamaged • *Luckily, the stuntman's helmet remained intact when he fell.* ❖ άθικτος

Reading — pages 136-137

11.10 spinning (n) /'spɪnɪŋ/
indoor cycling • *She keeps fit by doing spinning on the cycles at the gym.* ➢ spin (v) ❖ στατικό ποδήλατο

11.11 game (adj) /geɪm/
willing to try sth dangerous, new or difficult • *If you're game for a challenge, let's play tennis.* ❖ πρόθυμος

11.12 wingsuit (n) /'wɪŋsuːt/
a parachuting suit with flaps like wings • *The skydiver spread his arms wide and his wingsuit made him soar like a bird.* ❖ στολή με φτερά για ελεύθερη πτώση

11.13 have what it takes (expr) /hæv wɒt ɪt teɪks/
have the necessary skills, power, intelligence, etc. to do sth • *Do you have what it takes to do a bungee jump or are you too scared?* ❖ έχω τα απαιτούμενα προσόντα/χαρίσματα

11.14 touch down (phr v) /tʌtʃ daʊn/
land • *The parachutist jumped out of the plane and touched down on the ground five minutes later.* ❖ προσγειώνομαι

11.15 give the go-ahead (expr) /gɪv ðə gəʊ ə'hed/
give sb permission to do sth • *The pilot waited for the control tower to give the go-ahead before he took off.* ❖ δίνω το πράσινο φως

11.16 bear in mind (expr) /beər ɪn maɪnd/
consider • *Please bear in mind that the museums are closed on Mondays.* ❖ έχω υπόψη

11.17 bend (v) /bend/
move sth so it is not straight • *She bent her arm to scratch her shoulder.* ➢ bend (n) ❖ λυγίζω

11.18 upright (adv) /'ʌpraɪt/
vertically • *The teacher got out of the chair and stood upright in front of the board.* ❖ όρθιος

11.19 footboard (n) /'fʊtbɔːd/
a board where you can rest your feet • *You can rest your feet on the footboard in front of your seat in most coaches.* ❖ υποπόδιο

11.20 inner (adj) /'ɪnə/
on the inside • *The inner part of the wheel spins round more slowly.* ❖ εσωτερικός

11.21 handle (n) /'hændl/
part of an object that you use to hold it • *The handle of the cup broke and the hot coffee burnt me.* ❖ χερούλι

11.22 outer (adj) /'aʊtə/
on the outside • *The outer side of the door got covered in ice in the cold weather.* ❖ εξωτερικός

11.23 stride (n) /straɪd/
a step • *It was three strides from the bedroom to the bathroom in the tiny hotel room.* ❖ βήμα, δρασκελισμός

11.24 buckle (n) /'bʌkl/
a piece of metal or plastic you use to do up a belt • *The buckle on my belt broke so I can't do it up.* ➢ buckle (v) ❖ αγκράφα, κούμπωμα

11.25 binding (n) /'baɪndɪŋ/
sth you use to tie sth else with • *I cut the binding off the box and unpacked the things inside.* ➢ bind (v) ❖ δέσιμο

11.26 screw (n) /skruː/
a thin pointed piece of metal that you push and turn in order to fasten sth together • *Use two screws to attach the leg to the seat of the chair.* ❖ βίδα

11.27 bolt (n) /bəʊlt/
a small piece of metal that is used to join two things • *He attached the shelf to the wall with a strong bolt.* ❖ βίδα, μπουλόνι

11.28 utmost (adj) /ˈʌtməʊst/
greatest • *I took the utmost care not to break anything when I cleaned Grandma's glassware.* ➢ utmost (n) ❖ μέγιστος

11.29 adhere (to) (v) /ædˈhɪə (tʊ)/
follow • *You must adhere to the instructions in order to assemble the table correctly.* ❖ τηρώ, ακολουθώ

11.30 ensure (v) /ɪnˈʃɔː/
make sure • *Ensure that you have all the bolts and screws before you try to assemble the furniture.* ❖ διασφαλίζω, σιγουρεύω

11.31 reverse (v) /rɪˈvɜːs/
position sth backwards • *If you reverse the cushions on the sofa, they won't fit properly.* ➢ reverse (n) ❖ αντιστρέφω

11.32 incur (v) /ɪnˈkɜː/
If you incur sth unpleasant, it happens because of sth you have done. • *The footballer incurred a serious knee injury when he was kicked.* ❖ υφίσταμαι, επισύρω

11.33 firmly (adv) /ˈfɜːmli/
tightly; strongly • *Hold the screwdriver firmly so you can turn the screws more easily.* ➢ firm (adj) ❖ σταθερά

11.34 tighten (v) /ˈtaɪtən/
make tight • *She tightened her belt so her jeans would stay up.* ➢ tight (adj) ❖ σφίγγω
✎ Opp: loosen

11.35 fasten (v) /ˈfɑːsn/
attach • *Please fasten your seat belt for take-off.* ➢ fastener (n) ❖ δένω

11.36 at regular intervals (expr) /ət ˈregjələr ˈɪntəvlz/
regularly • *Inspectors come to the school at regular intervals.* ❖ σε τακτά (χρονικά) διαστήματα

11.37 maintenance (n) /ˈmeɪntənəns/
keeping sth in good condition • *Your old car needs regular maintenance to keep it running well.* ➢ maintain (v) ❖ συντήρηση

11.38 perception (n) /pəˈsepʃn/
the way you think about what sth is like • *Her perception of danger increased after she had an accident.* ➢ perceive (v), perceptive (adj) ❖ αντίληψη

11.39 embrace (v) /ɪmˈbreɪs/
accept sth with enthusiasm • *To embrace risks you need to be unafraid of danger.* ➢ embrace (n) ❖ αγκαλιάζω, δέχομαι

11.40 safety-conscious (adj) /ˈseɪfti-ˌkɒnʃəs/
careful not to put yourself in danger • *The safety-conscious skydiver checked his parachute carefully before the jump.* ❖ ευαισθητοποιημένος για την ασφάλεια

11.41 longtime (adj) /ˈlɒŋtaɪm/
for a long time • *A longtime fitness instructor, Rob has helped many people to get in shape.* ❖ μακροχρόνιος, βετεράνος

11.42 pursuit (n) /pəˈsjuːt/
an activity • *His favourite pursuit is mountain climbing.* ➢ pursue (v) ❖ ασχολία

11.43 natural ceiling (expr) /ˈnætʃərəl ˈsiːlɪŋ/
the natural limit of what is possible • *There is a natural ceiling that will limit how fast humans can run.* ❖ φυσικό όριο

11.44 hold sb back (phr v) /həʊld ˈsʌmbədi bæk/
stop sb doing sth • *Her fear of heights held her back from climbing to the top of the tower.* ❖ εμποδίζω

11.45 tolerance (n) /ˈtɒlərəns/
ability to bear sth • *He has a low tolerance for pain so he really complains if he gets hurt.* ➢ tolerate (v), tolerant (adj) ❖ ανοχή, ανεκτικότητα
✎ Opp: intolerance

11.46 crave (v) /kreɪv/
desire sth greatly • *Sometimes I crave chocolate; I just have to have some.* ➢ craving (n) ❖ λαχταρώ

11.47 perceive (v) /pəˈsiːv/
think of sb/sth in a particular way • *I don't understand why some people perceive maths to be a difficult subject.* ➢ perception (n) ❖ αντιλαμβάνομαι

11.48 thrill-seeking (adj) /ˈθrɪl-ˌsiːkɪŋ/
looking for excitement • *The thrill-seeking couple went on an extreme sports weekend.* ❖ που επιδιώκει συναρπαστικές εμπειρίες

11.49 minimise (v) /ˈmɪnɪmaɪz/
make as small as possible • *Wear your seatbelt to minimise the risk of injury if we have an accident.* ❖ μειώνω, ελαχιστοποιώ

11.50 precaution (n) /prɪˈkɔːʃn/
an action to stop sth dangerous happening • *We took all the necessary safety precautions before doing the parachute jump.* ➢ precautionary (adj) ❖ προφύλαξη

11.51 feasible (adj) /ˈfiːzəbl/
possible • *It wasn't feasible to continue climbing in the snow so we abandoned the attempt.* ➢ feasibility (n) ❖ εφικτός
✎ Opp: unfeasible

11.52 reassure (v) /rɪəˈʃɔː/
say sth to stop sb worrying • *The guide reassured us the museums were open, even though we had heard there was a strike.* ➢ reassurance (n) ❖ καθησυχάζω

11.53 be cut out (phr v) /biː kʌt aʊt/
be suited to • *Bobby is not cut out for sport because he is not the athletic type.* ❖ είμαι φτιαγμένος για κάτι

11.54 burning desire (expr) /ˈbɜːnɪŋ dɪˈzaɪə/
a very strong desire • *Her burning desire was to take part in the Olympics, so she trained hard every day.* ❖ μεγάλη επιθυμία, διακαής πόθος

11.55 be entitled (expr) /bɪ ɪnˈtaɪtəld/
have the right to have sth • *Pensioners are entitled to half-price tickets on public transport.* ❖ δικαιούμαι

Excitement
adrenaline
burning desire
rush
thrill-seeking
ultimate

Vocabulary pages 138-139

11.56 broadcast (n) /ˈbrɔːdkɑːst/
a TV or radio programme or transmission • *I watch the news broadcast every evening.* ➢ broadcast (v), broadcaster (n) ❖ εκπομπή

11.57 wits (pl n) /wɪts/
the ability to think quickly and decide correctly • *Thanks to his quick wits, he swerved the car away from the dog just in time.* ❖ ευστροφία, εξυπνάδα

11.58 come in handy (expr) /kʌm ɪn ˈhændi/
be useful • *A torch will come in handy in case there is a blackout.* ❖ είναι χρήσιμος

11.59 with a view to (expr) /wɪð ə vjuː tə/
with the intention of doing sth • *I saved all year with a view to going on holiday.* ❖ με σκοπό (να κάνω κάτι)

11.60 internship (n) /ˈɪntɜːnʃɪp/
a job that a student does to gain experience • *The medical student did his internship at the local hospital.* ❖ πρακτική

11.61 commentator (n) /ˈkɒmənteɪtə/
sb who describes a sport on the radio or TV • *The commentator explained which players were in each team.* ➢ commentate (v), commentary (n) ❖ σχολιαστής

11.62 interpreter (n) /ɪnˈtɜːprɪtə/
sb who translates what people are saying • *An interpreter translated what the Spanish coach said to the English reporters.* ➢ interpret (v) ❖ διερμηνέας

11.63 observer (n) /ɒbˈzɜːvə/
sb who regularly pays attention to certain events, situations, etc. • *International observers went to Iran to report on its nuclear programme.* ➢ observe (v) ❖ παρατηρητής

11.64 cover (v) /ˈkʌvə/
report an event for the media • *The football match is being covered by Channel 1 tonight at 9pm.* ➢ cover (n) ❖ καλύπτω

11.65 steer (v) /stɪə/
direct a car • *I steered the car left into a side road.* ➢ ❖ κατευθύνω

11.66 figure (n) /ˈfɪgə/
a famous person • *Messi is an admired figure in the world of football.* ❖ πρόσωπο

11.67 captivating (adj) /ˈkæptɪveɪtɪŋ/
fascinating • *The football final was a captivating match well worth watching.* ➢ captivate (v) ❖ συναρπαστικός

11.68 charming (adj) /ˈtʃɑːmɪŋ/
attractive • *The charming ballet was beautifully performed.* ➢ charm (v, n) ❖ γοητευτικός

11.69 dazzling (adj) /ˈdæzlɪŋ/
very impressive • *The fireworks display was a dazzling end to the evening.* ➢ dazzle (v) ❖ εκθαμβωτικός

11.70 pleasing (adj) /ˈpliːzɪŋ/
giving pleasure or satisfaction • *The warm climate in the Mediterranean is very pleasing in spring.* ➢ please (v) ❖ ευχάριστος

11.71 admirer (n) /ædˈmaɪərə/
sb who is impressed by sb/sth • *Admirers of the celebrity asked for his autograph.* ➢ admire (v) ❖ θαυμαστής

11.72 relay race (n) /ˈriːleɪ reɪs/
a running competition that includes four runners on each team who have to pass a baton to each other as their part of the race • *Each athlete ran 100m in the relay race and the team went once around the track.* ❖ σκυταλοδρομία

11.73 serve (v) /sɜːv/
start a tennis game by throwing a ball into the air and hitting it • *The tennis player served and his opponent hit the ball back.* ❖ σερβίρω

11.74 ace (n) /eɪs/
a perfect serve that the other player cannot return • *The serve was an ace that the other tennis player could not reach.* ❖ άσος

11.75 round (n) /raʊnd/
a series of games in a competition • *In round two of the cup, Italy will play France.* ❖ γύρος

11.76 set (n) /set/
a section of a tennis match • *The tennis player won the second set 6-4.* ❖ σετ

11.77 club (n) /klʌb/
a long thin metal stick you use to hit the ball in golf • *The golf player chose a club and expertly hit the ball onto the green.*
❖ μπαστούνι του γκολφ

11.78 bat (n) /bæt/
a long wooden stick that you use to hit a ball in some sports • *The baseball player hit the ball hard with the bat.* ➢ bat (v) ❖ ρόπαλο

11.79 drive (n) /draɪv/
the act of hitting a ball hard • *The excellent drive sent the ball 300 metres.* ➢ drive (v)
❖ εναρκτήριο χτύπημα (στο γκολφ)

11.80 steady (v) /ˈstedi/
become calmer • *John steadied, aimed and then threw the ball into the basket.*
➢ steady (adj) ❖ σταθεροποιούμαι, συγκεντρώνομαι

11.81 shoot (v) /ʃuːt/
aim and throw or kick • *Messi shot the ball right into the net.* ➢ shot (n) ❖ σουτάρω

11.82 toss (v) /tɒs/
throw • *The rugby player tossed the ball to his teammate.* ➢ toss (n) ❖ πετώ

11.83 buzzer (n) /ˈbʌzə/
an electrical device that makes a buzzing noise and is used to mark the end of periods of play in some sports • *It was a one-sided game and at the buzzer, the score was 110-36.*
➢ buzz (v) ❖ κουδούνι

11.84 lead (n) /liːd/
the first position in a race or competition
• *Smith is in the lead... he is going faster and he crosses the line first.* ❖ προηγούμαι

11.85 baton (n) /ˈbætən/
a stick that is passed from one person to another in a relay race • *The runners in the relay race passed the baton smoothly and won the race.* ❖ σκυτάλη

11.86 lane (n) /leɪn/
one of the parallel strips of track or water for runners, rowers or swimmers in a race • *Harvey is in lane 2 of the track.*
❖ διάδρομος

11.87 lap (n) /læp/
one circuit of a running track or one stage in a swim • *The 200m freestyle is four laps of the pool.* ➢ lap (v) ❖ γύρος

11.88 writhe in agony (expr) /raɪð ɪn ˈægəni/
twist your body because you are in a lot of pain • *The player is writhing in agony and it seems the injury is serious.* ❖ σπαρταρώ από τον πόνο

11.89 umpire (n) /ˈʌmpaɪə/
sb who watches a game of cricket or tennis and makes sure rules are not broken
• *The umpire said the batsman was out.*
❖ διαιτητής

11.90 diving (n) /ˈdaɪvɪŋ/
falling over on purpose (in football) • *The attacker was shown a yellow card for diving in the penalty box.* ➢ dive (v) ❖ βουτιά

11.91 dribbling (n) /ˈdrɪblɪŋ/
(in football) moving the ball with a number of short kicks • *Messi's amazing dribbling enabled him to get past three players and score a goal.* ➢ dribble (v) ❖ τρίπλα

11.92 conquer (v) /ˈkɒŋkə/
beat • *The king conquered his enemy and took control of the castle.* ➢ conqueror (n)
❖ κατακτώ

11.93 contend (v) /kənˈtend/
compete • *Two athletes are contending for a new world record.* ➢ contender (n)
❖ διαγωνίζομαι

11.94 bolt (v) /bəʊlt/
run fast • *The runner bolted across the line as fast as he could go.* ➢ bolt (n)
❖ τρέχω γρήγορα

11.95 dash (v) /dæʃ/
run fast • *He dashed down the track to finish the race in just 20 seconds.* ➢ dash (n)
❖ τρέχω γρήγορα

11.96 sprint (v) /sprɪnt/
run fast • *100m runners can sprint faster than any other athletes.* ➢ sprint (n)
❖ τρέχω γρήγορα

11.97 bounce (v) /baʊns/
move up and down after hitting a surface
• *The football bounced against the goalpost and rolled off the pitch.* ➢ bounce (n)
❖ αναπηδώ

11.98 bowl (v) /bəʊl/
throw a ball for the batsman to hit in cricket
• *The cricket player bowled and the batsman hit the ball perfectly.* ➢ bowler (n) ❖ κάνω ρίψη στο κρίκετ

11.99 pitch (v) /pɪtʃ/
throw a ball for a batsman to hit in baseball
• *The baseball player pitched well and his opponent missed the ball.* ➢ pitcher (n)
❖ κάνω ρίψη στο μπέιζμπολ

11.100 row (v) /rəʊ/
use oars to move a boat • *I rowed the canoe down the river.* ❖ κωπηλατώ

11.101 hinder (v) /ˈhɪndə/
make sth difficult for sb to do • *A leg injury hindered the player from playing well.*
➢ hindrance (n) ❖ εμποδίζω

11.102 overpower (v) /əʊvəˈpaʊə/
be stronger than; beat • *Sweden were easily overpowered by the German team, who won 4-0.* ❖ νικώ

11.103 thrash (v) /θræʃ/
beat completely • *Real Madrid thrashed Chelsea 6-1.* ➢ thrashing (n) ❖ συντρίβω, νικώ

11.104 **aspire** (v) /əˈspaɪə/
aim for • *The young boy aspires to greater things and dreams of being a football star.* ➢ aspiration (n) ❖ φιλοδοξώ

11.105 **hone** (v) /həʊn/
improve • *You can hone your talent with more practice.* ➢ honing (n) ❖ τελειοποιώ

11.106 **sharpen** (v) /ˈʃɑːpən/
improve • *You must sharpen your reactions so you can always hit the ball back to your tennis opponent.* ➢ sharp (adj) ❖ ακονίζω

11.107 **commit** (v) /kəˈmɪt/
give your time or effort to sth • *The coach committed himself to training the team every day.* ➢ commitment (n) ❖ αφοσιώνομαι

11.108 **dedicate** (v) /ˈdedɪkeɪt/
give your time to sth • *When you dedicate yourself to a sport you must train hard.* ➢ dedication (n), dedicated (adj) ❖ αφιερώνω

11.109 **devote** (v) /dɪˈvəʊt/
give your time or effort to sth • *The fans devoted every Saturday to supporting their team.* ➢ devotion (n), devoted (adj) ❖ αφιερώνω/-ομαι, αφοσιώνω/-ομαι

11.110 **disqualify** (v) /dɪsˈkwɒlɪfaɪ/
declare sb ineligible for competition because of an offence • *He was disqualified from the race when he made two false starts.* ➢ disqualification (n) ❖ αποκλείω/-ομαι

11.111 **obstruct** (v) /əbˈstrʌkt/
stand in the way • *The basketball player gets three free shots because a player from the other team obstructed her.* ➢ obstruction (n) ❖ εμποδίζω

11.112 **suspend** (v) /sʌsˈpend/
ban for a short period • *The athlete was suspended for three months for making racist remarks during a match.* ➢ suspension (n) ❖ αποβάλλω

11.113 **applaud** (v) /əˈplɔːd/
clap to show appreciation or enjoyment of sth • *The spectators applauded as the athletes took their places for the race.* ➢ applause (n) ❖ ζητωκραυγάζω

11.114 **revive** (v) /rɪˈvaɪv/
bring sb back to consciousness • *The player who got hit on the head was revived with some cold water.* ➢ revival (n) ❖ επαναφέρω

11.115 **root for sb** (phr v) /ruːt fə ˈsʌmbədi/
want sb to win • *The fans are rooting for their team and hope for a win.* ❖ επευφημώ

11.116 **in a matter of** (expr) /ɪn ə ˈmætər əv/
in only a few (years, hours, minutes, etc.) / little (time) • *They're leaving on a cruise in a matter of a few days.* ❖ σε λίγο

11.117 **remount** (v) /riːˈmaʊnt/
get back on a bike or horse after falling off • *The cyclist who fell remounted quickly and continued the race.* ❖ ξανανεβαίνω

11.118 **catch up** (phr v) /kætʃ ʌp/
reach sb in front of you by going faster • *The child ran to catch up with his friends in front of him.* ❖ προφταίνω

11.119 **pull out** (phr v) /pʊl aʊt/
stop taking part • *He had to pull out of the race because of an injury.* ❖ αποσύρομαι

11.120 **drop back** (phr v) /drɒp bæk/
fall behind the others • *The runner was clearly tired as he dropped back behind the others.* ❖ μένω πίσω

11.121 **miss out on sth** (phr v) /mɪs aʊt ɒn ˈsʌmθɪŋ/
not have the chance to do sth pleasant or good • *If you don't go to university, you'll miss out on a great opportunity in life.* ❖ χάνω ευκαιρία

11.122 **knock out** (phr v) /nɒk aʊt/
defeat sb in a competition so that they can no longer take part • *Italy knocked out Spain and will go on to play in the next match.* ❖ αποκλείω

11.123 **warm up** (phr v) /wɔːm ʌp/
exercise to prepare your body for a race • *Warm up by stretching before the race.* ➢ warm-up (n) ❖ κάνω προθέρμανση

11.124 **heat** (n) /hiːt/
a part of a competition whose winners then compete against each other in the next part • *He came last in the first heat so he is out of the competition.* ❖ γύρος

11.125 **quarter final** (n) /ˈkɔːtə ˈfaɪnəl/
one of the four games near the end of a competition, whose winners play in the two semi-finals • *In the quarter finals the teams playing are Germany against Spain, England against Italy, Greece against Sweden and Brazil against Paraguay.* ❖ προημιτελικός

11.126 **semi** (n) /ˈsemɪ/
one of two matches whose winners then play against each other in the final • *Greece won the semi and went on to play Portugal in the final.* ❖ ημιτελικός

11.127 **hamstring** (n) /ˈhæmstrɪŋ/
a tendon behind your knee • *He has hurt his hamstring, so cannot put weight on his knee.* ❖ ιγνυακός τένοντας

11.128 **snap** (v) /snæp/
break suddenly • *He snapped a tendon, which is a serious injury.* ➢ snap (n) ❖ παθαίνω ρήξη ή τράβηγμα τένοντα

11.129 come to a halt (expr) /kʌm tʊ ə hɔːlt/
stop • *The Formula One car came to a halt after only two laps because of engine failure.* ❖ σταματώ

11.130 stretcher (n) /ˈstretʃə/
sth used for carrying a sick or injured person who cannot walk • *They carried the injured player off the field on a stretcher.* ❖ φορείο

11.131 lean on sb (expr) /liːn ɒn ˈsʌmbədi/
rest on sb who helps you support your weight • *After I sprained my ankle in the park, I had to lean on my friend all the way back to my house.* ❖ στηρίζομαι σε κάποιον

11.132 spirit (n) /ˈspɪrɪt/
the set of ideas and beliefs that are typical of a particular group of people • *He showed Olympic spirit when he congratulated the winner wholeheartedly.* ❖ πνεύμα

11.133 the ball's in sb's court (expr) /ðə bɔːlz ɪn ˈsʌmbədiz kɔːt/
it is up to sb to make the next move • *He has agreed to their terms, so the ball is now in their court.* ❖ ρίχνω το μπαλάκι σε κάποιον, εσύ αποφασίζεις

11.134 be first out of the gate (expr) /bɪ fɜːst aʊt ɒv ðə geɪt/
be first to do sth • *John's company was the first out of the gate when it launched its new product.* ❖ είμαι ο πρώτος που θα κάνει κάτι

11.135 have sb in one's corner (expr) /hæv ˈsʌmbədi ɪn wʌnz kɔːnə/
have sb supporting you • *I hope I have the boss in my corner at the meeting because I need his support.* ❖ έχω την υποστήριξη κάποιου

11.136 drop the ball (expr) /drɒp ðə bɔːl/
make a mistake • *I'm sorry; I really dropped the ball on this one.* ❖ κάνω λάθος

11.137 fall at the first hurdle (expr) /fɔːl æt ðə fɜːst ˈhɜːdəl/
fail as soon as one encounters the first obstacle • *He fell at the first hurdle and left college after failing his first term exams.* ❖ αποτυγχάνω νωρίς και εγκαταλείπω

11.138 backer (n) /ˈbækə/
sb who supports sb/sth financially • *If you want to set up a business, you'll need a financial backer.* ➢ back (v) ❖ υποστηρικτής, χρηματοδότης

11.139 hit the bull's-eye (expr) /hɪt ðə bʊlz-aɪ/
be perfectly correct • *You hit the bull's eye when you guessed that she won the lottery.* ❖ πετυχαίνω διάνα

Talking about different sports

tennis	football
ace	diving
serve	dribbling
set	shoot
umpire	
	track and field
golf	baton
club	lane
drive	lap
	relay race
baseball	sprint
bat	
pitch	

Grammar pages 140-141

11.140 dime (n) /daɪm/
a ten cent coin • *This old tennis racket isn't worth a dime, so you should throw it out.* ❖ κέρμα των δέκα λεπτών

11.141 compliment (v) /ˈkɒmplɪment/
say sth nice to sb to praise them • *He complimented the chef on the delicious meal.* ❖ κάνω κομπλιμέντο

Listening page 142

11.142 bargain for sth (expr) /ˈbɑːgɪn fɔː ˈsʌmθɪŋ/
expect sth to happen • *We bargained on good weather for the cricket match and were not disappointed.* ❖ περιμένω να συμβεί κάτι, ποντάρω σε κάτι

11.143 get a kick out of sth (expr) /get ə kɪk aʊt ɒv ˈsʌmθɪŋ/
enjoy sth • *He gets a kick out of teasing me when my team loses.* ❖ τη βρίσκω

11.144 be on the other side of the fence (expr) /bɪ ɒn ðə ˈʌðə saɪd ɒv ðə fens/
be opposed to sb/sth • *I'm on the other side of the fence because I support West Ham, not Tottenham like you.* ❖ αντιτίθεμαι

11.145 rival (n) /ˈraɪvəl/
an opponent • *The tennis rivals played an exciting match in the final.* ➢ rival (v), rivalry (n) ❖ αντίπαλος

11.146 stray from the path (expr) /streɪ frɒm ðə pɑːθ/
not do what you should • *She strayed from the path and got into trouble with the police.* ❖ ξεστρατίζω, παραστρατώ

11.147 wriggle one's way out of sth (expr) /'rɪgl wʌnz weɪ aʊt ɒv 'sʌmθɪŋ/
try to avoid doing sth • *Kevin tried to wriggle his way out of tidying his room, but his mum insisted.* ❖ ξεγλιστρώ

11.148 have sb's best interests at heart (expr) /hæv 'sʌmbədiz best 'ɪntrests æt hɑːt/
care about sb's well-being • *Teachers say they have their students' best interests at heart when they set them tests.* ❖ ενδιαφέρομαι για το καλό/συμφέρον κάποιου

11.149 be in good hands (expr) /bɪ ɪn gʊd hændz/
be looked after by sb you can trust • *Dave is an excellent tutor so you are in good hands.* ❖ είμαι σε καλά χέρια

11.150 give sth up (phr v) /gɪv 'sʌmθɪŋ ʌp/
stop doing sth you do regularly • *You should give up eating sweets to lose weight.* ❖ κόβω μια συνήθεια

11.151 contestant (n) /kən'testənt/
sb who takes part in a competition • *Only ten contestants in this competition will continue to the next round.* ➢ contest (n) ❖ διαγωνιζόμενος

Speaking page 143

11.152 spectator (n) /spek'teɪtə/
sb who watches a sports event • *The spectators cheered when Ronaldo scored the winning goal.* ➢ spectacle (n) ❖ θεατής

11.153 not one's cup of tea (expr) /nɒt wʌnz kʌp ɒv tiː/
not sth one likes • *Tennis isn't my cup of tea but I love golf.* ❖ (δεν) είναι του γούστου μου

Writing: an informal letter pages 144-145

11.154 input (n) /'ɪnpʊt/
advice; ideas • *This group project needs input from all of us, not just me.* ❖ συμβουλές, ιδέες

11.155 changing room (n) /'tʃeɪndʒɪŋ ruːm/
a room where you change clothes for sport • *The players changed into their gear in the changing room.* ❖ αποδυτήριο

11.156 cramped (adj) /kræmpt/
a cramped room does not have enough room for the people in it • *The room is only six square metres, so it's rather cramped.* ❖ περιορισμένος

Phrasal verbs

be cut out	miss out on sth
catch up	pull out
drop back	take out
give sth up	touch down
hold sb back	warm up
knock out	

Video 11: Flying Pumpkins page 146

11.157 pumpkin (n) /'pʌmpkɪn/
a large orange coloured vegetable • *We cut the pumpkin into a scary face for Halloween.* ❖ κολοκύθα

11.158 contraption (n) /kən'træpʃn/
a strange machine • *Your old bicycle is a strange contraption.* ❖ μαραφέτι

11.159 spring (n) /sprɪŋ/
a spiral that bounces back to shape when pulled or pressed • *The door closes automatically as it is attached to a spring.* ❖ ελατήριο

11.160 wire (n) /'waɪə/
a long thin piece of metal • *Don't touch the wires in this electric cable because they are live.* ❖ καλώδιο, σύρμα

11.161 bucket (n) /'bʌkɪt/
a cylindrical container with a handle in which you can carry water • *The old woman drew water from the well using a bucket.* ❖ κουβά

11.162 take out (phr v) /teɪk aʊt/
destroy sth • *The explosives took out several buildings.* ❖ καταστρέφω

Vocabulary Exercises

A Complete the phrasal verbs in the correct form in these sentences.

1 The runner was so tired he _____ back and ended up in last place.
2 I don't want to _____ out on all the excitement of the final match.
3 If you had _____ up before the race, you wouldn't have pulled a muscle.
4 My team is sure to _____ out yours so we can get into the final.
5 The skydiver is _____ down safely in a field at this very moment.
6 My fear of crowds always _____ me back from going to football matches.
7 She was badly injured and had to _____ up a promising career in the sport.
8 Are you sure you are _____ out to be on the basketball team when you are only 1.60m tall?
9 Run faster and try to _____ up with those in the lead!
10 Did he have to _____ out of the race because of injury?

B Match the words and make nouns.

1 stunt   room   _____
2 ham   man   _____
3 quarter   cast   _____
4 make   race   _____
5 relay   final   _____
6 wing   up   _____
7 broad   string   _____
8 changing suit   _____

C Choose the correct answers.

1 Somebody who **is game** will probably
   a refuse to do something new.
   b agree to try something new.

2 You **give the go-ahead** if you
   a want somebody to walk in front of you.
   b allow somebody to do something.

3 A person who **gets a kick out of something**
   a feels a lot of pain.
   b enjoys it a lot.

4 Somebody who **drops the ball** will
   a let you down.
   b back you up.

5 If something **is your cup of tea** you
   a like it.
   b drink it.

6 You would **writhe in agony** if
   a you were in terrible pain.
   b you were extremely nervous.

7 Somebody who snaps a **hamstring** will have a painful
   a arm.
   b leg.

8 If you **adhere** to the rules, you
   a follow them.
   b break them.

D Circle the correct words.

1 I used a screw / spring to firmly attach the legs to the seats of the chairs.
2 The golf pro had very expensive bats / clubs.
3 The athlete ran fast down the second rung / lane of the track.
4 The footballer was suspended / revived for four games because of bad behaviour.
5 The referee / contestant pressed the buzzer to answer the question.
6 Panathinaikos has again thrashed / embraced their opponents in a 6-0 win.
7 The crowd in the stadium is rooting / donning for the underdog.
8 Today's match was a(n) utmost / captivating performance by both teams.

11 Grammar

11.1 Reported Speech: Statements/Πλάγιος λόγος: Καταφατικές προτάσεις

Όταν μεταφέρουμε τον ευθύ λόγο (direct speech) σε πλάγιο (reported speech), οι χρόνοι που χρησιμοποιεί ο ομιλητής συνήθως αλλάζουν ως εξής:

Present Simple	Past Simple
'He **likes** team sports,' she said.	She said (that) he **liked** team sports.
Present Continuous	Past Continuous
'He **is visiting** the city,' she said.	She said (that) he **was visiting** the city.
Present Perfect Simple	Past Perfect Simple
'She **has won** the race,' he said.	He said (that) she **had won** the race.
Present Perfect Continuous	Past Perfect Continuous
'I **have been working** hard,' she said.	She said (that) she **had been working** hard.
Past Simple	Past Perfect Simple
'She **assembled** the parts,' he said.	He said (that) she **had assembled** the parts.
Past Continuous	Past Perfect Continuous
'He **was warming up**,' she said.	She said (that) he **had been warming up**.

Άλλες αλλαγές στους τύπους των ρημάτων είναι οι παρακάτω:

can	could
'He **can** cycle fast,' she said.	She said (that) he **could** cycle fast.
may	might
'She **may** fly to Rome,' he said.	He said (that) she **might** fly to Rome.
must	had to
'You **must** follow your dreams,' the coach said.	The coach said (that) we **had to** follow our dreams.
will	would
'They **will** buy a new bike,' he said.	He said (that) they **would** buy a new bike.

Σημείωση:
1. Τα ρήματα *say* και *tell* χρησιμοποιούνται συχνά στο reported speech. Το ρήμα *tell* ακολουθείται από αντικείμενο (object).
   → The coach **said** (that) we should come early.
   → The coach **told us** (that) we should come early.

2. Μπορούμε να παραλείψουμε τη λέξη *that*.
   → She **said that** she was training daily.
   → She **said** she was training daily.

3. Μερικές φορές οι αντωνυμίες και τα κτητικά επίθετα πρέπει να αλλάξουν.
   → '**I**'m going to the changing rooms,' she said.
   → She said (that) **she** was going to the changing rooms.
   → 'That's **my** equipment,' he said.
   → He said (that) that was **his** equipment.

4. Οι παρακάτω χρόνοι και λέξεις δεν αλλάζουν στο reported speech:
   Past Perfect Simple, Past Perfect Continuous, *would, could, might, should, ought to, used to, had better*, καθώς και *must/mustn't* όταν αναφέρονται σε συμπέρασμα.
   → 'I **had been watching** the match,' she said.
   → She said (that) she **had been watching** the match.

11 Grammar

11.2 Reported Speech: Changes in time and place

Όταν μεταφέρουμε τον άμεσο λόγο σε πλάγιο, συχνά αλλάζουμε και κάποιες λέξεις που δηλώνουν χρόνο και τόπο.

Direct speech	Reported speech
'I'm checking the wheels **now**,' she said.	She said she was checking the wheels **then**.
'She's interviewing him **today**,' he said.	He said she was interviewing him **that day**.
'We can't go skydiving **tonight**,' he said.	He said we couldn't go skydiving **that night**.
'I missed the penalty **yesterday**,' he said.	He said he had missed the penalty **the previous day/the day before**.
'He started university **last week**,' she said.	She said he had started university **the previous week/the week before**.
'I'll read the contract **tomorrow**,' he said.	He said he would read the contract **the next day/the following day**.
'He's playing in the tournament **next week**,' she said.	She said he was playing in the tournament **the following week**.
'**This** is our new coach,' she said.	She said **that** was their new coach.
'The match started an hour **ago**,' he said.	He said the match had started an hour **before**.
'He's surfing **at the moment**,' she said.	She said he was surfing **at that moment**.
'Your new contract is **here** in the office,' she said.	She said his new contract was **there** in the office.

11.3 Reporting Verbs

Εκτός από τα ρήματα *say*, *tell* και *ask*, μπορούμε να χρησιμοποιήσουμε και άλλα ρήματα για να μεταφέρουμε με μεγαλύτερη ακρίβεια τα λόγια κάποιου. Παρατήρησε τους διαφορετικούς τρόπους σύνταξης.

ρήμα + απαρέμφατο με *to* (full infinitive)	
agree	'Yes, I'll watch the game with you,' she said. She **agreed to watch** the game with me.
claim	'I'm taking the necessary precautions,' she said. She **claimed to be** taking the necessary precautions.
decide	'I think I'll watch the game with you,' she said. She **decided to watch** the game with me.
refuse	'No, I won't watch the game with you,' she said. She **refused to watch** the game with me.
offer	'Shall I watch the game with you?' she asked. She **offered to watch** the game with me.
promise	'Don't worry, I'll watch the game with you,' she said. She **promised to watch** the game with me.
ρήμα + αντικείμενο + απαρέμφατο με *to* (full infinitive)	
advise	'If I were you, I'd keep away from hooligans,' he said. He **advised me to keep** away from hooligans.
encourage	'Come on, you can keep away from hooligans,' he said. He **encouraged me to keep** away from hooligans.
order	'Keep away from hooligans!' he told me. He **ordered me to keep** away from hooligans.
persuade	'You should try to keep away from hooligans,' he said. 'You're right,' I answered. He **persuaded me to keep** away from hooligans.
remind	'Remember to keep away from hooligans,' he said. He **reminded me to keep** away from hooligans.
warn	'Be careful! Don't get mixed up with hooligans,' he said. He **warned me not to get** mixed up with hooligans.

ρήμα + gerund (-ing)	
admit	'I took your tickets,' she said. She **admitted taking** my tickets.
deny	'No, I didn't take your tickets,' she said. She **denied taking** my tickets.
recommend	'You should buy new tickets,' she said. She **recommended buying** new tickets.
suggest	'Let's look for your tickets,' she said. She **suggested looking** for my tickets.
ρήμα + πρόθεση + gerund (-ing)	
apologise for	'I'm sorry I didn't clean the changing rooms,' he said. He **apologised for not cleaning** the changing rooms.
complain about	'I had to clean the changing rooms again!' he said. He **complained about having** to clean the changing rooms again.
insist on	Of course I'll clean the changing rooms,' he said. He **insisted on cleaning** the changing rooms.
ρήμα + αντικείμενο + πρόθεση + gerund (-ing)	
accuse sb of	'I believe you played very badly', he said. He **accused me of playing** very badly.
congratulate sb on	'You played a great game! Well done!' he said. He **congratulated us on playing** a great game.
ρήμα + that	
announce	'I'm going to run the marathon,' she said. She **announced that** she was going to run the marathon.
complain	'I don't have the strength to run the marathon,' she said. She **complained that** she didn't have the strength to run the marathon.
demand	'You must help me run the marathon,' she said. She **demanded that** I help her run the marathon.

11.4 Reported Questions

Όταν μεταφέρουμε ερωτήσεις από τον άμεσο στον πλάγιο λόγο (reported speech), οι αλλαγές στους χρόνους, στις αντωνυμίες, στα κτητικά επίθετα, στο χρόνο και τον τόπο είναι όπως και στις καταφατικές προτάσεις του πλάγιου λόγου. Όμως στις ερωτήσεις στον πλάγιο λόγο, το ρήμα παραμένει στον καταφατικό τύπο. Επίσης δε χρησιμοποιούμε ερωτηματικό.

Όταν η άμεση ερώτηση περιέχει ερωτηματική λέξη (who, why, how, when κλπ.), τη χρησιμοποιούμε και στην πλάγια ερώτηση.
→ '**When** did you become a sports announcer?' he asked.
→ He asked **when** I had become a sports announcer.

Όταν η άμεση ερώτηση δεν περιέχει ερωτηματική λέξη, χρησιμοποιούμε *if* ή *whether* στην πλάγια ερώτηση.
→ 'Is skydiving as exciting as they say?' she asked.
→ She asked **if/whether** skydiving was as exciting as they said.

11 Grammar

Grammar Exercises

A Rewrite these sentences in reported speech.

1. 'I often go to football matches.'
   He _____

2. 'This exercise instruction manual is mine.'
   She _____

3. 'I won't stay for the basketball game because I must hurry home.'
   He _____

4. 'I shall meet him tomorrow outside the stadium.'
   She _____

5. 'We shall train the players harder next week.'
   He _____

6. 'You must take up a new pursuit, Greg.'
   I told _____

B Circle the correct words.

1. Stan apologised for being / to be late.
2. The instructor advised us / to us to take it gently at first.
3. He admitted to cheat / cheating in the competition.
4. Dad insisted on getting / to get an apology from both of us.
5. My rivals accused me / accused of cheating.
6. We suggested going / that going to a baseball game.
7. Fiona offered to drive us / us drive to the event.
8. He congratulated the winners about / on their performance.

C Write the questions in reported speech.

1. 'Have you ever played tennis?'
   He asked _____

2. 'Why are you throwing in the towel?'
   He asked me _____

3. 'Why don't you take any exercise?'
   She asked me _____

4. 'When will the players be ready to compete?'
   She wanted to know _____

5. 'Did your team get into the final?'
   He asked me _____

6. 'What is your main ambition, Sandra?'
   I asked _____

7. 'Why don't you follow your team's progress, John?'
   I asked _____

8. 'What time must we be there?'
   She wanted to know _____

Exam Task

For questions 1-10, read the text below. Use the word at the end of some of the lines to form a word that fits the gap in the same line.

Motocross

Motocross is a sport that first started in the UK back in the 1930s. Not a (1) _____ for the faint-hearted, it is a tough sport requiring (2) _____ to ride motorbikes across rough terrain in all weather. Originally, the vehicles were regular motorbikes, but soon technical (3) _____ allowed lighter, more agile models to be used. A motocross rider needs a high (4) _____ for fear as the races are fast and dangerous. Riders go through plenty of training to (5) _____ their reactions when driving at high speeds. Some motocross riders branch out into freestyle motocross events where they perform (6) _____ stunts such as jumping over obstacles or through rings of fire. By attracting (7) _____, these events manage to promote motocross and help a new generation of riders who (8) _____ to taking part in thrill-seeking sports to experience the excitement of motocross in a small-scale arena. The international (9) _____ of motocross is that it is a European sport and as a result it has not taken off in the States. However, Supermoto, which was an offshoot of motocross in the 1970s, was recently revived in America and is growing into an (10) _____ event for many young motorbike riders.

PURSUE
CONTEST

SPECIFY
TOLERATE
SHARP

CAPTIVATE
ADMIRE
ASPIRATION
PERCEIVE

INSPIRE

12 Fast Forward

page 147

12.1 **fast forward** (expr) /fɑːst ˈfɔːwəd/
moving ahead at a faster pace than usual
• *Press fast forward on the DVD remote to go more quickly to the next scene.* ❖ γρήγορη προώθηση

Word Focus — page 148

12.2 **recoup** (v) /riːˈkuːp/
get back money you have given or spent
• *He recouped the money he spent on the company when profits increased dramatically.* ❖ ανακτώ, ξανακερδίζω

12.3 **light year** (n) /laɪt jɪə/
a very long time • *Manned space travel to distant planets seems light years away.* ❖ έτος φωτός

12.4 **title deed** (n) /ˈtaɪtl diːd/
a legal document proving your ownership of property • *Frank is the owner of this property so he has the title deed.* ❖ τίτλος ιδιοκτησίας

12.5 **helium** (n) /ˈhiːlɪəm/
a light gas that doesn't burn, often used to fill balloons • *The child's balloon was filled with helium.* ❖ ήλιο

12.6 **trespass** (v) /ˈtrespɑːs/
enter land or building without permission
• *The walkers trespassed on the farmer's land by crossing the field that was marked Private.*
➢ trespasser (n), trespassing (n) ❖ εισέρχομαι παράνομα

12.7 **fuel-laden** (adj) /ˈfjʊəl-ˌleɪdən/
heavily loaded with fuel • *The fuel-laden plane took off for its eight-hour flight to New York.*
❖ φορτωμένος με καύσιμα

12.8 **money-spinner** (n) /ˈmʌni ˈspɪnə/
a project that makes money • *His latest money-spinner is selling tickets for flights to the Moon.* ❖ σχέδιο για να βγάλω χρήματα

12.9 **plot** (n) /plɒt/
a piece of land • *He bought a small plot of land in the countryside.* ❖ κομμάτι γης, οικόπεδο

12.10 **footprint** (n) /ˈfʊtprɪnt/
a mark in the ground left by a foot or shoe
• *I made footprints in the mud as I walked across the field.* ❖ πατημασιά

Reading — pages 148-149

12.11 **state secret** (n) /steɪt ˈsiːkrɪt/
sth only the government knows about • *It's no state secret that NASA have sent a robot to Mars.* ❖ κρατικό μυστικό, απόρρητο

12.12 **allocate** (v) /ˈæləkeɪt/
give for a particular purpose • *The Ministry of Education has allocated money to schools to buy essential equipment.* ➢ allocation (n)
❖ κατανέμω, διαθέτω

12.13 **astronomical** (adj) /ˌɑːstrəˈnɒmɪkl/
enormous • *The banker received an astronomical bonus of three years' salary.*
❖ τεράστιος, αστρονομικός

12.14 **frontier** (n) /ˈfrʌntɪə/
an area where people have never lived before
• *Space is the last frontier, but one day people will establish colonies there.* ❖ σύνορο, όριο

12.15 **foundation** (n) /faʊnˈdeɪʃn/
an organisation that gives money to be used for a special purpose • *The Arts Foundation needs more funds to support young artists.*
➢ found (v) ❖ ίδρυμα

12.16 **settlement** (n) /ˈsetlmənt/
a place where people come to live and build their homes • *This village is on the site of an ancient settlement.* ➢ settle (v), settler (n)
❖ οικισμός

12.17 **commerce** (n) /ˈkɒmɜːs/
business • *He works in commerce as a sales representative.* ➢ commercial (adj) ❖ εμπόριο

12.18 **critical** (adj) /ˈkrɪtɪkl/
very important • *Funds are critical for the expensive project.* ❖ κρίσιμος

12.19 **concrete example** (expr) /ˈkɒŋkriːt ɪksˈɑːmpl/
a specific example • *A concrete example of space exploration is the Moon landing.*
❖ συγκεκριμένο παράδειγμα

12.20 **promising** (adj) /ˈprɒmɪsɪŋ/
likely to succeed • *The promising business venture is bound to be a success.*
➢ promise (v, n) ❖ υποσχόμενος

12.21 **manufacture** (v) /mænjʊˈfæktʃə/
produce; make • *This factory is where they manufacture steel bars for buildings.*
➢ manufacturer (n) ❖ κατασκευάζω

12.22 **lunar colony** (n) /ˈluːnə ˈkɒləni/
a settlement on the Moon • *Would you ever agree to live in a lunar colony?*
❖ σεληνιακή αποικία

12.23 **acre** (n) /ˈeɪkə/
a unit for measuring area (4,047 square metres)
• *This small plot is one acre in size.* ❖ μέτρο εμβαδού, (περίπου τέσσερα στρέμματα)

12.24 **ounce** (n) /aʊns/
a unit for measuring weight (about 28 grams)
• *You need four ounces of butter to make the cake.* ❖ ουγγιά

12.25 back down (phr v) /bæk daʊn/
admit you are wrong • *He knows he's in the wrong, but he refuses to back down.*
❖ υπαναχωρώ

12.26 license (n) /ˈlaɪsəns/
an official document giving permission for sth • *The restaurant doesn't have a license to sell alcohol.* ❖ άδεια
✎ Also: licence (BrE)

12.27 space agency (n) /speɪs ˈeɪdʒənsi/
an organisation that studies and sends people to space • *NASA, the American space agency, has sent a spacecraft to Mars.* ❖ διαστημική υπηρεσία

12.28 treaty (n) /ˈtriːti/
an agreement between countries • *The two countries signed a trade agreement.* ❖ συνθήκη

12.29 stick to one's guns (expr) /stɪk tu wʌnz gʌnz/
refuse to change your opinion • *Dad didn't want me to study drama but I stuck to my guns and applied to drama school.*
❖ δεν αλλάζω γνώμη

12.30 file (v) /faɪl/
give a document to an organisation so it can be officially recorded • *He filed a complaint against his neighbours for being noisy every night.* ❖ υποβάλλω

12.31 ownership (n) /ˈəʊnəʃɪp/
when sth belongs to you • *Gun ownership in America is legal, but many people disagree with it.* ➢ own (v), owner (n) ❖ ιδιοκτησία

12.32 individual (n) /ˌɪndɪˈvɪdʒuəl/
a person • *Each individual in this firm has something to offer.* ➢ individual (adj) ❖ άτομο

12.33 venture (n) /ˈventʃə/
a business that involves risks • *Her business venture succeeded and she made a lot of money.* ❖ επιχείρηση

12.34 part with one's cash (expr) /pɑːt wɪð wʌnz kæʃ/
spend or give away money • *He didn't buy the laptop because he couldn't part with his cash.*
❖ ξοδεύω ή δίνω τα χρήματά μου

12.35 slice (n) /slaɪs/
a thin piece cut from a larger piece • *I put two slices of cheese in my sandwich.* ❖ φέτα

12.36 pay for sth out of one's own pocket (expr) /peɪ fɔː ˈsʌmθɪŋ aʊt ɒv wʌnz əʊn ˈpɒkɪt/
pay for sth using personal funds • *I have to pay for a new phone out of my own pocket because mum hasn't got the money at the moment.* ❖ πληρώνω από την τσέπη μου

Vocabulary pages 150-151

12.37 pattern (v) /ˈpætən/
decorate • *He patterned the wall with a floral design wallpaper.* ➢ pattern (n)
❖ διαμορφώνω, διακοσμώ

12.38 shape one's future (expr) /ʃeɪp wʌnz ˈfjuːtʃə/
determine what will happen to you • *What you decide to study after school will shape your future.* ❖ διαμορφώνω το μέλλον μου

12.39 know what the future holds (expr) /nəʊ wɒt ðə ˈfjuːtʃə həʊldz/
know what will happen in the future
• *Nobody can know what the future holds.*
❖ ξέρω τι επιφυλάσσει το μέλλον

12.40 outcome (n) /ˈaʊtkʌm/
a result • *It is hoped the outcome of the Mars mission will be a success.*
❖ αποτέλεσμα

12.41 upshot (n) /ˈʌpʃɒt/
the result of a series of events • *The upshot of the team's successes is that they are first in the league.* ❖ τελικό αποτέλεσμα, κατάληξη

12.42 hunch (n) /hʌntʃ/
an idea based on a feeling • *I have a hunch that Fred will call today, but I could be wrong.*
❖ προαίσθημα

12.43 educated guess (expr) /æn ˈedʒukeɪtɪd ges/
a guess based on some information you already have • *The scientist made an educated guess about what the terrain on Mars would be like.* ❖ άποψη βασισμένη σε εμπειρία και θεωρητική γνώση

12.44 see sth coming (expr) /siː ˈsʌmθɪŋ ˈkʌmɪŋ/
predict • *'David has decided to drop out of university and become a fisherman.' 'Wow! I didn't see that coming!'.* ❖ περιμένω ότι κάτι θα συμβεί

12.45 omen (n) /ˈəʊmən/
a sign of what will happen in the future
• *Let's hope a rise in the stock markets today is a good omen for the end of the recession.* ➢ ominous (adj) ❖ οιωνός

12.46 mimic (v) /ˈmɪmɪk/
copy what sb does • *The child mimicked his mother and learned by copying her every move.*
➢ mimic (n) ❖ μιμούμαι

12.47 artificial intelligence (n) /ˌɑːtɪˈfɪʃl ɪnˈtelɪdʒəns/
computer technology where computers work in a similar way to human brains
• *Artificial intelligence is used to build computers that learn as they function.*
❖ τεχνητή νοημοσύνη

12.48 humankind (n) /ˈhjuːmənˌkaɪnd/
people • *Humankind is thought to be the only species with a sense of its own demise.*
❖ το ανθρώπινο είδος, ανθρωπότητα

12.49 genetic engineering (n) /dʒəˈnetɪk endʒɪˈnɪərɪŋ/
the science of changing the genetic structure of organisms • *Genetic engineering could find a way of creating humans that live longer.*
❖ γενετική μηχανική

12.50 wireless telecommunications (pl n) /ˈwaɪələs telɪkəmjuːnɪˈkeɪʃnz/
the transfer of information between two or more points that are not connected by an electrical conductor • *Wireless telecommunications have made mobile phones a reality.* ❖ ασύρματες τηλεπικοινωνίες

12.51 speech recognition (n) /spiːtʃ rekəgˈnɪʃn/
the ability of a computer to recognise what sb is saying • *This computer carries out my spoken commands thanks to a speech recognition program.* ❖ αναγνώριση ομιλίας

12.52 eternity (n) /ɪˈtɜːnɪti/
a very long time; the whole of time without any end • *It seemed like an eternity while I was waiting for the bus in the rain.* ➣ eternal (adj) ❖ αιωνιότητα

12.53 infinity (n) /ɪnˈfɪnɪti/
endless space and time • *Numbers never end so you could go on counting to infinity.* ➣ infinite (adj) ❖ άπειρο

12.54 posterity (n) /pɒˈsterəti/
people who will live in the future • *We must save the environment for ourselves and for posterity.* ❖ απόγονοι

12.55 immortal (adj) /ɪˈmɔːtəl/
living for ever • *The Greek gods were immortal.* ➣ immortality (n) ❖ αθάνατος
✎ Opp: mortal

12.56 intended (adj) /ɪnˈtendɪd/
meant • *The intended result was to make a lovely cake but this mess looks like something else.* ➣ intend (v) ❖ επιδιωκόμενος

12.57 perpetual (adj) /pəˈpetʊəl/
continuing forever in the same way • *The robber lived in perpetual fear of being caught by the police.* ❖ διαρκής

12.58 timeless (adj) /ˈtaɪmləs/
not changing as the years go by; not becoming old-fashioned • *The most stylish clothes are timeless and have nothing to do with fashion.* ➣ time (v, n) ❖ διαχρονικός

12.59 pioneering (adj) /paɪəˈnɪərɪŋ/
introducing new ideas for the first time • *Bill Gates is a pioneering businessman who helped create the technology we know today.* ➣ pioneer (v, n) ❖ πρωτοποριακός

12.60 preceding (adj) /prɪˈsiːdɪŋ/
happening before sth else • *The programme preceding this one finished five minutes ago.* ➣ precede (v) ❖ προηγούμενος

12.61 visionary (adj) /ˈvɪʒənri/
having new ideas for the future • *Visionary people see a future where living on other planets is possible.* ➣ vision (n) ❖ διορατικός

12.62 looming (adj) /ˈluːmɪŋ/
having a threatening appearance • *Bad weather was looming and the sky was as black as night.* ➣ loom (v) ❖ που εμφανίζεται (απειλητικά)

12.63 menacing (adj) /ˈmenəsɪŋ/
threatening • *They were scared of his menacing manner and knew he meant to do them harm.* ➣ menace (v, n) ❖ απειλητικός

12.64 anticipated (adj) /ænˈtɪsɪpeɪtɪd/
expected • *The anticipated storm hit the area as predicted in the night.* ➣ anticipate (v), anticipation (n) ❖ αναμενόμενος

12.65 fated (adj) /ˈfeɪtɪd/
bound to happen • *He was fated to meet his death on that long journey.* ➣ fate (n) ❖ προδιαγεγραμμένος, γραμμένος από τη μοίρα

12.66 rational (adj) /ˈræʃənəl/
based on reason • *She is a rational person so she will definitely accept a reasonable explanation.* ➣ rationale (n) ❖ λογικός
✎ Opp: irrational

12.67 unexpected (adj) /ʌnɪksˈpektɪd/
not predicted • *We had an unexpected visit from Kay who dropped by to surprise us.* ➣ expect (v) ❖ απροσδόκητος, απρόοπτος

12.68 unforeseen (adj) /ʌnfɔːˈsiːn/
not predicted • *The unforeseen market crash was a shock to all investors.* ➣ foresee (v) ❖ απρόβλεπτος

12.69 disposable (adj) /dɪsˈpəʊzəbl/
which can be thrown away • *We used disposable plates at the picnic and threw them away in the bin.* ➣ dispose (v), disposal (n) ❖ μίας χρήσης

12.70 inescapable (adj) /ɪnɪsˈkeɪpəbl/
impossible to escape; bound to happen • *It's an inescapable fact they we will all die one day.* ➣ escape (v, n) ❖ αναπόφευκτος

12.71 inevitable (adj) /ɪnˈevɪtəbl/
impossible to avoid • *He drove so carelessly that the accident was inevitable.* ➣ inevitability (n) ❖ αναπόφευκτος

12.72 showpiece (n) /ˈʃəʊpiːs/
a very good example of sth that a government or organisation wants people to see • *The museum will be the new showpiece of the city when it opens next year.* ❖ έξοχο δείγμα, έκθεμα

12.73 infrastructure (n) /ˈɪnfrəˌstrʌktʃə/
facilities that make a place function • *Funding for the infrastructure of the city should lead to more building and road systems.* ❖ υποδομή

12.74 ongoing (adj) /ɒnˈɡəʊɪŋ/
continuing • *Ongoing space exploration has sent a rocket to Mars, where information is being gathered.* ❖ συνεχιζόμενος

12.75 boast (v) /bəʊst/
have sth that you are proud of • *Greece boasts some of the most beautiful islands in the world.* ❖ περηφανεύομαι, καυχιέμαι

12.76 initial (adj) /ɪˈnɪʃl/
first • *The initial plan was to go to Italy but we changed our minds and went to France.* ➣ initially (adv) ❖ αρχικός

12.77 **set the pace** (expr) /set ðə peɪs/
create an example for others to copy
• The athlete in the lead set the pace for the 1500m heat. ❖ καθορίζω το ρυθμό

12.78 **geneticist** (n) /dʒəˈnetɪsɪst/
sb who is an expert in genetics • She is a geneticist and she studies rare human genes. ❖ γενετιστής

12.79 **trend** (n) /trend/
a tendency • The trend for humans to be taller may be due to better nutrition.
➢ trendy (adj) ❖ τάση

12.80 **upper** (adj) /ˈʌpə/
in a higher position than sth else • The upper limit for buildings in this area is six storeys, no higher. ❖ ανώτερος

12.81 **far-fetched** (adj) /ˌfɑː-ˈfetʃt/
very unlikely to be true • His story about breaking the world record is far-fetched, and I don't believe him. ❖ απίθανος, εξεζητημένος

Time
eternity
immortal
infinity
light year
perpetual
timeless

Grammar   pages 152-153

12.82 **investment** (n) /ɪnˈvestmənt/
when you spend a large amount of time or energy on sth • Becoming a doctor means a huge investment of your time and energy for many years. ➢ invest (v), investor (n) ❖ επένδυση

12.83 **privacy** (n) /ˈprɪvəsi/
being alone; freedom from public attention • I have six brothers and sisters, so I don't get much privacy at home. ➢ private (adj)
❖ προστασία της ιδιωτικής ζωής, ησυχία

12.84 **rover** (n) /ˈrəʊvə/
a remotely operated vehicle used to explore Mars • The data from the soil sample collected by the rover on Mars was studied by NASA scientists. ❖ τηλεκατευθυνόμενο διαστημικό όχημα, ρόβερ

12.85 **outdo** (v) /ˌaʊtˈduː/
do better or more than sb/sth else • She outdid everyone else in the competition and won first prize. ❖ ξεπερνώ

12.86 **set one's sights on sth** (expr)
/set wʌnz saɪts ɒn ˈsʌmθɪŋ/
decide you want sth and try to get it • He has set his sights on becoming a doctor. ❖ βάζω στόχο

12.87 **prestige** (n) /presˈtiʒ/
respect and admiration given to sb, usually because of high quality or success • The opera singer has gained international prestige.
➢ prestigious (adj) ❖ κύρος

12.88 **at stake** (expr) /ɑːt steɪk/
at risk • The scientist's reputation would be at stake if the experiment failed.
❖ που διακυβεύομαι

12.89 **beam** (v) /biːm/
send (radio or television) signals over a long distance • The images were beamed to Earth from space. ➢ beam (n) ❖ εκπέμπω

12.90 **humanity** (n) /hjuːˈmænɪti/
people • Caring for the environment is something all of humanity should be involved with. ❖ ανθρωπότητα

12.91 **solar system** (n) /ˈsəʊlə ˈsɪstəm/
the planets around a sun • Earth is the only inhabited planet in our solar system.
❖ ηλιακό σύστημα

12.92 **requisite** (adj) /ˈrekwɪzɪt/
necessary • He had the requisite training to be an astronaut so he was accepted on the space mission. ❖ απαιτούμενος

12.93 **equation** (n) /ɪˈkweɪʒn/
a mathematical statement showing that two amounts are equal • One of the most famous equations in the world is $E = mc^2$. ❖ εξίσωση

12.94 **particle physics** (n) /ˈpɑːtɪkl ˈfɪzɪks/
the study of the very small parts that make up an atom • He is studying particle physics at university. ❖ πυρηνική φυσική

12.95 **lose one's temper** (expr) /luːz wʌnz ˈtempə/
get angry • Sharon lost her temper and shouted angrily at Jack when he broke her new phone. ❖ χάνω την ψυχραιμία μου

Listening   page 154

12.96 **not break the bank** (expr)
/nɒt breɪk ðə bæŋk/
not cost a lot of money • That dress is lovely, and it won't break the bank either!
❖ δεν είναι ακριβός

12.97 **omission** (n) /əˈmɪʃən/
not including sb/sth when they should have been included • There are some very serious omissions in the book so I don't think you should use it as a source.
❖ παράλειψη, αμέλεια

12.98 **biodiesel** (n) /ˈbaɪəʊdiːzəl/
fuel made from agricultural products • It is feasible that in the future cars will run on biodiesel rather than petrol.
❖ βιοντίζελ

12.99 **demonstration** (n) /demənˈstreɪʃn/
showing how to do sth or how sth works • The lecturer gave the chemistry students a demonstration of the experiment to show them how to do it. ➢ demonstrate (v)
❖ επίδειξη

Writing: an essay (2) pages 156-157

12.100 primitive (adj) /ˈprɪmətɪv/
belonging to a very simple society • *They live in a primitive house with no electricity or running water.* ❖ πρωτόγονος
✎ Opp: advanced; sophisticated

12.101 pessimistic (adj) /pesɪˈmɪstɪk/
believing that bad things will happen in the future • *He is pessimistic and thinks he has failed his exams.* ➢ pessimism (n) ❖ απαισιόδοξος
✎ Opp: optimistic

12.102 optimistic (adj) /ɒptɪˈmɪstɪk/
believing that good things will happen in the future • *She feels optimistic that she will do well in all of her exams.* ➢ optimism (n), optimistically (adv) ❖ αισιόδοξος
✎ Opp: pessimistic

12.103 doom (v) /duːm/
be sure to fail, die, etc. • *Unfortunately, their efforts were doomed to failure.* ➢ doom (n, v) ❖ καταδικάζω

12.104 seek to do sth (expr) /siːk tə du ˈsʌmθɪŋ/
try to do sth • *The teenager is seeking to become more independent.* ❖ προσπαθώ να κάνω κάτι, επιδιώκω

12.105 defining feature (expr) /dɪˈfaɪnɪŋ ˈfiːtʃə/
aspect that describes what sth is • *A defining feature of humans is their curiosity about the world around them.* ❖ χαρακτηριστικό στοιχείο

12.106 materialise (v) /məˈtɪərɪəlaɪz/
happen in the way you expect • *Her hopes of becoming an astronaut never materialised.* ❖ πραγματοποιούμαι

12.107 greed (n) /griːd/
desire to have more than you need • *Because of greed he would not share his good fortune with his poor neighbours.* ➢ greedy (adj) ❖ απληστία

12.108 altruism (n) /ˈæltruɪzm/
caring about others, even when this is at a cost to yourself • *The doctor showed true altruism when he left his job to work with war refugees.* ❖ αλτρουϊσμός

Video 12: Space Walk page 158

12.109 pressurised (adj) /ˈpreʃəraɪzd/
If a container is pressurised, the air inside it is kept at a controlled pressure. • *The marine biologists were safe inside the pressurised submarine as they dived to the depths of the ocean.* ➢ pressure (n) ❖ συμπιεσμένος

12.110 vacuum (n) /ˈvækjuːm/
a space with no gas inside it • *Astronauts would never survive in the vacuum of space without a special suit.* ❖ κενό αέρος

12.111 shuttle (n) /ˈʃʌtl/
a spacecraft which goes beyond the Earth's atmosphere and returns like a plane • *The shuttle was the first craft to leave the earth's atmosphere and return.* ❖ διαστημικό λεωφορείο

12.112 radiation (n) /reɪdɪˈeɪʃn/
dangerous energy sent out from some substances • *The radiation in the earth was being measured with a Geiger counter.* ➢ radioactive (adj) ❖ ραδιενέργεια

12.113 tough (adj) /tʌf/
strong • *Jeans are made of tough material that doesn't rip easily.* ➢ toughness (n) ❖ σκληρός

12.114 orbit (n) /ˈɔːbɪt/
the path travelled by an object moving around another, larger object • *The space station is in orbit around the Earth and is actually visible from the ground.* ➢ orbit (v) ❖ τροχιά

Vocabulary Exercises

A **Complete the table.**

Nouns	Adjectives
astronomy	1
promise	2
immortality	3
time	4
vision	5
menace	6
threat	7
anticipation	8
fate	9
pioneer	10
disposal	11
optimism	12

B **Match.**

1 Who has the title
2 The project could be a money-
3 Can you give me a concrete
4 It's no state
5 I would live on a lunar
6 This software uses state-of-the-art artificial
7 Do you think genetic
8 Count the planets in our solar

a example to illustrate what you mean?
b deed to this plot of land?
c spinner that should make us rich.
d colony if I had the opportunity.
e engineering is ethical?
f secret that he's a millionaire.
g system, please, children.
h intelligence.

C **Read the definitions and complete the words.**

1 a business that involves risks   v _ _ _ _ _ _
2 believing bad things will happen in the future: p _ _ _ _ _ _ _ _ _
3 a space with no gases in it: v _ _ _ _ _
4 an agreement between countries: t _ _ _ _ _
5 endless space and time: i _ _ _ _ _ _ _
6 impossible to avoid: i _ _ _ _ _ _ _ _
7 very unlikely to be true: f _ _ - _ _ _ _ _ _ _
8 facilities that make a place function: i _ _ _ _ _ _ _ _ _ _ _ _
9 a place where people come to live and build their homes: s _ _ _ _ _ _ _ _
10 a tendency: t _ _ _ _

12 Grammar

12.1 Clauses of Reason

Για να δείξουμε την αιτία μιας συγκεκριμένης κατάστασης, μπορούμε να χρησιμοποιήσουμε τις παρακάτω λέξεις: *so, because of, for, because, owing to, due to, as, since, seeing that/as, with*.
→ **Since** we are eating healthier food, we should also be getting more exercise.
→ Some people are against space exploration **because** it requires huge sums of money.
→ **With** so many things to see in Shanghai, we'll never feel bored.
→ Why don't we check out the Maglev, **seeing that/as** it's the fastest train in the world?

12.2 Clauses of Purpose and Result

Για να δείξουμε τον σκοπό μιας συγκεκριμένης κατάστασης, μπορούμε να χρησιμοποιήσουμε τις παρακάτω λέξεις: *so that, in order to, so as to, for* και το full infinitive (απαρέμφατο με *to*).
→ We can use technology **in order to / so as to** fight poverty.
→ Telescopes are used **to observe / for observing** outer space.

Για να δείξουμε το σκοπό μιας συγκεκριμένης κατάστασης, μπορούμε να χρησιμοποιήσουμε τις παρακάτω λέξεις: *so, such a(n), so many, so much, so few, so little, too/not enough + to*.
→ The Moon landing was **such an extraordinary event (that)** the whole world watched it on TV.

12.3 Clauses of Contrast

Μπορούμε να εκφράσουμε αντίθεση με τις παρακάτω λέξεις: *despite, in spite of, despite the fact that, in spite of the fact that, however, nevertheless, although, though, even though, whereas, while*.
→ **Even though** biodiesel is an eco-friendly fuel, it isn't widely available.
→ **In spite of** the huge cost, space programmes continue to be supported by governments.

12.4 *Neither ... nor*

Neither ... nor σημαίνει 'ούτε ... ούτε'. Τα υποκείμενα που συνδέονται με το *neither ... nor* συντάσσονται με ρήμα ενικού ή πληθυντικού αριθμού, ανάλογα με το υποκείμενο που βρίσκεται πιο κοντά στο ρήμα.
→ **Neither** Adrian **nor** Carlos **wants** to take part in the space flight.
→ **Neither** Ed **nor** his classmates **were** able to solve the mathematical equation.

12.5 *Either ... or*

Χρησιμοποιούμε *either ... or* (είτε ... είτε) για να πούμε ότι μπορούμε να διαλέξουμε ανάμεσα σε δύο πιθανές επιλογές.
→ Our annual budget will finance **either** educational programmes **or** space programmes.
→ **Either** John **or** Bill can come with us.

Χρησιμοποιούμε *not ... either ... or* για να εκφράσουμε άρνηση και προς τις δύο πιθανές επιλογές.
→ I do**n't** believe **either** my brother **or** my sister will become teachers.
→ I was**n't** especially good at **either** chemistry **or** biology.

Χρησιμοποιούμε *not either* μετά από αρνητική πρόταση.
→ He isn't interested in training to become an astronaut and I'm **not either**.
→ I wouldn't buy a plot on the Moon and my friends would**n't either**.

Grammar Exercises

A **Complete the sentences with the correct prepositions.**
1. We are unable to continue the research owing _____ lack of funds.
2. The astronaut had to leave the programme because _____ ill health.
3. She went to university _____ order to study astrophysics.
4. I am much poorer _____ my unwise business deal, which lost me money.
5. _____ spite of the weather, he studied the night sky every winter night.
6. This program is used _____ predict future weather patterns.
7. _____ the reputation of the school at stake, I want our team to win that cup!
8. I carried on playing in spite _____ the fact that I had a hamstring injury.

B **Complete the sentences with one word in each gap.**
1. _____ it is such a long report, you can have another week to do it.
2. I moved abroad _____ there were no jobs at home.
3. Let's share the cost _____ as we are both a bit short of cash.
4. This speech recognition program is too hard _____ understand.
5. Your idea to live on the Moon is _____ silly that I am astonished you mentioned it.
6. She wanted to learn to fly _____ she applied for lessons.
7. _____ he is over fifty, he can still train to become an astronaut.
8. _____ the fact that she has vertigo, she climbed up the tower.

C **Circle the correct words.**
1. Neither John nor Larry **like / likes** physics homework.
2. 'Which did you prefer of the first two *Star Wars* movies?' 'I didn't like **neither / either** of them.'
3. Either Jane **nor / or** Chris is going to help me with my report.
4. **Nor / Neither** of my brothers has ever flown.
5. Neither my sister nor my friends **send / sends** me emails regularly.
6. **Either of / Either** the kids could have broken your vase.
7. I asked my brothers to watch a film with me, but **either / neither** of them could.
8. Neither Robert **nor / or** Stuart went to the film premiere.

12 Grammar

Exam Task

For questions 1-6, complete the second sentence so that it has a similar meaning to the first sentence, using the word given. Do not change the word given. You must use between three and six words, including the word given.

1 I couldn't answer the first question or the second question in the exam.
   EITHER
   I couldn't answer _____ question in the exam.

2 In the end, the investor withdrew from the project.
   DOWN
   In the end, the investor _____ the project.

3 When he heard I had failed, he got angry, just as I had expected.
   TEMPER
   When he heard I had failed, _____, just as I had expected.

4 I knew you were going to do that so it's no surprise.
   SAW
   I _____ so it's no surprise.

5 I'm telling you Fred isn't an athletic type and Joe isn't one either.
   NEITHER
   I'm telling you that _____ an athletic type.

6 Even though we live in Frankfurt, neither my mum nor my dad can speak German.
   OF
   Even though we live in Frankfurt, _____ German.

Alphabetical Word List

An alphabetical list of all the words that appear in the companion follows. The number next to the entry shows where the word appears.

A

a bite to eat   10.17
a frog in one's throat   2.92
a host of   2.99
a hot potato   5.112
a little bird told me   2.91
a pain in the neck   3.144
abject poverty   8.127
aboard   10.23
abridged   9.8
absent-minded   3.51
absorb   5.149
acceleration   1.174
accessible   2.65
acclaim   1.10
accompany   3.14
accomplish   1.65
accomplished   1.161
account   8.29
accountant   8.114
accrue   1.63
ace   11.74
achievement   1.2
acidic   5.48
acquire   7.39
acre   12.23
adaptable   1.100
addictive   2.8
adhere to   11.29
admirer   11.71
admit defeat   1.70
admit defeat   10.95
adolescent   2.24
adrenaline   11.4
advantageous   8.59
advent   2.98
affluent   8.67
agility   7.8
agricultural   10.110
air one's views   2.13
air raid siren   9.36
aisle   4.49
all rolled into one   4.119
alley   8.138
allocate   12.12
allure   4.65
alternative   3.126
alternative to   6.97
altruism   12.108
amnesia   3.2
anaesthetise   10.133
anchor   10.19

anglerfish   7.137
animate   4.72
anorexic   3.45
anterograde amnesia   3.7
anthropologist   2.33
anticipated   12.64
antioxidant   5.21
antiquity   7.76
apathy   9.39
apparatus   7.46
appealing   1.144
appetising   5.61
applaud   11.113
appliance   7.114
application   4.24
appoint   1.158
apprehensive   1.104
approach   1.175
apt   8.32
army of ants   6.104
arrowhead   10.10
artefact   7.104
artificial   7.33
artificial intelligence   12.47
aspect   1.147
aspire   11.104
assemble   7.85
assembly line   7.80
assess   10.101
asset   1.156
assumption   7.50
astronomical   12.13
at a guess   2.84
at a moment's notice   4.90
at regular intervals   11.36
at stake   12.88
at the expense of   8.136
attention deficit disorder   3.106
attribute   1.160
auction   8.142
audition   4.95
auditorium   5.141
authenticity   9.105
authority   9.104
automated   7.20
aviation   7.35
aviator   7.40

B

baby boomer   1.56
back down   12.25
backer   11.138

backing singer   9.66
backstage   4.50
backup   8.3
ban   5.152
banish   5.30
bank balance   8.81
bank statement   8.82
bank teller   8.57
banquet   5.52
bare-bones   1.6
bargain for sth SB   11.142
bark   3.70
barren   6.111
barrier   1.28
bartering   8.8
bat   11.78
baton   11.85
battery hen   5.136
be at each other's throats   3.99
be at odds   6.157
be cut out   11.53
be entitled   11.55
be first out of the gate   11.134
be in good hands   11.149
be in the money   8.90
be in two minds   6.134
be made redundant   8.38
be married off   4.41
be on the go   9.18
be on the other side of the fence   11.144
be on the tip of your tongue   3.103
be pushed for time   6.136
be up in arms   6.63
be up to scratch   1.143
beam   1.40
beam   12.89
bear in mind   11.16
beat   5.86
beat   9.41
beat down   6.82
bed of snakes   6.103
bedspread   5.144
bend   11.17
beneficial   3.40
berry   6.73
beverage   5.83
bewilderment   3.15
binding   11.25
biodiesel   12.98
biodiversity   6.139
bird of prey   1.166

bite sb's head off   3.97
bitter   2.27
bivouac   1.5
bizarre   6.129
black market   8.75
blanch   5.55
bland   5.59
blast   2.50
bleak   10.130
blend   5.40
blistering   6.41
blockbuster   4.9
blood bank   3.52
blood donor   3.53
blood pressure   3.55
blood transfusion   3.57
blood vessel   3.56
blow one's own trumpet   9.86
blow over   6.86
blow sb away   1.108
blow up   6.83
blowy   6.52
blunder   3.3
blustery   6.53
boast   9.87
boast   12.75
bodily function   3.82
bold   1.71
bolt   11.27
bolt   11.94
bomb   9.100
bond   8.9
bony   3.44
boom   8.66
born and bred   10.7
bother   2.57
bounce   11.97
bounce back   10.84
bowl   11.98
box clever   1.133
box office   4.107
brand   9.93
brand new   10.103
breadline   8.1
break a leg   4.102
break through   1.109
breakthrough   2.37
breed   1.141
breezy   6.54
brew   5.98
brief   10.20
bright   6.44

137

bright spark 1.134
bring about 1.57
bring down 2.70
bring on 3.115
bring to mind 8.23
broadcast 11.56
broaden one's horizons 2.108
bronze 7.102
browsing 10.81
bruise 3.87
bucket 11.161
bucket down 6.84
buckle 11.24
budgeting 8.121
bumblebee 7.34
bunch 2.30
burden 2.55
burn the candle at both ends 10.89
burning desire 11.54
bustling 8.60
buzzer 11.83
by a mile 1.119
by heart 9.81
by-product 6.5

C

candid 1.96
captivating 11.67
captivity 2.124
capture 4.33
carpenter 9.101
carry out 10.24
carving 9.47
cash flow 8.117
cast 4.80
cat's got your tongue 2.93
catapult 8.17
catch up 11.118
cater for 9.16
catwalk 4.43
cautious 1.92
chain of events 6.22
challenger 1.168
change one's tune 9.82
changing room 11.155
chant 3.152
charcoal 5.148
charity 6.117
charming 11.68
chart 7.131
chart 9.28
cheat death 2.29
check out 9.12
cheer sb on 1.145
chest of drawers 9.102
chew 5.28
chic 4.64
chick flick 4.58

chickpea 5.133
chip in 8.69
chop 5.38
chop and change 10.8
chunk 3.19
circulation 8.40
clay 9.48
clean sth out 5.123
clear 6.33
clear up 6.85
clerical staff 1.150
climb the corporate ladder 10.70
climb up the career ladder 10.109
club 11.77
cognition 5.5
coin 7.97
coincidental 6.18
colleague 10.71
combination 4.135
come down with 3.73
come in for 2.15
come in handy 11.58
come over 1.148
come to a halt 11.120
come up against 1.110
commemorate 6.133
comment 2.1
commentator 11.61
commerce 12.17
commission 9.59
commit 11.107
commute 10.36
compile 4.70
compliment 11.141
component 7.63
composition 6.12
comprise 8.44
computerised 7.48
conceited 1.105
concept 9.60
concrete example 12.19
condiment 5.2
conduct 3.119
conductor 7.61
confidential 2.110
confine (to) 2.12
conquer 11.92
conservation 2.128
considerate 1.101
consist of 6.11
construction 7.25
consult 3.26
consumption 5.22
contaminating 5.151
contemplation 6.154
contempt of court 4.110
contend 11.93
contented 3.49

contestant 11.151
continental 6.107
contract 3.123
contraption 11.158
contributor 4.13
control panel 7.79
controversial 4.109
convenience 10.125
conventional 3.125
coordinator 2.119
cope 3.147
copper 7.60
core 9.22
corporate sponsor 1.20
correspondence 1.151
corrode 7.65
corrupt 2.78
cosmopolitan 10.53
cost an arm and a leg 9.11
cost effective 7.21
couch-bound 10.79
counterfeit 8.41
counterpart 5.23
courgette 8.36
courteous 1.153
courtesy of 9.13
cover 11.64
cover one's costs 8.28
cover version 9.70
covering 5.70
CPR 3.130
crack 5.87
craft 7.110
craftsman 8.140
crafty 1.82
cramped 11.156
crash 8.48
crave 11.46
craving 5.6
crawl 2.20
credit 8.30
credit card fraud 2.112
credit crunch 8.2
credit limit 8.88
credit rating 8.89
creepy crawly 3.142
crevasse 1.51
crew 4.86
crime rate 10.62
crippling 8.101
critical 12.18
criticism 2.11
crucial 4.73
crusader 10.37
crush 1.30
cube 7.55
cuisine 5.35
culinary 5.36
culminate 9.27
culprit 10.77

cultivate 5.68
culture vulture 9.1
cunning 1.83
curiosity 7.126
curl up 7.24
currency 8.22
custard 5.147
cut (sth) off 2.46
cut down on 5.11
cut in 2.71
cut out 5.132
cutting edge 7.88
cutting-edge 4.26
cuttlefish 5.129
cyborg 2.32
cylinder 7.56

D

dandruff 3.104
daring 4.40
dash 11.95
date 8.139
dated 4.122
day-care 10.35
dazzling 11.69
deafening 9.117
debit 8.31
debt 8.19
debut 9.74
decibel 9.29
dedicate 11.108
dedicated 10.30
deem 4.74
defend 2.49
defining feature 12.105
deforestation 3.153
defy 4.30
dehydrated 3.34
delicate 3.46
delirium 3.41
demise 6.123
demonstration 12.99
denomination 8.42
dense 7.71
deny 4.21
depict 1.146
deposit 8.116
deprived 9.25
derive 7.77
derive 8.105
descent 1.18
despair 8.14
desperate 4.23
detention centre 9.7
deter 5.33
detractor 2.76
devaluation 8.7
devastation 10.47
device 2.105

devoid (of)   10.57
devote   11.109
diabetes   3.150
diced   5.102
digest   5.117
dime   11.140
dine out   5.90
director   4.12
dirt   6.56
dirt cheap   8.129
disability   9.21
discard   7.51
discipline   10.123
discrete   7.141
discriminate   1.54
disgraceful   5.118
dishcloth   5.66
disinterest   10.112
disorder   3.43
dispense   3.133
disperse   6.88
displace   7.59
disposable   12.69
disprove   7.100
disqualify   11.110
dissolve   5.77
distance   2.42
distinguish   1.55
distinguished   9.17
disturb   1.138
diving   11.90
do away with sth   7.31
do one's best   1.126
do sth on a shoestring   8.99
do the trick   1.124
do without   10.85
domain   2.69
dominance   1.135
dominant   4.27
don   11.2
donation   3.61
doodle   9.46
doom   12.103
double-edged sword   2.115
down-and-out   8.119
downgrading   8.6
download   9.30
down-to-earth   8.126
drama queen   4.103
draw   6.148
dress rehearsal   4.79
dressing room   4.75
dribbling   11.91
drill   6.58
drive   11.79
drizzly   6.39
drop back   11.120
drop the ball   11.136
drought   6.90
drove of cattle   6.101

drowning   7.139
dry up   6.87
dull   6.47
dumb down   1.131
dump   6.55
dyke   6.166

E

eager   10.34
ease   9.118
easel   9.49
eat on the hoof   5.135
eat up   5.1
eatable   5.74
ecstatic   4.36
edgy   9.115
edible   5.75
editor   4.106
educated guess   12.43
eel   7.138
efficient   7.84
elaborate   6.165
electrifying   4.34
element   6.32
elevation   6.116
embrace   11.39
emerge   6.25
emit   6.30
emotional   3.33
enable   1.44
encounter   2.101
endangered   2.122
endeavour   9.20
endure   6.23
engineer   7.109
enhance   8.46
enlist   4.44
enquiring mind   7.128
ensure   11.30
entail   1.149
entrepreneur   1.60
enviously   4.92
equation   12.93
erase   9.19
erode   7.66
erupt   7.72
essentials   1.21
establish   3.60
eternity   12.52
ethnic   5.79
evaluation   7.124
evil-doer   4.115
evolution   1.58
evolve   2.97
excavation   10.25
exceed   1.169
excel   10.68
exchange rate   8.10
exclusive   1.12

execute   1.46
exhilarating   4.11
expand   7.69
expedition   1.13
exploitable   4.61
explosive   7.68
exposure   5.31
extend   7.70
extensive   3.154
extinct   2.123
extra   4.87
extract   5.78
extravagantly   8.95
eyebrow   4.126

F

façade   9.122
face   1.49
face the music   9.83
facet   7.140
failing eyesight   3.83
faint-hearted   4.48
fair   1.88
fair   6.45
fake   8.134
falcon   1.164
fall at the first hurdle   11.137
fall behind   8.115
fall through   1.112
fall to   4.28
famished   5.50
farewell   8.74
far-fetched   12.81
fashion   6.81
fast forward   12.1
fasten   11.35
fated   12.65
fatty acid   5.4
fearlessness   1.43
feasible   11.51
feast   5.51
feast for the eyes   4.120
feature-length   4.19
feel sth in one's bones   6.119
female lead   4.76
ferric   6.16
ferrous   6.15
festive   5.140
fever   3.69
fibre   3.140
field notes   10.26
field work   10.13
fierce opposition   4.25
fight off   3.74
figure   11.66
file   12.30
filling   10.131
film buff   4.1
filter   7.52

filthy rich   8.128
fine   6.46
firmly   11.33
fit   3.89
fizzy   5.24
flair   1.162
flamboyantly   4.84
flavouring   5.76
flawless   7.78
flaxseed   5.20
flea   3.124
flea market   8.76
fledgling   10.74
flee   4.39
flexible   7.22
floating   6.171
flood   6.158
flourish   8.65
fluid   8.78
follower   2.16
food chain   6.140
food voucher   8.11
footage   4.2
footboard   11.19
footprint   12.10
for my money   8.91
forbidding   6.109
forefront   7.87
foremost   8.64
forgery   8.43
forgetful   3.48
fork out   8.70
formation   6.9
formative years   10.12
fortification   10.5
fossil fuel   6.98
foundation   12.15
founder   1.61
foyer   4.51
fraction   7.81
fragile   10.38
fragrant   6.150
frame   7.28
free-for-all   9.10
free-range   5.137
fresco   9.57
frontier   12.14
frustrated   4.104
fuel-laden   12.7
fulfil   10.111
full of beans   5.110
fund   8.51
fundamental   4.128

G

gadget   2.106
galley   10.1
game   11.11
gaping   1.50

gather 10.14
gauze 3.88
GCSE 2.23
gear 10.22
gemstone 7.74
gender 1.27
genetic engineering 12.49
genetically modified 3.105
geneticist 12.78
get a kick out of sth 11.143
get ahead 1.113
get around 3.146
get back at 2.72
get by 10.67
get cold feet 3.98
get one's money worth 8.92
get one's wires crossed 7.89
get the green light 1.127
get there 1.122
geyser 7.112
give sth up 11.150
give the go-ahead 11.15
give way 7.23
glimpse 7.133
glitch 7.91
global warming 6.155
gloomy 6.48
go all out 1.125
go blank 2.80
go for it 1.116
go off 5.130
go on 1.29
go places 1.128
go without a hitch 1.121
gobble 5.45
graduate 10.60
grain 5.119
grant 7.101
graphic artist 9.106
grate 5.39
graveyard 3.118
gravity 4.31
greed 12.107
greenhouse gas 6.21
groggy 2.41
ground-breaking 1.34
gruelling 2.4
guild 8.68
gulp 5.126
gum 3.110
gusty 6.34
guts 2.85
gutsy 1.72

H

habituation 5.32
haggling 8.12
hail 1.45
hamstring 11.127

handicrafts 9.107
handle 11.21
hands down 4.124
hang on 1.114
hard to come by 10.98
hardback 7.3
hardship 10.66
hard-up 8.26
harness 1.170
harness 6.10
harshly 8.102
harvest 5.69
hassle-free 3.141
hat trick 2.77
have (got) a lot of one's plate 1.117
have a change of heart 3.96
have deep pockets 8.98
have egg on one's face 5.106
have money to burn 8.123
have one's cake and eat it too 5.99
have sb in one's corner 11.135
have sb's best interests at heart 11.148
have sth at one's fingertips 2.116
have what it takes 11.13
head (for) 10.18
headstrong 1.97
heal 3.62
healer 3.155
heart-rending 4.37
heartthrob 4.69
heart-warming 4.20
heat 11.124
heat stroke 3.139
hectic 10.48
helium 12.5
helping 5.63
hide out 6.128
highbrow 9.3
highlight 1.26
high-powered 10.124
hinder 11.101
hippodrome 10.4
hit rock bottom 10.90
hit the bull's eye 11.139
hit the road 10.64
hold sb back 11.44
home turf 1.33
hone 11.105
honourable 1.74
hospitality 6.143
hostile 6.108
hours on end 2.34
house-bound 8.133
hue 7.105
humanity 12.90
humankind 12.48
humid 6.49

hunch 12.42
hunter-gatherer 6.71
hysteria 3.42

I

ideal 2.54
identify 2.66
identity theft 2.111
ignorant 1.106
illiterate 4.45
imbalance 3.91
immersed 4.35
immortal 12.55
impact 10.126
impartial 1.89
impetuous 1.93
impose 7.136
in a matter of 11.116
in agony 3.81
in character 4.85
in confidence 2.81
in good shape 10.15
in harmony 9.77
in tandem with 8.4
in the region of 8.113
in working order 10.45
incident 5.128
income 10.65
inconclusive 6.135
incorporate 10.122
incur 11.32
indifferent 6.95
individual 12.32
industrial 1.35
industrious 1.64
inequality 3.92
inescapable 12.70
inevitable 12.71
infectious 3.116
infinity 12.53
inflate 1.171
inflation 8.5
inflexible 1.107
infrastructure 12.73
inhabit 4.93
initial 12.76
initiative 10.100
injure 3.64
ink 9.51
inner 11.20
innovation 7.82
input 11.154
insect repellent 3.145
insignificant 3.23
insist 1.66
insistence (on) 6.100
inspire 1.14
install 2.94
instant 1.36

instigate 9.5
instruction manual 7.93
intact 11.9
intellect 9.26
intended 12.56
interact 2.35
interactive whiteboard 10.119
interest rate 8.37
interfere (with) 6.99
internal organ 3.84
internship 11.60
interpreter 11.62
interval 4.52
intravenous 3.54
inundated 4.3
invest 8.55
investment 12.82
ioniser 5.150
iron 6.14
irrigation screw 7.10
irritable 10.82
irritating 2.9
itinerary 2.95

J

jaw 1.142
juggle 10.6
justification 7.125
juvenile 6.131

K

kaftan 8.141
keep your chin up 3.101
keep your head above water 10.91
kiln 7.4
knock out 11.122
know what the future holds 12.39
knuckle down 1.115

L

lace with 5.15
lagoon 6.142
laid-back 6.124
land a part 10.108
landfall 6.69
landfill 6.64
landscape 9.56
landslide 6.70
lane 11.86
lap 11.87
lashes 4.127
launch 1.25
laundry 8.103
lavish 8.125
lay the foundations 7.127
layer 4.132

lead 11.84
lead vocalist 9.67
leading 8.61
leading man 4.100
lean on sb 11.131
leap 1.39
learned 2.3
leftovers 5.81
legal tender 8.13
legitimate 2.63
lend a hand 10.31
let alone 8.39
let-down 4.121
license 12.26
life expectancy 10.135
light year 12.3
light years ahead 7.90
limb 7.42
line up 9.97
line one's pockets 8.97
lines 9.98
liquefied 7.73
listings 9.24
literally 3.20
literary 2.10
live in the fast lane 10.115
live off the land 6.72
live on 5.91
live out of a suitcase 10.61
loan 2.67
lollipop 3.114
lonesome 6.120
longtime 11.41
look down on sb 5.120
looming 12.62
lose one's temper 12.95
low-lying 6.156
luminous 6.1
lunar colony 12.22
lunatic 7.5
lung 7.95
lure 1.172
lyrics 9.37

M

MA 10.121
machinery 7.14
magma 6.2
mainstream 9.72
maintenance 11.37
make a big deal out of sth 9.91
make a fortune 8.83
make a killing 8.124
make a loss 8.84
make a profit 8.85
make a song and dance about sth 9.90
make ends meet 8.122
make for 10.16

make up 4.15
make up one's mind 10.39
make-up 11.3
malaria 3.67
malfunction 7.116
mansion 7.27
manual labour 7.15
manufacture 12.21
marine 10.9
marshland 6.161
materialise 12.106
max out 2.68
maze 5.18
MDF 7.7
mechanical 7.49
medication 3.93
medieval 3.117
mediocre 1.73
menacing 12.63
mental 2.127
merciless 1.78
metropolitan 10.55
microbe 6.3
microphone stand 9.68
middling 9.73
migrate 6.76
mimic 12.46
mind-blowing 1.37
mine 6.59
miniature 2.39
minimalist 4.57
minimise 11.49
minor 3.24
miracle 3.71
misinformation 2.113
miss out on sth 11.121
miss the mark 4.123
mission 9.4
mixed blessing 3.21
modest 1.102
molar 10.132
molten 6.6
money is no object 8.118
money-spinner 12.8
monitor 3.1
monitor 7.62
mood-altering 10.83
morals 2.53
mortally 3.66
mortgage 8.54
mosquito 3.143
mother tongue 10.118
motionless 4.129
mould 4.130
mouldy 5.57
mount 8.20
movement 9.61
mug 8.107
muggy 6.50
munch 5.44

mundane 7.19
muscular 3.36
mushroom 9.14
music to one's ears 9.85
mussel 5.127
mutual 8.62

N

nail 7.113
nap 6.115
napkin 5.67
native 2.118
natural ceiling 11.43
natural resource 6.152
navigate 5.17
nestle 6.145
neuron 3.4
newcomer 10.58
nibble 5.43
nickel 7.2
noble 1.75
no-brainer 1.130
nomad 6.75
nomination 7.1
not break the bank 12.96
not one's cup of tea 11.153
not rocket science 7.94
nuclear reactor 7.111
nugget 8.108
nurse 3.27
nutrient 5.115
nutritious 3.39

O

oats 5.109
obedience 1.140
obesity 5.8
objective 1.90
objects of art 9.108
obligatory 2.121
oblivious 3.12
observation 2.48
observer 11.63
obsess 10.80
obstacle 1.4
obstinate 1.98
obstruct 11.111
occupation 10.40
occurrence 7.134
odour 5.143
off 5.58
offend 2.56
offset 2.117
oil 9.52
oil spill 6.67
old money 8.79
omen 12.45
omission 12.97

on board 10.21
on display 9.78
on occasion 2.83
on tour 9.23
ongoing 12.74
opening act 9.71
opening night 4.81
oppressive 6.43
optimistic 12.102
orbit 12.114
ordeal 2.22
ounce 12.24
out of bounds 2.104
out of context 2.82
outcome 12.40
outdo 10.69
outdo 12.85
outer 11.22
outskirts 6.66
overcast 6.35
overcome 1.3
overpower 11.102
owe 8.53
ownership 12.31
oxidation 6.7
ozone layer 6.27

P

pace 10.94
pack away 5.89
painfully 2.89
palette 9.50
parachute 1.167
paramedic 3.132
parched 3.35
parliament of owls 6.105
part with one's cash 12.34
particle 7.96
particle physics 12.94
pass out 3.75
paste together 4.18
patroller 1.42
pattern 12.37
pave the way 7.129
pay for sth out of one's own pocket 12.36
pay homage to 6.132
peak condition 5.131
peckish 5.10
pedestrianise 10.59
per capita 5.80
perceive 11.47
perception 11.38
performing artist 9.110
performing arts 9.69
periodic table 7.64
perpetual 12.57
persevere 1.123
persist 1.67

personable   1.159
pessimistic   12.101
phenomenally   9.96
phishing   2.60
phonograph   7.9
photosynthesis   6.4
pianist   9.32
pick at   5.92
pick up   3.76
picturesque   6.144
pig out   5.7
pile on   5.13
pilot project   9.2
pioneering   12.59
pitch   11.99
pitiless   1.79
plague   3.111
plant   7.83
plaster   9.53
platter   5.65
play by ear   9.75
play havoc   5.16
playwright   9.9
pleasing   11.70
plight   9.6
plot   12.9
plug (into)   2.40
plummet   8.47
plunge   8.18
poach   5.54
pocket   1.32
pocket money   8.80
polish off   5.93
pollutant   6.62
polluter   6.61
polymer   8.45
pop art   9.63
portion   5.62
portray   4.46
posterity   12.54
potential   3.156
pound   5.14
pouring   6.36
poverty   7.29
practise   3.28
prayer   3.157
precaution   11.50
preceding   12.60
precise   3.22
premiere   4.99
preoccupied   1.137
prescribe   3.29
pressurised   12.109
prestige   12.87
preventative measure   3.127
pricey   9.94
pride of lions   6.106
primate   2.125
principal   6.118
privacy   12.83

privilege   10.127
procedure   3.58
processed food   5.12
proclaim   7.30
project   4.117
prolonged   6.89
promising   12.20
promotion   10.96
property   1.139
prophecy   7.13
prospect   10.113
prosperous   8.63
prosthetic   7.41
protest   2.25
provincial   10.49
provoke   2.19
pterosaur   4.5
publicity   4.96
pull off   1.111
pull out   4.97
pull out   11.119
pull through   5.121
pull together   10.86
pulse   9.42
pulses   5.134
pump   6.160
pumpkin SB   11.157
purchase   8.27
purify   7.53
purist   2.100
purity   7.75
pursue   10.102
pursue one's dream   1.15
pursuit   11.42
push the panic button   7.92
put down (a deposit)   8.71
put sb off   9.99
put up with   5.124

Q

quarter final   11.125
quench one's thirst   5.25
quest   1.23

R

radiation   12.112
radical   6.163
rail   10.106
raisin   5.111
rank   4.71
rash   1.94
rat race   10.114
rational   12.66
ravage   3.6
rave (about)   4.113
ravenous   5.49
reach   2.107
reaction   2.18

read music   9.43
realise one's ambitions   1.62
realm   10.3
reasonable   10.54
reassure   11.52
recall   3.9
recession   8.15
reckless   1.95
reclaim   6.168
reclining   6.125
recollection   3.16
record label   9.31
recoup   12.2
recover   3.63
recovery   10.63
recreation   6.162
recreation   6.172
rectangle   7.57
reflect   10.41
reflective   7.107
refuge   6.79
regard   2.129
regardless (of)   6.164
regretful   4.105
rehearse   4.68
reinforced   7.6
reinvent the wheel   7.86
relate   2.52
relay race   11.72
release   4.67
relieve   3.30
reluctance   4.108
remains   2.103
remark   2.47
remarkable   1.19
remodel   7.43
remount   11.117
renovate   5.125
representative   9.113
reproduction   9.55
reptile   4.29
reputation   7.130
requisite   12.92
resemble   6.127
resist   2.58
resistance   1.173
resolve   1.68
respectively   8.106
respond   3.31
restrict   7.120
resuscitation   3.134
retail industry   8.132
retire   10.120
retrograde amnesia   3.8
reveal   4.66
revenge   2.75
revenue   8.135
reverse   11.31
revive   11.114
revolution   1.59

revolutionise   7.44
rigorous   10.29
rim   11.8
rinse   10.33
riot   4.118
rival   11.145
roast   5.108
roasting   6.37
rodent   3.122
root   3.149
root   11.115
root canal   10.137
rotten   5.145
round   11.75
rover   12.84
row   4.53
row   11.100
ruin   10.72
run the risk   5.26
run yourself into the ground   10.92
rung   11.7
runner-up   1.16
running sore   3.86
rural   10.116
rush   11.5
ruthless   1.80

S

sadden   6.121
safe and sound   6.92
safeguard   3.129
safeguard   3.131
safekeeping   10.27
safety-conscious   11.40
sales figures   8.86
sales tax   8.87
sample   3.120
sand dune   6.169
sane   3.37
satellite   7.106
satellite dish   10.105
savings account   8.109
savoury   5.9
scale   9.95
scale the heights   1.1
scales   8.104
scam   2.62
scan   7.122
scatty   3.50
scorched   6.110
scraps   5.82
screech   2.26
screw   11.26
scroll   2.7
scrumptious   5.60
scrutiny   9.103
sculpted wall   9.112
sea lion   10.136

seam 7.17
seamstress 7.16
searing 6.113
seasick 3.79
second to none 2.21
sector 7.37
secure a deal 1.11
sedentary 10.50
see sth coming 12.44
seek 6.78
seek to do sth 12.104
selfless 1.81
sell sth for a song 9.84
semi 11.126
sentimental 1.86
sequence 4.116
serve 11.73
serving 5.64
set 4.54, 11.76
set one's sights on sth 12.86
set out 2.17
set sb back 8.72
set the pace 12.77
set to music 9.40
set up 8.35
settlement 12.16
sever 2.6
severe 3.121
sewing machine 7.18
shade 4.131
shaman 3.148
shanty town 8.100
shape one's future 12.38
share 2.2, 8.50
sharp 5.85
sharpen 11.106
shed 5.29
shelter 6.80
sheltered 10.43
shield 6.28
shift 6.24
shine light on sth 7.132
shockwaves 8.16
shoot 4.16, 11.81
shopping district 10.97
short (of sth) 8.112
shout at the top of your lungs 3.100
showbiz 4.83
showery 6.40
showpiece 12.72
shuttle 12.111
shuttlecock 1.165
side-effect 3.135
sift through 4.17
sign up (for sth) 2.45
silkscreen 9.65
simmer 5.37
sing like a canary 2.88

sing like a canary 9.88
sing sb's praises 9.89
single 9.33
sink 6.159
sip 5.42
siren's call 10.76
sizzling 5.113
skim 5.114
skin tone 4.125
slam 2.51
slash 10.129
sleep deprivation 3.113
slice 12.35
slip 6.68
slip of the mind 3.13
slog it out 10.107
sly 1.84
smash 8.49
smashing 3.94
smooth sailing 8.131
smuggle 5.146
snail 10.32
snap 11.128
snatch 1.31
soaked 6.93
soar 6.114
sociable 10.56
socialite 9.64
soft drink 5.84
soil 6.57
solar panel 7.117
solar radiation 6.29
solar system 12.91
solely 7.98
solid 4.134
solitary 10.51
solo artist 9.34
soothing 3.109
soundtrack 4.7
sour 5.46
space agency 12.27
spark 6.8
spasm 3.90
specification 11.6
spectator 11.152
spectrum 3.5
speculate 8.56
speech recognition 12.51
spending spree 8.120
spew 6.31
sphere 7.58
spiced 5.101
spinning 11.10
spiral out of control 7.115
spirit 11.132
splash out 8.73
split 5.105
split an atom 7.99
splitting headache 3.95

spoil 10.73
spoilt 5.104
spontaneous 1.52
spot on 7.32
spotty 2.31
sprain 3.32
spread 5.53
spring 11.159
sprint 11.96
stable 5.72
stage 9.15
stage fright 4.78
staggering 1.8
stale 5.56
stall-holder 8.25
stand out 9.114
standing ovation 4.82
stand-up comedy 4.98
staple 5.73
star-studded 4.111
startlingly 6.112
state secret 12.11
state-of-the-art 4.32
static 2.96
steady 11.80
steel bar 7.26
steer 11.65
stem from 3.108
sterilise 7.54
stick to one's guns 12.29
sticky 6.38
still 4.6
still life 9.58
stimulate 7.45
stimulating 2.126
stir up 2.73
stock market 8.77
stove 6.147
straight from the horse's mouth 2.87
strain 10.88
stray from the path 11.146
street artist 9.109
streetwise 1.132
stretcher 3.136
stretcher 11.130
strict 10.117
stride 11.23
strive 4.94
stroke 9.44
struggle 4.47
stubborn 1.99
stunning 6.146
stunt 1.38
stunt 5.3
stuntman 11.1
subject 9.62
subject to 6.19
subjective 9.92

submarine 10.11
submit 4.14
subsistence farming 5.138
subspecies 6.122
substitute 7.36
succinct 3.138
suffice 6.74
sufficient 5.27
sugary-sweet 4.10
sulphur dioxide 6.60
sultry 6.51
sum 8.52
summit 1.24
supplement 5.116
surface 7.108
surgery 3.59
survival of the fittest 6.141
susceptible 10.75
suspend 1.41
suspend 11.112
sustainable 7.118
swallow 3.68
swap 5.19
sweep 8.130
sweltering 6.42

T

tagged 10.2
take after sb 5.122
take in 5.142
take out 3.77
take out 11.162
take sb aback 2.28
take the bull by the horns 8.21
take to 2.74
tandem 1.7
tart 5.47
task sb with sth 3.25
taste 4.8
tear-jerker 4.59
tender age 4.38
terminal 3.85
terminal velocity 1.163
terrace 9.123
territory 6.77
the ball's in sb's court 11.133
the best thing since sliced bread 5.100
the down side 9.119
there's no use crying over spilt milk 5.103
thespian 4.101
think outside the box 10.99
thrill 2.59
thrill-seeking 11.48
thrive 6.26
throw in the towel 10.93
throw money around 8.94

throw money at   8.93
throw up   3.78
tide   6.170
tie up loose ends   10.44
tighten   11.34
tighten one's belt   8.96
tile   7.119
timeless   12.58
timid   1.91
tin   7.103
tint   9.45
title deed   12.4
title role   4.77
to a lesser extent   10.78
to sb's face   2.86
to the accompaniment of   4.88
tolerance   11.45
tonsils   10.104
tooth decay   3.112
top-notch   1.9
topping   5.71
toss   11.82
touch down   11.14
touchy   1.85
tough   12.113
tower of giraffes   6.102
track down   4.42
trader   8.24
traffic congestion   9.120
trait   1.152
tranquillity   6.153
transaction   8.33
transform   7.12
transmit   3.151
trash   11.103
traumatise   2.44
trawler   10.46
treacherous   2.5
treaty   12.28
tremendous   1.155
trend   12.79
trespass   12.6
tribe   3.72
trigger   6.13
triumphant   1.103

trompe l'oeil   9.121
troubleshooter   1.69
tuck in   5.94
tug at sb's heartstrings   4.62
tumble down   1.47
turmoil   6.20
turn a blind eye   3.102
turn back the clock   9.116
turn sb down   8.110
tusk   10.134
twist   4.112

U

ultimate   1.17
ultrasound   7.121
umpire   11.89
unaware   6.94
under construction   2.79
under contract   9.76
under fire   1.120
under new management   9.80
underdog   4.63
underestimate   6.151
undergo   10.28
undernourished   3.47
under-privileged   1.154
understudy   4.91
uneventful   10.42
unexpected   12.67
unforeseen   12.68
unofficial   8.34
unprecedented   2.109
unravel   4.4
unrivalled   2.43
unrushed   6.126
unsophisticated   10.52
unstable   7.67
unsuspecting   2.61
upbeat   1.87
upbringing   1.53
upper   12.80
upright   11.18
upshot   12.41
urban   6.138

urge   5.34
urgent   3.158
usher   4.55
utensil   7.47
utmost   11.28
utterly   3.107

V

vaccination   3.137
vacuum   12.110
vain   1.76
valid   2.64
values (pl n)   2.38
vast   3.17
VAT   8.111
vendor   8.137
venture   12.33
venue   5.139
verify   8.58
verse   9.38
version   6.17
vertical   1.48
veteran   4.22
viable   6.96
victim   7.135
vigorously   5.88
virtually   2.36
virtuous   1.77
virus   3.18
vision   1.22
visionary   12.61
visual   4.114
vivid   3.11
void   2.14
voluntary   2.120

W

wake up and smell the coffee   5.97
walk of life   10.128
wall mural   9.111
warm up   5.95, 11.123
wary   2.114
wasteland   6.65

watercolour   9.54
wear sb down   10.87
weary   6.91
weird   6.130
well   6.149
wellbeing   3.128
whet one's appetite   5.41
whip up   5.96
whistle   9.35
wholesome   3.38
wild applause   4.89
windmill   6.167
windscreen wipers   7.11
wing   9.79
wings   4.56
wingsuit   11.12
wipe out   3.10
wire   11.160
wireless telecommunications   12.50
wisdom tooth   3.80
wise up   1.129
with a view to   11.59
withdraw   2.102
without reservation   1.157
wits   11.57
wobble   1.176
woe   4.60
work against the clock   6.137
work around the clock   1.118
workforce   7.38
worthy   7.123
worthy cause   1.136
wouldn't say boo to a goose   2.90
wound   3.65
wrap   4.133
wriggle one's way out of sth   11.147
writhe in agony   11.88

Y

you are toast   5.107